Q2Q

ALSO FROM THE EDITORS

Q2Q: Queer Canadian Theatre and Performance: New Essays on Canadian Theatre Volume 8

Q2Q

QUEER CANADIAN
PERFORMANCE TEXTS

EDITED BY PETER DICKINSON,
C.E. GATCHALIAN, KATHLEEN OLIVER,
AND DALBIR SINGH

PLAYWRIGHTS CANADA PRESS
TORONTO

LIBRARY AND ARCHIVES CANADA CATALOGUING IN PUBLICATION
Q2Q : queer Canadian performance texts / edited by Peter Dickinson, C.E. Gatchalian, Kathleen Oliver, and Dalbir Singh. -- First edition.

ISBN 978-1-77091-915-0 (softcover)

    1. Sexual minorities--Drama. 2. Homosexuality--Drama. 3. Canadian drama (English)--21st century. 4. Homosexuality in the theater--Canada. 5. Sexual minorities' writings, Canadian. I. Dickinson, Peter, 1968-, editor II. Gatchalian, C. E., 1974-, editor III. Oliver, Kathleen, 1964-, editor IV. Singh, Dalbir, 1979-, editor V. Title: Queer performance texts.

PS8309.H64Q28 2018   C812'.608035266   C2018-902033-4

Playwrights Canada Press acknowledges that we operate on land, which, for thousands of years, has been the traditional territories of the Mississaugas of the New Credit, the Huron-Wendat, the Anishinaabe, Métis, and the Haudenosaunee peoples. Today, this meeting place is still home to many Indigenous people from across Turtle Island and we are grateful to have the opportunity to work and play here.

We acknowledge the financial support of the Canada Council for the Arts—which last year invested $153 million to bring the arts to Canadians throughout the country—the Ontario Arts Council (OAC), the Ontario Media Development Corporation, and the Government of Canada for our publishing activities.

Canada Council Conseil des arts
for the Arts du Canada

ONTARIO ARTS COUNCIL
CONSEIL DES ARTS DE L'ONTARIO
an Ontario government agency
un organisme du gouvernement de l'Ontario

Ontario
Ontario Media Development
Corporation

CONTENTS

ACKNOWLEDGEMENTS

First and foremost, we thank the artists included in this collection for sharing their work. Our appreciation, as well, to the authors of each of the individual framing introductions.

Playwrights Canada Press staff have been a joy to work with. We thank Annie Gibson, Blake Sproule, and Jessica Lewis for their support of this book, and of Canadian playwriting and theatre criticism more generally. Blake and Andrew Wilmot helped smooth out the rough patches of our manuscript with their diligent copy-editing.

Jan Derbyshire came up with the Q2Q handle by which this book and its companion essay volume have been launched into the world. We owe her huge thanks for this.

Finally, as editors, Peter, Chris, and Kathleen wish to acknowledge the special role played by Dalbir in shepherding this book into print, particularly his hard work liaising with all of the writers and staying on top of new copy as it came in. Thank you, Dalbir; we could not have done this without you.

INTRODUCTION:
QUEER WORKS/WORKING QUEER

PETER DICKINSON, C.E. GATCHALIAN,
KATHLEEN OLIVER, AND DALBIR SINGH

What becomes a queer Canadian play or performance text most in the second decade of the twenty-first century? Is it characters that are recognizably lesbian, gay, bisexual, trans, Two-Spirit, queer, or genderqueer? Or maybe it is storylines, themes, and dramatic conflicts that register as familiar queer narrative arcs: illicit desire, coming out, family abandonment, migration to the city, romance, marriage, having children, home renovation. But in our newly liberated (or is it neoliberal?) post-Stonewall, "post-AIDS," post-post queer world, how does one keep so many different plotlines (from going) straight? And how important is it for audiences to get all the jokes?

In assessing what makes queer performance queer, let alone queerly Canadian, it is useful to supplement complicated questions of who and what a given work represents with how it actually works, including how it works on us: stylistically, affectively, and ideologically. Let us start—of course—with the how of queer theatrical style.

On the one hand, a phrase like "queer theatricality" seems both obvious and tautological. After all, we've long been taught, including by critics of the Western dramatic canon (we're looking at you, Plato!), that to be theatrical is to be queer, and vice versa. But what does this actually look like in terms of performative aesthetics? Often queer theatricality is associated with excess; it is too sentimental, too outrageous, too ridiculous, too camp, too sexual, too confrontational, too political, too "too." But if a poetics of queer excess carries with it no immediately recognizable or translatable value within a hetero-patriarchal economy of white, middle-class entertainment, that means its fluid forms—and the ideas conveyed by those forms—can potentially escape commodification within that economy. The only categorical statement that can be made about the workings of a queer theatrical style in the plays and performance texts included in this volume is that such workings resist categorization.

Katie Sly and Jonathan Seinen's *Charisma Furs*, Shawn Wright's *Ghost Light*, and Sunny Drake's *No Strings (Attached)* are all, on some level, versions of solo autobiographical performance; but whereas Sly and Wright both tell their stories in their own voices, Drake adopts a fictional persona. And while Sly and Drake employ movement and physical theatre, material objects, music, and, in Drake's case, projections as theatrical supplements, Wright relies only on his body and voice. *androgyne*, by d'bi.young anitafrika, and *Dear Armen*, by lee williams boudakian and Kamee Abrahamian, both combine text/spoken word, movement, and music to explore specific cultural histories of queer and gender non-conforming individuals; however, these recognizable and presumably transferable queer forms are additionally filtered through specific diasporic storytelling traditions: African griot/Jamaican dub; and Armenian folktales, singing, and dancing. Donna-Michelle St. Bernard's *Give It Up* gives us an impossible and necessarily unfulfilled butch-femme love story that also stands as an allegory for a nation's interrupted and arrested history. Even the most formally "conventional" play in this collection, Minh Ly's *Ga Ting*, self-consciously exploits that most queerly theatrical of genres: melodrama.

If one understanding of the mimetic tradition of theatrical representation is that a successful dramatic production works by having audience members find positive likenesses of themselves on stage with whom to identify, root for, pity, or mourn, then queer theatre—like much feminist theatre—might be said to "unmake" such taken-for-granted affective attachments through a negative dialectical process. Feminist theatre critic Elin Diamond, drawing on Brecht, Walter Benjamin, and Theodor Adorno, has noted that this process of defamiliarization does not deny the operations of referentiality on stage; it merely attempts to unfix the naturalization of certain dominant frames of reference-making based on the passive registering of a superficial correspondence between, say, an actor's body and a character's behaviour.[1] In the case of queer theatre and performance, we can see this unfixing at work in the ongoing questioning of the supposed coherence of normative expressions of gender, sexuality, and desire (i.e., that the hero always gets the girl, or that she even wants to be gotten by him in the first place). But to understand how, even as eager and receptive spectators of queer theatre and performance, we are to be as affectively unsettled as uplifted by what we see on stage, we need to acknowledge the frequency with

---

1 Elin Diamond, *Unmaking Mimesis: Essays on Feminism and Theatre* (New York: Routledge, 1997), viii–ix.

which this work trades in ambivalent and even deliberately degrading emotional relays and embodied intimacies.

Given the historical stigmatization of queer sexualities, it is unsurprising that queer theatre artists are comfortable working with and through feelings of shame, embarrassment, abjection, pain, and disgust. From Sly's stories of growing up poor and queer in *Charisma Furs* to the slow exposing of the long buried family hurt and suffering that lurks underneath Jimmy's romantic neediness in Drake's *No Strings (Attached)*; from the frequent expressions of guilt that pepper Shawn Wright's discussions of his relationship with his mother to Matthew's contention that the Lees are ashamed of their dead son's sexuality in Ly's *Ga Ting*; from grappling with cultural taboos around gender difference and same-sex desire in anitafrika's *androgyne* and boudakian and Abrahamian's *Dear Armen* to the wrenching physical and psychological conflict between self-preservation and allegiance to a cause in St. Bernard's *Give It Up*, the plays collected in this anthology resist giving their audiences easy emotional resolution or consolation. At the same time, they challenge us to remain disinterested or uninvested in the subject matter by forcing us to evaluate why we feel the way we do, and who else might feel this way. In this regard, the difficult affective work set in motion by these plays and performances overlaps with the project of queer cultural analysis undertaken by critics like Ann Cvetkovich, Heather Love, and Mel Chen. These critics are interested in how the group experience of queer "trauma," queer "loss" and "damage," and queer "toxicity"[2] can paradoxically help to consolidate and collectivize sexual minorities and subcultures. This coalition-building happens not from a conservative, knee-jerk response of "we're not really like that," but rather from the more thoughtful—and painful—working through of the intolerance of that response, a que(e)rying of the self, and its various disavowals and exclusions, that any queer subject who has had to grapple with internalized homo/transphobia will be well equipped to undertake.

Another way of saying this is that to work the idea of "queer" in theatre and performance is to engage in a project that is expressly political. On the one hand, it may be taken as a given that the politics of queer performance are de facto oppositional and antinormative, not least with respect to entrenched models of

---

2   See, respectively, Ann Cvetkovich, *An Archive of Feelings: Trauma, Sexuality, and Lesbian Public Cultures* (Durham, NC: Duke University Press, 2003); Heather Love, *Feeling Backward: Loss and the Politics of Queer History* (Cambridge, MA: Harvard University Press, 2009); and Mel Chen, *Animacies: Biopolitics, Racial Mattering, and Queer Affect* (Durham, NC: Duke University Press, 2012). All three critics are building on the pioneering work of Eve Kosofsky Sedgwick on the performativity of "queer shame"; see Sedgwick, *Touching Feeling: Affect, Pedagogy, Performativity* (Durham, NC: Duke University Press, 2003), 35–66.

gender, sexuality, and desire. And yet as the works gathered in this collection demonstrate, queerness is as much a politics of relationality as it is of resistance— a way of being with or beside one another despite our differences, rather than against one another because of them. It's a way of working across our unequal social histories and inheritances that does not seek to smooth over conflict, but rather makes room for the restiveness of contradiction, including the possibility that what we understand to be institutionalized norms of sex and gender and romance and family might not just be subjected to queer political critique but might also be shown, through performance, to be capacious enough to include queer subjects.[3] It is striking just how many lines are crossed in the plays and performance texts that follow: lines that are material and metaphorical; that are generational and geographical; that are cultural and historical; that are temporal and spatial; fictional lines in the sand between characters and the real lines of the stage that traditionally separate performers from audience members. Via these and additional transversal methods, each piece can be seen as working an intersectional queer politics into its specific performance practices.

In Donna-Michelle St. Bernard's *Give It Up*, Yolanda and Adanma are young female resistance fighters who find themselves sharing the same jail cell in the final years of Angola's civil war. During that decades-long conflict, which only officially ended in 2002, it is estimated that more than 20,000 children were impressed into armed or domestic service by government forces and the opposition group UNITA (National Union for the Total Independence of Angola), with underage girls often forcibly kidnapped and married to UNITA militants. Rather than submit to that fate, Yolanda and Adanma have become "Sarahs," members of an all-female rebel movement led by a charismatic leader with whom it is suggested both women are in love, and whom they are now in danger of betraying as a result of their imprisonment and torture. But as with her earlier portraits of the sisters Gigi and Lola in *Gas Girls*, and Nila and Salome in *Salome's Clothes*— texts that, like *Give It Up*, form part of the playwright's 54-ology project[4]—St. Bernard builds tension by showing how the biopolitical effects of power and circumstance are meted out differently on the bodies of her protagonists. Yolanda

---

3   Once again it was Eve Kosofsky Sedgwick who first highlighted the importance of queer's transitivity—that is, its tendency to work "across" different conceptual formulations and subject positions; see her *Tendencies* (Durham, NC: Duke University Press, 1993), xii. Sedgwick also discusses the nondualistic and relational possibilities of "besideness" in *Touching Feeling*, 8–9.

4   St. Bernard's 54-ology project is her ambitious attempt to examine each country on the continent of Africa "through a different piece of performance work." See https://54ology.wordpress.com/.

and Adanma should be natural allies, but in fact they don't even like each other. They do, however, need each other, and their relationship is queer not just in the way they have chosen to live aslant of patriarchy and heteronormativity, but in the recognition that if they are to remain true to the liberation movement to which they belong, then they must come to terms with what each is and is not capable of doing both for and in the name of that movement.

The "doing" of belonging is explored in a resolutely DIY and intensely personal way in *Charisma Furs*, Katie Sly's memoir of their queer youth: the highs (winning a soccer game), the lows (getting by on social assistance), and the high of being made to become low (submitting to a dominatrix for the first time). Co-created with Jonathan Seinen, the piece literally and metaphorically strips the craft of theatre down to its bare essentials. A performer tells their story to an audience, and through the reciprocal acts of talking and listening there is established the basis for other yet-to-be imagined contexts of shared assembly. In this respect, it is perhaps no accident that craft-making—from learning how to make an origami box to learning how to give and receive pleasure—figures so prominently in *Charisma Furs*. Often maligned as the poorer cousin to conceptual artistry (cf. Aristotle on *techne* vs. *poiesis*), craft is in fact central to feminist and queer self-fashioning. Katie receiving instruction on how to be a responsive (and responsible) sub; Katie instructing the audience in the power of co-presence: by such sustained techniques of the body do the performance practices of gender and theatre align as repositories of repertory knowledge-making and knowledge transfer.[5]

At the other end of the generational spectrum is renowned Canadian actor Shawn Wright's *Ghost Light*, his funny, affectionate, and moving ode to the memory of his mother, Regina. Like Nana in Michel Tremblay's similarly themed *For the Pleasure of Seeing Her Again*, Wright's "Mumma" is a force of nature, a devoutly Catholic Acadian woman who is also the leading lady of the St. Rose Parish Players, an amateur dramatic troupe in Saint John, New Brunswick. And yet while mother and son share a love of the stage, outside of the theatrical spotlight they don't quite know how to star in their own lives. In Wright's case this includes owning up to his sexuality, with the weight of his religious upbringing combined with his own internalized homophobia, preventing him from coming out to his mother until after she is dead. But the rituals of the theatre, like those of the church, can be powerful things, and in this play Wright is not so much exorcising his ghosts as incorporating them, giving voice to Regina and letting her

---

5   On this very topic, see Ben Spatz, *What a Body Can Do: Technique as Knowledge, Practice as Research* (New York: Routledge, 2015).

tread the boards once again so that each may repeat for the other not just their most ennobling and triumphant roles but also their most flawed and complex.

Minh Ly's *Ga Ting* also explores the complex bonds of family, both biological and chosen. However, the play is not your typical domestic melodrama. On a business trip to Toronto, the white Matthew visits Hong and Mai Lee, the Chinese immigrant parents of Matthew's dead boyfriend, Kevin, with whom he lived for three years in Vancouver. Matthew, excluded from Kevin's funeral, wants some closure to his grief, and as a result of his visit Mai in turn becomes increasingly curious about Kevin's life with Matthew. Making liberal and canny use of Cantonese (translated via English surtitles), the play foregrounds through its content and form the multiple audiences it is hailing, as well as the very different points of entry to the story for said audiences. To this end, *Ga Ting* begins by exploiting over the meal Mai has prepared for Matthew the awkwardness of the protagonists, upending various cultural stereotypes for comic effect. Soon, however, things turn serious as Matthew accuses the Lees of alienating their son by not supporting his choice of career as an artist, and by refusing to talk about his sexual orientation or his bipolar disorder. Hong, meanwhile, blames Matthew for Kevin's death by keeping him in Vancouver and introducing him to a "depraved" gay lifestyle (the circumstances of Kevin's death remain deliberately ambiguous). However, Ly does not allow his characters—or his audience—to remain stuck in the familiar and righteously superior position of their individual grief; indeed, one of the many emotional rewards of this play is discovering how its temporal structure (making use of flashbacks and flashforwards) reveals the reorientation of empathy—between characters, and from audience members—to be a necessary consequence of our shifting relationships to a lost love.

Garo Berberian, the protagonist of lee williams boudakian and Kamee Abrahamian's *Dear Armen*, knows about loss. Garo is a researcher and writer "interested in the stories of women and queers who are often or not at all represented in literature or history books." A second-generation Armenian-Canadian who is also genderqueer, Garo's desire to know more about their own ancestry leads them to the story of Armen Ohanian, an Armenian dancer, actress, writer, and lifelong communist whose melding of modern and "Oriental" dance techniques made her a star among post-World War I European audiences eager for representations of exoticism. Garo is keen to claim Ohanian as a dissident queer role model, but their thesis advisor insists that their evidence is "weak" (Ohanian divorced her first husband and is said to have had an affair with Natalie Barney). However, the silences and gaps in the historical record around non-Western queer women, far from stymying Garo, paradoxically become a generative way to address what remains unspoken in their own family, not least in terms of their relationship with their aunt, Morkoor. That is, just as Ohanian wrote in her memoirs that what she was giving Western audiences in her dancing was an Orientalist fantasy, and that through such masking of her real self she was able to obtain a degree of freedom and independence, Garo's rejection of their aunt's version of what a real Armenian woman should be and do allows both of them to begin the process of reinventing that "most important thing": a bond of kinship that is testament to the larger survival of a culture.

What does it mean to be a hopeless queer romantic in today's digital hook-up culture? And how does one negotiate the online codes of that culture—which remain perniciously gender normative (and white)—when one is trans and socially activist? These are just two of the questions tackled by Sunny Drake in *No Strings (Attached)*, his hilarious and moving one-person show about dating in the age of geosocial networking apps like Grindr and Craigslist and OK Cupid. Via the meta-theatrical frame of a fictional twelve-step meeting of fellow "Romance-aholics" (the audience), we are introduced to our protagonist, Jimmy, who casually describes himself at the top of the show as an "Effeminate-Queer-Pansy-NonMonogamous-SparklyPrincess-SomewhatSlutty-Kinky-Transsexual-Man," but whom we quickly learn is also still very hung up on his ex, Brian. The ethical complications of subscribing to a collectivist, radically non-normative, polyamorous queer sexual politics, while still harbouring personal abandonment issues, is mercilessly sent up by Drake in successive parodies of our over-sharing culture: extended texting sequences with Jimmy's sponsor, Sunny; fantasy interludes in which we're transported to a reality-style game show from hell; arguments with one's online self about the accuracy of dating profiles. In the end, what Drake reveals through the rawest elements of Jimmy's testimonial, as well as the stage magic that accompanies them, is that even as bodies become ever more liberated from repressive regimes, ongoing self-care must remain the cornerstone of sexual progress.

That such progress can be hampered by the added weight of culturally specific taboos around gender presentation and sexual desire, and that, moreover, the overcoming of such taboos is additionally complicated by the persistence of institutionalized racism is the subject of d'bi.young anitafrika's *androgyne*. The piece focuses on the relationship between andro and gyne, two childhood friends from Jamaica who have both immigrated to Canada, and who now live blocks away from each other in the Toronto suburb of Scarborough. Both characters are attracted to other "womxn," but their deep affection for each other is shadowed by memories of parental opprobrium, internalized social stigma, economic precarity, and the daily terrors of living as a black queer female in a racist, homophobic, and misogynistic culture. As such, it takes the length of the play for the kiss that gyne introduces in poetic form in an early scene to be completed physically by andro at the end. And even then the fragile relationship the couple has managed to forge, *together,* is threatened by that which each, *separately,* is unable to name about themselves in the other's presence.

In choosing these plays for this collection, we have attempted to model our own intersectional methodology, focusing on work that reflects a range of subject matter and styles but also aiming for as much inclusivity as possible in terms of gender, geographical, and racial representation. Despite our best intentions, gaps do remain. In particular, we regret that we were unable to include work from Québec, or by a Two-Spirit writer. At the same time, we see this volume joining a burgeoning list of queer Canadian theatre resources (many of them published by Playwrights Canada Press) that, taken together, begin to address the real diversity of our community.[6] But there is still a lot of work to be done. And that includes on the other side of both the proscenium arch and this printed page. Indeed, what will continue to become queer Canadian theatre and performance most—today and into an as yet unmapped future—is audiences and readers. So what are you waiting for?

Let's get to work.

---

6   See Rosalind Kerr, ed. *Lesbian Plays: Coming of Age in Canada* (Toronto: Playwrights Canada Press, 2006); Sky Gilbert, ed., *Gay Monologues and Scenes* (Toronto: Playwrights Canada Press, 2007) and *Perfectly Abnormal: Seven Gay Plays* (Toronto: Playwrights Canada Press, 2007); Susan G. Cole, ed. *Outspoken: A Canadian Collection of Lesbian Scenes and Monologues* (Toronto: Playwrights Canada Press, 2009); Jean O'Hara, ed. *Two-Spirit Acts: Queer Indigenous Performances* (Toronto: Playwrights Canada Press, 2013); and Moynan King, ed., *Queer/Play: An Anthology of Queer Women's Performance and Plays* (Toronto: Playwrights Canada Press, 2017).

GIVE IT UP

DONNA-MICHELLE ST. BERNARD

This play is for Kern, Mom, and our merciful Lord.

ACKNOWLEDGEMENTS

Give it Up was developed with moral and material support from:

lemonTree creations playwright residency (alongside its companion piece, *The Smell of Horses*)
National Arts Centre playwright residency 2014
Obsidian Theatre Company through the Ontario Arts Council's Theatre Creators' Reserve Program
Cahoots Theatre's Hot House Creators Unit 2011/2012
Stratford Festival of Canada's 2011 Playwrights Retreat

THE SPACE LEFT BEHIND: AN INTRODUCTION TO DONNA-MICHELLE ST. BERNARD'S *GIVE IT UP*

LAINE ZISMAN NEWMAN

A feminist does not lend her hand; she too curls her fist . . .
When a hand curls up as a feminist fist, it has a hand in a movement.
—Sara Ahmed, "A Feminist Army"[1]

Set in Angola, Donna-Michelle St. Bernard's *Give It Up* follows the experiences of two young girls, Yolanda and Adanma, participating in a civil resistance as soldiers (referred to as "Sarahs"). Throughout the play, the women are imprisoned, interrogated, and violently abused in a military camp, while being guarded by the only other character present on stage, Saad, a boy soldier.[2] The relationship between the two main characters is complex and develops more so through the tension between them than through their affection or tenderness. Histories, values, and relationships are revealed through the friction of their forced presence in the same space. Never depicted as "fast friends" or companions, their kinship is circumstantial. They are part of a larger whole, an army, which both characters value as essential to liberation.

As part of St. Bernard's 54ology—a series of performances and artistic creations that look at each country in Africa—space is essential to *Give It Up* from the outset of the production. The play itself is birthed from the locale from which it is inspired. Though the static stage depicts a single room, the play maps the journeys that have brought these women to their present place, and the imagined

---

1   Sara Ahmed, "A Feminist Army," *Feminist Killjoys*, October 19, 2016. https://feministkilljoys.com/2016/10/19/a-feminist-army/.

2   Saad's story is expanded in St. Bernard's companion work, *The Smell of Horses*, which depicts his arrival to a remote military outpost and the challenges he endures under his superiors.

futures of their potential release from it. Rather than considering the politics of the country depicted in the performance and unpacking the geographies of war, I am interested in how St. Bernard builds the space of the performance through the bodily presence in the room: how a single room is changed through the embodied senses of the two girl soldiers, how the audience's perception of the space is developed through the characters' articulation of those senses. I offer one interpretation of the play here. I do not intend to be prescriptive, but instead describe the impression that this play left upon me. Your reading may, and likely will, be different. We all experience this story differently, as we all experience our sense of sight and hearing differently. There is so much that exists in the silent moments of this text, and as I will suggest, there are many stories that unfold in the seemingly empty spaces from which Donna-Michelle St. Bernard compels her audiences to seek out and learn.

A SENSE OF SPACE.

Sara Ahmed argues that bodies, inseparable from the spatiality of their sexuality, gender, and race, are not detached from the space in which they perceive; rather they are "shaped by their dwellings and take shape by dwelling."[3] Spaces, too, are shaped by the people within them; who is granted mobility, who and what is within reach, and who is alongside you, all change how a space is experienced and perceived. This reciprocal relationship between bodies and the spaces they inhabit demonstrates how space is contingent on the physical ways particular bodies pass through or reside within them. Our reception of space, as audience members in the theatre, is likewise influenced through such engagement. Our orientation in the space where we read the play, where we view the play, or where we sit down to reflect upon it all alter how we interpret these characters and their stories. By directing attention toward sensation in a confined space, St. Bernard gives us access to her characters' struggles as living, breathing people. We are unable to disconnect from the bodily implications of their immobility, confinement, and torture. Their physical senses and the articulations of these senses are essential to the construction of space and the ways in which the audience imagines it. When their senses are limited, the space of the performance becomes smaller, more confined. The walls thicken as the characters are denied sight. The space beyond the walls becomes more present as we hear the violent responses to torture happening outside of the room. In this way, the space of

---

3   Sara Ahmed, *Queer Phenomenology: Orientations, Objects, Others* (Durham, NC: Duke University Press, 2006), 9.

the play is developed through the senses that are deprived within it and bodies that are confined to it.

OUT OF SIGHT. CERTAINTY OF SOUND.

We begin in a small room. It is made smaller by the blindfold on Yolanda's face. The emphasis on Yolanda's lack of sight makes us, as receivers of this story, more aware of our own senses and urges us to actively acknowledge our surroundings. In this opening sequence, Yolanda begins to question her senses: Did she really just hear a door open? Yes. Her assurance that her senses have not deceived her insists that we trust our own—we listen more closely. This ability, to hear what we cannot see, to use our senses to move beyond the confines of space, heightens and intensifies throughout the performance. The characters' immobility within the room shifts as their senses open doors beyond walls. To be clear, I am not proposing a romanticization of a lack of sight as inherently enabling insight. On the contrary, in the context of the play, the characters' interrogation and abuse is predicated upon the attempted elimination of agency through bodily control and constraint. This is a disorientation device, changing the ways in which the Sarahs' bodies inhabit and experience space through sensorial control. As audience members, we too are disoriented and attempt to move outside of the space through what we hear beyond the walls. The affective perception, that an outside exists within this space, recurs throughout the performance as the memory of trees and connections to the world beyond these walls are brought into the room through the stories told—as sources of inspiration and the continuing hope of a possibility of release.

The distress and violence off stage seep into the room through audible sounds of trauma. At times, the characters try to stunt this ability to hear what cannot be seen. Unable to listen to the pain and violence Yolanda endures, Adanma attempts to sing to block out the sounds. She hears what is on the other side of the walls and knows the impending violence that exists beyond the space. The sounds the characters hear, and the memories of sounds from before their capture, are sensorial and embodied markers of time and space. When Adanma recalls what drew her to the Sarahs, she remembers the soldier's brutality through sounds. She recounts hearing her neighbour's demise one night: "the door splinters, things breaking, angry laughter." The memory is not disconnected from her experienced body but attached to and inextricable from her senses. This focus on embodied and internalized trauma is emphasized in the next sentiment, when Adanma wakes up the next morning and remembers: "Their house was a face with a black gaping mouth, broken teeth, no soul." The sounds of the space are personified: the demolished door; a mouth, destroyed objects; broken teeth, and the sounds of the soldiers' angry laughter ripping the soul from what once housed a family. Even in those memories articulated throughout the performance, it is the sounds of trauma and tragedy that the characters are unable to strip from their minds.

The audience is listening, but is also deprived of the ability to watch the violence that is taking place. That which Yolanda endures at the hands of her captors occurs off stage. By removing them from view, St. Bernard does not exploit the pain her characters experience nor does she feign an ability to adequately represent the ways such violence manifests. Most of us cannot ever imagine the atrocities and real-life experiences tortured women endure each day. To attempt to recreate or fictionalize them on stage has the potential to trivialize the lived experiences of those who have been and continue to endure violence and death at the hands of oppressors, and those who sacrifice their safety to fight and resist this oppression. But the moments of stillness in the play, where we can hear but not see, allow us to engage with concepts and realities beyond the stage. These pauses take us outside of the text, to reconcile with the reality that these kinds of experiences exist in everyday life.

A SARAH. SARAH.

While there is a clear focus on the individual characters' senses and physicality, as the play continues it becomes evident that these senses belong to a larger body—a collective, an army of soldiers, who maintain a sense of self while devoting their lives to a struggle bigger than themselves. Here, I am interested in the way in which "Sarah," the name of the soldiers involved in the resistance, is used in the play. At times, the characters refer to each other as "a Sarah": I am a solider; I am a member of a group with a purpose; I act on behalf of a whole. Other times, however, the characters simply refer to each other as "Sarah": A person; a proper noun; an individual with their own emotions, motivations, experiences, and limitations. The characters hold both identities simultaneously. They are each Sarah and *a* Sarah, sometimes to conflicting degrees. I am a human being; I am a part of a whole.

I began this introduction with a quotation from Sara Ahmed's 2016 blog entry, "A Feminist Army." Here, Ahmed discusses the concept of a "call to arms," and asks us to hear "the arms in this call, or to hear the arms as calling." Our resistance is embodied: our arms, a part of the whole. Just as "Sarah" is one person, she is attached to a body of resistance—to "a Sarah," the body that exists, that takes space, even after an individual arm is severed. Ahmed explains that the arm exists beyond the end of life: "The arm gives flesh to this persistence. The arm has to disturb the ground, to reach up, to reach out of the grave, that tomb, that burial." I want to think here about how St. Bernard's attention to the physical presence and senses of the characters on stage can be conceived of as an allusion to the individual within the whole, as a means of seeing the person within the collective. We are compelled to recognize the individual Sarah, but we never lose sight of *the* Sarah: the solider in an army, resisting and fighting within an assembly. To experience sensation as an individual within a whole is to experience the resistance of a collective.

One of the most notable articulations of space in *Give It Up* comes at the end of the play, when the audience is asked to fill empty space with a story. Upon revealing that she has sacrificed herself to their captors rather than leaving behind a fellow Sarah to be tortured, Yolanda describes both herself and Adanma as "only the torn corner of a page." She then describes herself as "the space that is left behind, telling nothing but undeniably absent [. . .] the empty space that lets you know that the story you are reading is incomplete." This statement reminds us to fill the emptiness. The absence of a story tells us a story. When we cannot see, when we cannot hear, when our senses are left with no tangible object on which to hold, we must continue to fill the void with the stories of those who can no longer speak, the stories of those whose only archive are the walls that once held them. In reading *Give It Up*, we should refuse the erasure of these stories, and take with us a commitment to fill empty spaces with the histories of resistance that remain unrecorded and unnamed.

Give it Up premiered in a workshop presentation by New Harlem Productions at the 2012 Stratford, ON, SpringWorks Festival with the following creative team:

Yol: nisha ahuja
Ada: Virgilia Griffith
Saad: Christian Feliciano

Director: Clare Preuss
Music Composition and Arrangement: Pamela Gilmartin

The play later received a staged reading at Theatre Passe Muraille's BUZZ Festival in 2012, was staged in the Stratford Festival's Playwrights Lab in September 2013, was workshopped in a Canada Council for the Arts supported residency at Canada's National Arts Centre in 2014 with English Theatre ensemble members, and received a workshop reading by StageLeft Productions for PACT Con 2016. Contributing artists included Pamela Gilmartin, Clare Preuss, Keira Loughran, Miranda Edwards, Sarah Kitz, nisha ahuja, Neema Bickersteth, Virgilia Griffith, Christian Feliciano, Karl Ang, Carmen Grant, Nehassaiu deGannes, Petrina Bromley, Christine Brubaker, Dmitry Chepovetsky, David Coomber, Eric Davis, Leah Doz, Sheldon Elter, Quancetia Hamilton, Eliza-Jane Scott, Joey Tremblay, Jillian Keiley, Sarah Garton Stanley, Michele Decottignies, Jenna Rodgers, Cheryl Foggo, Chantelle Han, Onika Henry, Chris Dovey, Cole Alvis, Indrit Kasapi, and Bob White.

CHARACTERS

Yol: Yolanda. Girl soldier. Butch.
Ada: Adanma. Girl soldier. Femme.
Saad: Guard. Boy soldier. Tenderfoot.

SETTING

Period: Early 2000. Civil war is about fifteen years deep, nothing new.

Set: A small room, a chair and table pushed to the walls. A small hole in one of the walls, a long crack in another, climbing up from the ground. An errant stick lies in the corner. A door leads out to a hallway; the hallway leads to other doors.

STYLE NOTES

Staging violence: The violence in this play should live in the effects of torture, not in witnessing torture itelf. The instances of harm that take place on stage and the sounds of Yol's torture should not be overly graphic.

Ada's songs: These songs are sung by Ada to accompany/drown out sounds of Yol's torture, but quickly find a strange harmony with them. Each of Ada's songs is articulated only as an intention. In creating this work I have been inspired by the music of Tracy Chapman and Pamela Gilmartin.

Context: This play is a part of the 54ology, inspired by stories of girl soldiers in Angola.

1. THE SPARROW HAS LANDED

YOL sits on the floor, blindfolded, knees up, back to the door. SAAD watches her silently for a long time. He leaves. The door opens and ADA is pushed in. As the door closes, ADA stands looking at YOL's back, then paces around her as she speaks, finally sits back to back, facing the door. ADA breathes audibly.

YOL: So they have another. Will you speak?

Pause.

No, not yet. Oh well. We can wait.

They wait.

Of course there are possibilities.

Pause.

One is that you are afraid. You may think that I am only here as a prop, to elicit your sympathy, and your confidence. I promise you this is not the case. I don't want you to tell me anything. It will be better for both of us if you don't.

They wait.

Another possibility is that you are here to elicit my sympathy . . . and my confidence. I have nothing to tell you. No secrets eating their way through my chest, nothing I've overheard that is aching to erupt from my heart through my lips, nothing I've seen that is causing me nervous indigestion.

They wait.

It is possible that you can't talk. People have been known to lose tongues, teeth . . . you? Or that you were born a mute? That one is less likely. There is the possibility that you are just sitting there, dragging out the silence . . . You'll let me work myself into an anxious state, babbling at the wall until I begin to question whether I really heard the door open or not. But I can feel you there, breathing. Nothing to say? That's fine. It's possible that you are standing over me now. Before the end of my next sentence you will bring your fist down on my head.

Pause.

Not that then, or my timing's just off.

They wait.

Whoever you are, I'm sorry for you if they were cruel.

ADA: Sarah.

YOL shifts.

Yes, it's me. It's—

YOL: Don't say your name.

ADA: There's no one here.

YOL: Still.

ADA: Yes . . . You're blindfolded.

YOL: You're not?

ADA: Let me take it off.

YOL: It will only make them angry.

ADA: Why only you?

YOL: Sloppy.

ADA: With all their training?

The door opens and SAAD enters, looks sharply at each of them, and exits.

YOL: I've said nothing.

ADA: I know. I was careless. I didn't cover myself well enough. She is still safe, though. They haven't got her yet.

YOL: As far as you know.

ADA: As far as I know. On the other hand, she could be close by . . . in the room next to this one, even. We wouldn't know it until we hear her voice from the yard, screaming in the night.

YOL: She wouldn't scream.

ADA: No.

They wait.

YOL: I have been too long alone here. I can't go on without speaking, even if it's only to you. If I cannot speak in here, I will find myself speaking in there, and then—

ADA: That's okay. Talk about something small, very small.

YOL: My shoes are too small. The left one is just pinching the edge of the little toe, on the underside.

ADA: Kick it off.

YOL: I did. They keep putting it back on, and it hurts even more after the relief of having it off. That short one has the keenest instinct for exploiting irritants. It's perverse. I'm going to change them. You know which shoes I will imagine I'm wearing?

ADA: No. Which shoes will you imagine?

YOL: A pair of yours. The red sneakers you wore to the rally in Kuito. You know the ones I mean?

ADA: Yeah. I like those shoes. They lasted for years and they never got uncomfortable. Got them second hand in the first place.

YOL: She always said you had a good eye.

ADA: Think they'll feed us?

YOL: Maybe. Depends how long we're supposed to last. Food bodes well, I think.

ADA: Mm.

ADA goes over to the table.

Maybe they will lay my hand here, and hammer my fingers.

YOL: Talk about something small.

ADA touches the table.

ADA: Small. So small. I think these little black circles are cigarette burns. So, we know that's part of it.

YOL: Nothing is certain. Sit down.

ADA: Just wait. You were here before me. You've had a chance to smell out the contents of every corner before settling yourself there. I'm only just getting my eyes back, just making out the walls. How do I know you haven't got some reason for choosing that spot? Just wait.

YOL: Do what you like.

ADA: I will.

ADA *stands over* YOL *for a moment, then sits again.*

YOL: Small things. The watch digging into my wrist, she gave it to me.

ADA: Don't.

YOL: I know. I won't.

ADA: I hope they don't have her.

YOL: Stop it.

ADA: Are you worried that I will weaken myself with these thoughts? It helps me to think of her.

YOL: It doesn't help me. You don't have to think of her out loud.

Silence.

ADA: They must have something on us, but I don't know what it could—

YOL: There is nothing to have. It's no crime to travel from one town to the next; they only think they own the roads. It's no crime to bring a friend a message from home. You must stop feeling guilt before they smell it on you. Try to be as innocent as you are ignorant.

ADA: They'd better come for me soon.

YOL: You remember that time she sent you down to get five recruits from the quarry?

ADA: Oh, come on.

YOL: But it was too dirty, so you went to the mall instead.

ADA: And came back with ten new girls.

YOL: Girls is right. Not one over seventeen years old.

ADA: You loved it.

YOL: Your little pageant was a pleasant distraction, but I trained ten girls who were gone in a week. I fully expected you'd leave with them.

ADA: If I had, I wouldn't be here now.

YOL: You regret it?

ADA: This is what we have to do.

YOL: No, it's what we've chosen to do.

ADA: Right. I'm choosing this.

YOL: What kind of life would you have if it wasn't this?

ADA: I don't know.

YOL: *(sneering)* A husband? Kids?

ADA: Maybe. Why not?

YOL: Could you really, in these times?

ADA: Do you know what's happening out there? They're living. They're having lives. They're not thinking about us in here, in the bush, on the long road. When this is all over, maybe we'll have made something possible for them, but what about us?

YOL: Are they living? Good. I'm happy. I'm happy for them.

ADA: Oh, you're happy. Good. Good for you. Great. We should all be so lucky.

YOL: Sarah, this is the hardest part. We don't know what's coming next; we make sacrifices, sometimes we resent them. You have it especially hard. You are young, pretty, there are other things for you to be doing now than this. I know it doesn't seem fair.

ADA: Why do you always have to talk as if you were born in it? This is my fight, too.

YOL: You joined long after me, you know.

ADA: So what.

YOL: So why does it bother you so much to be reminded of it?

ADA: It doesn't. Am I bothered? I'm sure you're every bit as essential to the movement as she believes.

YOL: She loves you, too.

ADA *laughs.*

For different reasons. She loves all of us. All who choose to struggle are worthy . . . I love you, too. Are you cold? Let me rub your wrists.

ADA: Don't you dare be kind to me.

YOL: We should all be kind to each other. Isn't that the point? Whether we like each other or not.

ADA: My point, personally, is to do the next necessary thing. And then the one following that. My point was to get to her position, to warn her that the action has been compromised, to deliver this message and not to think beyond that.

YOL: Well she's safe. At least you made it to the post. At least one of us delivered the message.

ADA: No.

YOL: What do you mean?

ADA: I didn't get there. She doesn't know yet. In two days she will move; fifteen Sarahs will move with her and soldiers will be expecting them.

YOL: What? But—

ADA: What do you want from me?

YOL: She's out there.

ADA: I went to warn her.

YOL: Do you know what will happen if they take her?

ADA: Yes. I know. Do something. What do we do now? Do something.

YOL: Me?

ADA: Sarah. What is the next necessary thing?

YOL: Worthless.

The door opens and SAAD *enters. Both tense, ready to go.* SAAD *takes* YOL's *arm.*

SAAD: Come with me.

ADA: Hey. Is there a bathroom?

SAAD: Are you joking?

YOL: We're real funny in here.

SAAD: I don't get it.

YOL: Can't you see us laughing?

ADA: Am I supposed to go on the floor, like an animal? Listen, if you be nice to me, I can be nice to you.

ADA makes a clumsy attempt at seduction. SAAD *is impassive.* ADA *peters out in the face of* SAAD's *unexpected disinterest.*

SAAD: Do you know what you're here for?

ADA: No, what?

SAAD: . . . I was just asking if you knew.

YOL: You don't know.

SAAD: Yes I do.

YOL: They didn't tell you.

SAAD: I know as much as I need to know.

YOL: Need to know only? That what they told you?

SAAD: They told me what a trigger is for, and where to put the bullets. You can believe they told me that. They told me how to treat a mouthy bitch.

YOL: Kid, if you're gonna carry a gun, they can at least treat you grown-up.

SAAD hardens.

Pause.

SAAD: Come on.

YOL blanches, but goes with SAAD. ADA flattens herself against the wall and sings. [ADA's intention: La la la la. I can't hear you.]

SAAD looks in and she stops abruptly.

2. THE ELEPHANT, TOO

SAAD opens the door and pushes YOL in again, a little worse for wear. Her blind-fold is gone. This time she circles ADA, looking at her bitterly before sitting in a corner. ADA does not want to look at her.

ADA: You again?

YOL: . . .

ADA: Just you?

YOL: . . .

ADA: How was it?

YOL: What a question.

ADA: I may as well know. It'll be me soon.

YOL: Don't be hungry for it.

ADA: I just want it over with.

YOL: What's the matter? Sweet talk doesn't melt doors? . . . There is no over. It starts, and then it just keeps going on . . . Talk about something. Something small.

ADA: Her hands are small. And those little red gloves she always wears, with the hole in one finger that she won't repair.

YOL: I made those gloves.

ADA: Who made the hole?

YOL: She did that. We were at Benguela, waiting for Fatima. It was cold, salted wind coming off the water, crouched in the bushes and soldiers kept passing very close by, loud with drink, every stumble almost landing them on top of us. Had to hold that hand all night to keep her from chewing right through to the bone.

ADA: Talk about something else.

YOL: Huh. Like shoes? I'm afraid I only have the one pair. The topic is exhausted for me.

ADA: Even here you are better than me.

YOL: What can I say? You don't want me to talk about her. She is all we have in common. She is the reason we are here.

ADA: You can blame her. I won't.

YOL: That's not what I'm saying. Just . . . you and I, that subject is unbearable, and yet there is little else to talk about.

ADA: Perhaps you can think of a way for us to get out of here.

YOL: You think we can?

ADA: I think you can. You're good at that.

YOL: I thought maybe you'd / already—

ADA: Given up? Not with the chance to see her again.

YOL: You see how it returns to her?

ADA: You're sure they can't hear us?

YOL: I'm sure of nothing. Sometimes I think I can hear them. They're laughing. One of them laughs loudly.

ADA: Do you hear them now?

YOL: No. Not now.

ADA: Say it with me then.

YOL: We shouldn't.

ADA: Quietly then.

ADA & YOL: *(like a prayer)* We girls will be women
We women will make war
In the name of our children
Yet to come

We girls will be women
We women will restore
In the name of our nation
Yet to come

No more of self, of home
I am Sarah
No more of family, of friends
We are Sarah

> *A short silence. Footsteps. The door opens and SAAD enters. ADA tenses, ready to go. SAAD looks at YOL.*

SAAD: Come.

YOL: No flowers? This is our third date.

SAAD: That's the wrong attitude.

> *YOL goes out with SAAD, looking back briefly. They stop just outside the door.*

YOL: Are you going to watch this time? You don't have to stand outside the door like that. You have my permission to watch what they are doing to me, what you are a part of.

SAAD: It's not yours to give.

YOL: Look at me. Do you know someone who has eyes like these? She is watching you, too. I give her permission to see what you are doing to me.

SAAD: They told me you were wicked, not to let you speak to me. All that you say must be reported.

YOL: I will be sure to return the favour when I am out of here.

SAAD: It will go better for you if you speak only to answer questions. Come.

> *The door closes. A few seconds pass in silence. YOL cries out.*

> *ADA sings. [ADA's intention: Yeah, okay. We're both suffering.]*

3. ARE YOU BEING SERVED?

*Footsteps are heard outside the door. ADA and YOL jolt awake and move away
from each other. SAAD opens the door and pushes in a bowl with a slice of bread
dissolving in water. They eye the bowl and hesitate.*

YOL: Leave it.

ADA: You said—

YOL: I said leave it. Do you know what rat poison tastes like? Truth serum?
Drain cleaner?

ADA: Maybe it's all over. Maybe they have her. How long have we been here?

YOL: Hours, not days. They hide the light to disorient you. It feels longer than it
is when you have no way to measure time's passing.

ADA: They'll come for me next. I feel it.

YOL: Listen, you have nothing to prove. You don't have to be brave.

ADA: Why are you saying that? I can take it. I've had the same training you've
had. I know what to do when they begin.

YOL: The training is nothing. When the first needle is pushed under your nail,
you will forget everything. When the first bone shatters . . . We shouldn't have
let you—

ADA: Nobody let me. I chose. I'm a Sarah, too. I'm not just some pet.

YOL: These ones, they're just boys. Don't have the heart for it. They haven't developed a taste, either for cruelty or efficiency. And they have no imagination. Their
captain returns tonight. He won't be squeamish.

ADA: You don't scare me.

YOL: Understand: she's still out there. There's still a chance, but someone has
to get word to her.

ADA: Because I failed.

YOL: Because we both did. No more of self.

ADA: You'd protect me?

YOL: Us. The mission. I'd protect that. Eat.

*YOL takes a piece of bread from the water, squeezes it out, smells and tastes it,
then hands ADA the squashed little dough ball.*

4. TEA AND SYMPATHY

SAAD removes YOL again. ADA is alone in the room. She listens at the door to SAAD pacing back and forth. Scritches tentatively at the door. Hears him pause and go on. Scritches some more, hears him stop. She murmurs at the door. It is implied, physically, that she is trying to seduce him. He opens the door a crack and his hand appears around it. ADA strokes it. SAAD balks at the intimacy and slams his own hand in the door by mistake. Hurt, he pushes the door open again so that ADA is thrown back, then slams it shut and goes back to pacing, nursing his hand.

5. MISCARRIAGE OF JUSTICE

SAAD opens the door and pushes YOL in again. As the door closes she spits something near to ADA.

YOL: Here. Take this piece of leather and push it between your teeth when they take you.

ADA: Take care of yourself and leave me out of it.

YOL: I am taking care of myself. I'm the one that will have to listen to what they do to you.

ADA: They won't take me. That pleasure is all yours.

YOL: What have you done?

ADA: Look at you. You actually think I folded already, without a hand laid on me. Relax. I did better than that. I told them I was pregnant.

YOL: That might not have been the best idea.

ADA: Of course not. You didn't think of it.

YOL: Who says I didn't?

ADA: Oh, so you did think of it.

YOL: Who wouldn't? A bit obvious. And even more obviously a mistake.

ADA: Works at the border.

YOL: This isn't the border, dummy. Maybe if you hadn't skipped the workshops—

ADA: They needed me elsewhere.

YOL: Every day. While the rest of us were on work rotation, they needed you to sew curtains instead of doing any heavy lifting, any heavy learning. Did you think it was a game? We were trying to prepare you for this.

ADA: You know so much. Does it hurt less when you know things?

YOL: Do you know why war is so full of rape? Why men throughout history have cut off breasts? Dragged fetuses from bellies and strewn them in the streets? They're not going to get sentimental about your impending motherhood; they are trying to end us. And you tell them that you are making more of us to end—you make yourself an even greater threat. If you were any part of this you would know. If you were one of us . . . I'm going to have to hurt you.

Picks up a stick from the corner.

ADA: You're threatening me?

YOL: Call it a kindness. Now shut up and do as I say.

YOL moves her hands between ADA's legs.

ADA: Don't touch me!

YOL: Shh. Hurry. There's no time.

ADA cries out in pain. Blood runs down her legs. She holds herself and moans. The guard is heard hurriedly approaching.

SAAD: That blood?

YOL: Haven't you seen it before?

SAAD: What's she done?

YOL: Nothing. It's gone.

SAAD: Why?

YOL: Hysterical. Miscarried. This one's not strong. She could never carry a child.

SAAD: Clean her up.

SAAD throws a rag, exits.

YOL: You have a way of making others responsible for you. Why did you come? I wonder if she thought you would. Did she show you her gun?

YOL laughs. ADA blushes.

I can see it. She stood like this, rested it on her thigh. You are very pretty.

And I'll bet you looked at her as you would a strong young man, measured her out with your eyes, licked your lips, asked if you could touch it, reached out with thin, trembling fingers and a jolt ran through you—fingers, arms, heart, spine, belly . . . First you thought you would like to be her, then you came to think you would like to have her. Girls like you, even in the cause, can't shake the idea that owning a person, that being owned is what love means. So she called to you. Why did you come?

ADA: Who cares?

YOL: I do. We have never talked as friends, have we? Just exchanged orders or shot looks from corners to cut each other down. We have never tried to be understood. At this moment, we are the last people anywhere, ever. I am the last one to look at you, to listen to you. Talk about something that matters.

Waits.

ADA: I came because things didn't stop changing. My father left. He went to the Congo to work the mines. The old men came to speak with my mother. I saw their eyes wander over me, but I still had two healthy brothers. Then they went. Younger men came to visit, those who had begun to profit from the fighting. Then the soldiers . . . their eyes. Not blurry and patient like the old men, or even hungry like the young men. Colder, like they were placing me in a list. They would not come visiting with small gifts for my mother like the others. I heard . . . late one night, my neighbour. She smiled at one of them during the day. Stupid. Night had barely fallen. I heard the door splinter, things breaking, angry laughter. She cried. I never heard anyone cry so long. How did she keep it up? In the morning their house was a face with a black gaping mouth, broken teeth, no soul. I packed a small bag and I came to her. I didn't want them to . . . First time I held a gun I knew I could feel what they felt. I could see how others became small in its sight, how I could become big enough that no man could . . . and now . . . did you—have they . . . ?

YOL: It will be different for each of us.

ADA: What do they ask in there? *(whisper)* What do they ask?

YOL: My name is Yolanda. I come from east region. I am without a husband or parents. I am going to Kuito to look for work. No. No. Yes. I don't know. Please repeat the question. No, I don't know. I can't remember. Sixteen. Yolanda. East region. Kuito. Farm. I don't know.

ADA: Yolanda, did they . . . ?

Footsteps. SAAD returns to take YOL.

YOL: No.

Involuntary.

SAAD: More lip? I'm not going to get trigger-happy and end this for you. Why do you provoke me?

YOL: Because you're sloppy, soldier. You're an accident.

SAAD: Then let me be very intentional.

SAAD inflicts harm on ADA.

ADA: Who are you? What are you? Don't you feel?

SAAD looks at YOL and she goes with him. After a few moments ADA hears YOL's voice faintly from the other room. ADA listens, strains, then moves her ear up next to the wall to hear better. After a while she retrieves the piece of leather and fits it into her mouth, closing her eyes, terrified. She sings through clenched teeth.

ADA sings. [ADA's intention: I am so scared for me.]

6. EENIE, MEENIE

SAAD opens the door and pushes YOL in again. She seats herself beside a crack in the wall and examines it closely. ADA comes to her and strokes her hair.

YOL: Stay away from me.

ADA: Don't you have better things to do than hate me right now?

YOL: Stop talking.

ADA: I won't. This isn't a situation you can control. Can you handle that? You are not the boss of me. Of anybody. You are powerless, just like me. You were caught, just like me and they're gonna keep torturing you—

YOL slaps ADA.

YOL: Shut the fuck up you stone . . . you . . . pebble.

Sulky silence. The door opens. YOL goes at ADA with renewed violence. They tussle. SAAD smiles and shuts the door.

Now sit in that corner and be quiet if you know what's good for you. Listen, they don't know there are two of us. They know they're looking for a Sarah. A girl about our age, travelling the road to Huambo. They want to find her and stop her. As far as they are concerned one of us is dangerous and the other is ignorant. Innocent. Once they know which one of us is a Sarah, they will let the other go. Do you understand? If it is not me, they want me to give you up, so you can tell them where she is. Or the other way around.

ADA: So if I tell them it's you . . .

YOL: You can go.

ADA: Oh.

YOL: I don't hate you.

ADA: Oh please.

YOL: I don't. You frustrate me; I don't hate you.

ADA: Oh please.

YOL: Why do you do that?

ADA: What?

YOL: I'm trying to have an honest— Look, we shouldn't talk at all. That's the point. We don't know each other.

ADA: And you want to solve that by not talking?

YOL: No, I mean they don't know that we know each other. So we don't. Get it? We don't both have to die here.

ADA: But one of us will.

YOL: Yes.

ADA: Oh.

YOL: And until then . . . this was always a possibility. Didn't you know that?

They both look at her broken feet.

ADA: What will they ask?

YOL: . . . They will say her name and they will watch you. They will say Sarah Sarah Sarah, and they will watch you. They will hold the back of your head so gently, cradled in the palm like an egg . . .

ADA: Sarah Sarah Sarah. Why don't they come for me?

YOL: Who knows? Maybe they think it's you. Maybe they think a real Sarah could never stand to see an innocent be tortured in her place, that she'd have to stand up and . . . but you seem to be taking it well.

ADA: Not fair. You're hardly an innocent.

YOL: No.

ADA: Or maybe they just think it's you. No one ever looks at me and thinks I'm the type who could stand the life.

YOL: She liked that about you.

ADA: She said so?

YOL: Sure.

ADA: She hardly said anything to me.

YOL: But she was always looking.

ADA: Was she?

YOL: You know she was. You lived for it.

ADA: She hardly said anything.

YOL: To anyone.

ADA: At night, in the camp, with your heads close together as sisters sharing secrets, the two of you—

YOL: We made plans. Discussed strategy. Always the Sarahs. No more of self.

ADA: Oh. Are you cold?

YOL: Yes.

ADA: Come.

> ADA *goes to* YOL *and wraps herself around her. They sleep.* SAAD *presses himself to the wall in the hallway.*

SAAD: My name is Saad.
I am a man. I come from Cruzeiro.
When I was at school my best friend was Jonas.
I have a mother.
I have a sister.
Their eyes are . . .
Their eyes were . . .
I feel. I do feel.
What I feel right now is . . .
I am hungry.

> SAAD *takes something from his pocket and focuses on eating it. He removes a small notebook from his pocket and reviews its contents.*

> ADA *sings. [*ADA's *intention: I am so worried for us.]*

7. YAY/BOO

YOL: They'll come in here and call to one of us.

ADA: And they will say, "We're letting you go."

YOL: But then they will follow her.

ADA: Only until they see that she is harmless.

YOL: Harmless, but also useless. They will silence her.

ADA: With a bribe. They'll hand her a bag of rice and a stack of bills.

YOL: And when she accepts it, they will charge her with treason.

ADA: And—

YOL: And she will be shot.

ADA: But there were two to begin with, so all is not lost.

YOL: Yes. One of us will stay here.

ADA: She will be strong, will tell them nothing.

YOL: As a result, their cruelties will expand and multiply.

ADA: Until they exhaust themselves and go away.

YOL: Leaving her alone in the dark.

ADA: The peaceful, peaceful dark. Alone.

YOL: Where soon enough, someone will come upon her, helpless.

ADA: Which one of us do you imagine is helpless?

YOL: Neither.

ADA: Exactly.

YOL: But one of us has a higher opinion of our captors' honesty.

ADA: About what?

YOL: Everything. Anything. Their plans.

ADA: You don't think they'll let one of us go.

YOL: I just don't assume it.

ADA: That makes no sense. If they have the one they want—

YOL: As far as they know.

ADA: As far as they know, why would they care about the other one?

YOL: Look, a tigress prowls the jungle, up here on this hill. That tiger has been known to snatch up children from town; and a group of townsfolk have formed a hunting party, well armed but ill-informed. They know the tiger will move, will likely come toward the water as the sun comes down. Over here, there is a bush full of little birds who have overheard the hunters talking. One—only one—flies up to warn the tigress. Will the hunter not shoot it down? And now that a ruckus has been made, a spray of birds bursts out of the bush—will he not shoot them, too? His gun is loaded and his fire stoked by fear for his children. Will he not then shoot at anything that moves?

8. MINEY MO

Footsteps. SAAD opens the door. YOL stands. SAAD ignores her and takes ADA's arm. She sets her jaw, then collapses into him, urinates. SAAD is disgusted. ADA is ashamed. YOL looks away. SAAD throws ADA down and pulls out a handkerchief, dabs at the spot on his pants, exits.

SAAD: . . .

YOL: That was good. You surprise me.

ADA: I didn't mean to.

YOL: It's okay. I had to . . . in there. They break you with shame. Here.

YOL removes her wrap, takes bread from the water and sets it aside. Saves one bowl and washes ADA with water from the other, then washes her wrap and replaces it with her own. ADA speaks as she washes.

ADA: Have you ever been in love?

YOL: You know I have.

ADA: I mean before her . . . I didn't think so.

YOL: And you? I suppose you are in love all the time.

ADA: It doesn't mean any less.

YOL: I suppose not. I was once in love with a tree.

ADA: How?

YOL: The shape of it. I couldn't look away when it was on the horizon, and I saw nothing else when I closed my eyes. The top of it rose above the roof of the house outside my window like it needed to be seen as much as I needed to see it.

ADA: Has anyone ever loved you?

YOL: When it flowered I knew that it preened for me, and when I came to the camp I missed it more than I missed my mother. I ached for it.

ADA: But you left. You came to her.

YOL: What was I to do?

ADA: Don't you have anyone?

YOL: My brothers . . . they got cold eyes, too. I am so tired. The next time he takes me might be the last. And if you are left behind I don't know what they'll do. We're out of time. We need a plan. I think—

Footsteps are heard. SAAD *opens the door and looks at them both for a long time. He takes* YOL. ADA *begins to sing softly.*

ADA *sings. [*ADA's *intention: I am so scared for you.]*

9. TAPPING OUT

YOL *returns; won't look at* ADA.

YOL: Don't say anything. I don't hate you yet but I will. Please. Not a word.

There is silence. They avoid each other in the small room. YOL *nurses new wounds. She has now taken the worst of it.* ADA *is about to speak several times but shows restraint; she is affected by* YOL's *appearance.*

ADA: Look. Here. This crack in the wall is only a little sapling. If they keep us here, we will watch it blossom and grow. Its roots run miles and miles from home to here. It has struggled up from the ground through this wall to reach you. Hear me? Look and you will recognize it. This sapling is a new start for a very old tree—it is your tree, preening for you once more.

YOL: My tree. It's in here with us.

ADA: Yes!

YOL: Then there is no one left outside to remember me. If we live in the memories of those who love us, then I died when I entered this place.

ADA: Don't let them take me, Yolanda! / Please do something!

YOL: NO NAMES! What do you want from me?

ADA: You said you had a plan. Before you left. You said we could do something. Please. I don't care if you hate me or not. You can't let them do . . . that, to me . . . I'm not like you.

YOL raises a hand to strike ADA, her fingers making pained claws. Malicious pause. A small victory. She lowers her hand.

YOL: Well at least now you know what you're like.

ADA: I don't care. I can live with that. I want to live.

YOL pauses.

ADA weeps softly.

. . .

. . .

. . .

YOL: This is what will happen next. One of us will go to her. One of us will stay here, and one of us will go to her, warn her . . . be with her.

ADA: And which *(chokes)* . . . which of us has earned freedom?

YOL: You are like a small child—do you know that? Your convoluted sense of justice only has your self at its centre.

ADA: I am only wondering how we will decide—

YOL: There is nothing to decide. It's been done. I . . . I couldn't take any more. But telling did not stop them. They did what they wanted.

ADA: And you leave me to that! You see now what you are like. How, a fellow Sarah, how could you bring your lips to shape the words? How did you condemn me and then come back in here to look at what you have ended? To look at the goat you have led to slaughter? You are rare. Oh god, look at your eyes. Your eyes are so hard.

YOL: Are they? I guess it really is done then.

ADA: I'll tell them. You won't get one mile before I tell them. You, you, confessed to me here in this room. You apologized for lying, for giving me up to save yourself. Said your mission was too important, begged my forgiveness. You won't get half a mile. They'll bring you back and we will both die here.

YOL: And when one of us doesn't warn her, they will all die out there. For your spite. You would.

ADA: I will. You think you can leave me here to be forgotten? We are the same. We are both written on the same page; we will both be torn out of the story and never thought of again.

. . .

. . .

YOL: You were right about one thing. Whatever you are, I couldn't let them do that to you—to anyone. Not if I could do something to stop it. They're not coming for you. I gave myself up, Sarah—Adanma. Because one of us has to go on. Because the way this thing works is, we each have to do what we are capable of. I know that I could never walk out of here leaving another Sarah behind. And I know that you can. For once, you are more capable than me. Does it feel good?

It's true that you and I are only the torn corner of a page. The difference between us is that you are the scrap of a torn corner that is discarded and never thought of again. Me? I am the space that is left behind, telling nothing but undeniably absent. I am the empty space that lets you know that the story you are reading is incomplete.

ADA: You—

YOL: Now stop talking and listen. There is still time if you hurry. Don't go to the post. They may still follow. Go to town and buy cigarettes. She is in an apartment above the cleaners. Sing out as you pass her. Wait to see the curtain move, then light your cigarette, puff twice, and crush it out. She will understand. She will cancel the compromised operation and meet you at the next post. Do it without hesitation.

ADA: And she will come to me.

YOL: Yes, she will come. To you. And you will sit in the dark and hold her hand to still her, and she may whisper to you, heads close together like sisters with secrets . . . but I will always be the one who died for her. I will always be the one she loves.

ADA: So.

SAAD opens the door and takes YOL without looking at ADA. A struggle is heard. Silence, ADA listens, hums. Another ruckus. SAAD returns stealthily, pushes the door open slightly, retreats, coughs. ADA waits a while, then tentatively looks out the door, exits.

10. FREEDOM NOW

A dark street. ADA *walks under a window and sings.*

ADA *sings. [*ADA's *intention: I am the winner/loser.]*

A curtain is pulled back. She smokes, crushes out the cigarette, and walks on. Singing, to herself now, she winds the piece of leather around her wrist and walks away.

ADA *sings.*

Fin.

CHARISMA FURS

KATIE SLY AND JONATHAN SEINEN

For Cathy Gordon, who gave this work a chance.
For Chris Gatchalian and his work as a diversity advocate.
For Jonathan Seinen and Kjell Cawsey, who took care of me.
For Mistress Amanda, who pulls souls out of obscurity and into themselves.
For the girls I grew up with.
For all of us who have been deeply alone.

—KS

ACKNOWLEDGEMENTS

Special thanks to Indrit Kasapi, Cole Alvis, Jordan Tannahill, William Ellis, Kjell Cawsey, Cathy Gordon, **the frank theatre company**, and Buddies in Bad Times Theatre.

A/THE QUEER REAL:
CHARISMA FURS
C.E. GATCHALIAN

On two occasions in *Charisma Furs*, co-written by Katie Sly and Jonathan Seinen, Katie directly asks the audience, "Can I be really real with you?" At first glance, the play's take on the real—or, more accurately, the queer real—is postmodern and non-totalizing. Rather than the queer real, the play gathers its energies around "a queer real"—the intensely personal, unabashedly specific real of the play's performer and co-author, Katie Sly.

These are the play's "facts." Katie—whose pronouns are they/them/theirs—is white, genderqueer, and bisexual. They like origami. Their job requires them to write computer code. Born in Montréal, now living in Toronto, they have recently ended a six-year relationship with a depressed male partner whom they financially supported. There is mention of another partner who was physically violent with them. Their childhood, mired in "white-trash" poverty, was dominated by a mentally ill mother and an abusive stepfather. While the present-day Katie (performing the play) is proudly and defiantly genderqueer, the Katie described in the play is more reticent about their identity, disliking their long hair "that waves out in the wrong places" and "the church clothes" their grandparents gave them so that "I'd have something they'd be comfortable being seen with me in." Growing up they were not athletic but had a special liking for soccer. They find solace—and transcendence—in Alice Munro and rope bondage.

This grounding into particulars is what gives *Charisma Furs* its visceral lyricism, as well as, paradoxically, its fragility and openness: by focusing on the stark specifics of Katie's life story, it effectively creates a space in which the audience can insert themselves and their own experience—their own unapologetically personal queer real. On the theoretical level, too, the play—guided in this respect by co-author Jonathan Seinen, who also directed the original production—offers a compelling paradigm for contemporary queer text-based dramatic work: fragmented and autobiographical, necessarily non-appropriative and non-colonizing.

We can trace the impetus for the play's excavations of the real to this revelatory passage two-thirds into the play:

> At the age of twelve I realized that the world my mom was describing to me was not the objective, real world. Like she would think that our local paper had coded messages to her in it, most often about how she was going to be the next prime minister . . . Which is why I am always asking very simple questions, like: Who am I? Where am I? What's real? Because I had that moment at the age of twelve of going, "Oh, oh, this person who is supposed to show me the world can't even see it." Can't see that she's not going to be the next prime minister, and can't see my stepdad for who he is.

The play contains at least four levels of reality. There is Katie before the show begins, making origami with the audience; there is Katie, mic in hand, talking directly to the audience, stand-up style; there is the audio recording of Katie's voice, elaborating on aspects of their personality at various points during the play; and there is Katie uttering staccato confessional verse, by turns pleading, whimsical, matter-of-fact, and angry. How do these four versions of Katie measure up against the Katie who's performing the play? What of the materials that are omitted from the narrative? How much of what we are being told is literally real, and how much—if any—is artistically embellished? And does it even matter? This imbrication of multiple reals—and questions about what constitutes the real—is at once destabilizing and liberating, atomizing and syncretic.

But *Charisma Furs* has the courage to question even that, and break through, at the end, the postmodern limits it has hitherto played inside. For at the core of this play is a hunger one could justifiably identify (dangerous though it might be) as "universal": a hunger for spirit, for transcendence, for the divine. (The militantly secular might prefer the term "power"—and, indeed, *Charisma Furs* has the range to explicitly bring that idea into the fold as well. In any event, this aspect of the play leans into the literal Spanish and Portuguese meaning of the word *real*: "royal.") Regardless of the term, what Katie attains, through rope bondage with a dominatrix in New York City, is the kind of *holistic* uplift virtually all of us crave. Seeing beauty in the supposedly ugly, freedom in the apparently oppressive, serene normativity in the ostensibly perverse, *Charisma Furs* shines a light on the potential of queer magic to square the circle we call truth.

Charisma Furs was initiated by Katie Sly and Jonathan Seinen during an artist residency with Toronto's lemonTree creations, which culminated in a workshop presentation in September 2014 at their 196 Spadina Avenue studio. Following this creation period, *Charisma Furs* was awarded support from the Ontario Arts Council's Theatre Creators' Reserve (TCR) program through recommender Buddies in Bad Times Theatre. In May 2015, a second round of development and presentation took place at Videofag as part of a residency. At that time, the creative team was joined by stage manager Kjell Cawsey.

The premiere of *Charisma Furs* took place during the 2015 SummerWorks Performance Festival, as part of the Live Arts Series curated by Cathy Gordon, in the upstairs Rehearsal Hall of Toronto's Factory Theatre. It featured the following cast and creative team:

Performer: Katie Sly
Director: Jonathan Seinen
Creators: Katie Sly and Jonathan Seinen
Stage Manager: Kjell Cawsey

Charisma Furs was subsequently produced at the rEvolver Festival in Vancouver, BC, in May 2016; an excerpt was presented at New York City's HOT! Festival in July 2016; the full performance was again presented in Toronto at the Storefront Theatre's Solo Sessions in December 2016; and it was produced at UNO Fest in Victoria, BC, in May 2017.

CHARACTER

Katie

NOTE

Charisma Furs is a solo performance piece, performed by Katie Sly.
All non-italicized text below is spoken by Katie. Katie's pronouns
are them/they/their.

The performance space, surrounded by audience seating, has a microphone on a stand, a circle of white vinyl on the floor, and a free-standing mirror wrapped in brown kraft paper. There are origami boxes of many different sizes and colours scattered around the room. On two separate walls are two drawings on kraft paper: on one wall is a KATIE-sized robot drawing, and on the other is a KATIE-sized squirrel drawing.

KATIE is sitting on the vinyl circle in the centre of the space as the audience arrives. They welcome audience members while making origami boxes. They invite audience members to join them and make their own boxes.

When the time is right, KATIE stands, smiles at the audience, and changes the lighting in the room.

KATIE: Thank you for being here.

Ginuwine's "Pony (Esta Remix)" starts playing.

KATIE walks past each audience member, making eye contact and flirting with them. When the chorus hits, they start dancing as if they're in a club.

After the first chorus, they grab the microphone; the music cuts out. KATIE holds the mic in a "stand-up comedian" style.

So. Does anyone actually need music made after the year 2000? Like as a child born in the late '80s, early '90s—boom! age-mystique—yeah, I only want the music I listened to when I was a little thuglet in the back of school buses. I only want "Gangsta's Paradise." I only want—

Ginuwine's "Pony (Esta Remix)" plays for a moment.

Ginuwine's "Pony." Which is why it's a Friday night and I'm getting ready to go to a party that plays *that song* every hour, on the hour. There is No No Pony.[1]

And as a child born in the late '80s, early '90s, if I'm real with you, if I'm really real with you—

KATIE *selects one audience member and really asks the question.*

Can I be really real with you?

Okay. No matter how evolved my queer politics get, I just wanna be a Fucking Hot Bitch in a hip hop video. Correspondingly, I am wearing denim short shorts my ass is just falling out of, and this grey tank top—except, "tank top" . . . Too strong a term. Like if we look it up on Aritzia's website right now it will be called a "bralet." A bralet. Like what the fuck does that mean? You know what? Who the fuck cares. Bralets for thuglets! Yes! Tell everyone!

So I'm at the party, and I see this mousy guy. Just like all the straight guys there he's wearing some element of plaid *(check-mark sound and gesture),* grey jeans *(check-mark sound and gesture),* and he's petite, handsome in a scrawny way, and he's dancing in this way that you have to admire, 'cause it's like extremely committed, but completely out to lunch—like his arm is in the air and his hips are just like a washing machine.

KATIE *moves across the room like a washing machine in its wash cycle.*

And he's moving across the dance floor like this. And I'm transfixed. And I watch him—and then I notice him notice me noticing him . . . and the washing machine changes directions—like those behaviour studies that tell you that someone is interested in you if their feet are facing you; his whole tripod is facing me, one foot, two feet—

KATIE *dangles the mic between their legs to punctuate the point.*

But he's a demure skinny little white guy so he's not going to make a move.

So I do.

I move up him, put my arm around him, ask, "Is this okay?" You know, consent politics.
He says, "Yeah!"
And then my request starts playing.

---

1   No No Pony is a long-standing dance party, which takes place in the basement of Parts & Labour in Toronto. This party is a reoccurring fundraiser for the Toronto-based theatre company Nobody's Business. Despite the fact that No No Pony's decor is littered with unicorns and that one-half of Nobody's Business founders is the talented and very out Johnnie Walker, No No Pony has become known as a straight hook-up party.

Next's "Too Close" starts playing. KATIE *dances for a bit.*

And then out of nowhere, this scrawny little white guy is making out with me—like holy shit, he has got it going on. Kind of. It's like a Muppet eating a cookie, you know?

KATIE gobbles the microphone like Cookie Monster eats a cookie.

This is a weird make-out technique! Okay! But then—then he moves that technique to my neck. And oh yeah *(shudders deliciously),* yeah that technique works there.

So I say, "What's your name?"
"Josh. What's your name?"
"Katie."
"Cool. Cool. Cool. Let's go to the bathroom."

Music pauses.

Now I'm a pretty open-minded person. I go to sex clubs. I've had sex with strangers in sex clubs while strangers are making out with strangers to the sex I'm having with strangers in sex clubs so it's *strange* . . . that I'm taken aback. But even in a sex club, I will talk to a person for about half an hour before I have sex with them. That conversation will not be yelled over beats so it will be an actual conversation. And possibly most importantly, I will have seen their naked body, so not only will I have a vibe on who they are as a human being, but I will have seen the goods I am about to interact with, you know what I'm saying?

KATIE eyes an audience member's member for a moment.

This guy, this guy at this sweaty basement dance party, I've got nothing on this guy.

Music plays again.

But I am pretty into his Brut, or Axe, or whatever he's wearing, so I tell him, "The problem with the bathroom is that's a short shitty fuck, and I'm the kinda person you fuck for hours."
"So we should get outta here."
"You have a place?"
"Kind of."

What the fuck does that mean?

"It's far."
"How far?"
"Far."

"How far?"

"Far."

"How far?"

"North York."

Pause.

Now North York from downtown Toronto . . . that's a long-ass subway ride with someone I've never really talked to. Like what are we gonna talk about as we pass through Summerhill Station? Maybe, maybe we'll discover we both love *Buffy the Vampire Slayer*, but more likely we will be talking about the weather.

So I put my hands on his chest, look up at him, and I say, "Buddy, that's way too far!"

And we dance for a few more minutes. And I say, "There's nothing more you really wanna know about me, is there?"

KATIE moves to the microphone stand and replaces the mic.

They go up to the free-standing mirror wrapped in kraft paper and trace their own body on the paper. While they do this, we hear the following recording of KATIE's *voice:*

"When someone disappoints me, or betrays me, or disrespects me, disrespects me especially, my body alights with this buzz, this hum, this electricity, like a neon tube, and I'm hot, and I know this can't stand, and I decide to destroy the relationship, because there's nothing else I can really attack, and once I destroy it, I feel an immense sense of satisfaction and wellness."

KATIE sits on the floor and makes an origami box.

Computers were created to do things people no longer want to do.
And the job of a developer is to tell machines what to do, in terms the machines can understand.
I write computer code.
It's really comforting.
Either you get the machine to do what you want it to, or you don't.
There's little subjectivity.
It's success or failure.
A binary value.
A zero or a one.
Either the companion robot winks at you when you want it to, or it doesn't.

KATIE eyes the robot drawing on the wall.

And I'm not near building a companion robot.

Not yet.

    KATIE continues origami box-making.

But, as infinitely complex as computer processes are, they are also infinitely simple, because machines actually only speak one language.

And there are small machines, within the big machines, that understand the coded languages developers write and translate the coded languages into the one universal language that all machines can actually understand, and actually do something with.

Zeros and ones.

So everything is a process. A process of translation. A process of synthesization. A process of transformation.

    They finish the box and hand it to someone in the audience.

I'm never not writing code.

    Sigur Ros's "untitled #1" starts playing. KATIE *goes to the kraft paper where they have traced their body, and they rip a hole at the drawing's head, revealing a mirror underneath.* KATIE *continues to rip the head out of the drawing, and they talk to their reflection.*

I want you
You who ripped out my heart
I want you
You who tied my shoelaces
I want you
You who left me for the girl with cocaine
I want you
You who I thought would cradle our child
I want you
You who I cannot forgive
You who it would be stupid to forgive
You who made me feel like I'd found home
You whose cunt I invited to ride my face
You whose come I gulped down like light beer
You who was afraid to dance in public
You who stole a shopping cart and then dumped it in the St. Lawrence River
You who told me I was the most beautiful thing in the world
You who said my laugh was a creek gurgling joy

You who was rude to my friends

You who embarrassed me in front of my friends

You who embarrassed me on the street

You whose fingers always smelled like fried chicken

You who will never take off your corded camp bracelets

You who glowed like a neon marquee

You who called me a dirty slut during role-play

You who I cried into in the bathtub

You who made me feel like there's a reason I exist

You who was a benevolent mirror

You who made me hate my body without you

You who tried to make yourself sound cooler than me

You who gave me a birthday card with a gender-neutral robot on it

You who my rib cage screams for

I want you

You who I'll never see again

You who I cannot trust

> *Fade out on Sigur Ros's "untitled #1."* KATIE *moves to the kraft paper drawing of a squirrel. While they interact with the drawings on the wall, we hear the following recording of* KATIE:

"*I envy animals really deeply. Every time I see a squirrel jump from one branch to another branch, I'm like, damn it! Why? Why not me? Jesus, what the hell were you thinking? Okay, so, squirrels, jumping, animals.*"

> KATIE *purrs at the squirrel drawing, then sits on a chair in the audience.*

I spent a lot of my childhood in an area of Montréal called Verdun. If you were Francophone, it was mostly working class. If you were Anglophone, it was mostly—what do I call it? Like low class? Welfare class? Like, I was on welfare, every other kid that I knew was on welfare, like maybe one or two kids had parents who had a job, but not really.

And everyone was on the hustle.

And people would own things, like cars, but those cars would have to be in someone else's name, because you couldn't own assets worth over $1000 and be on social assistance. Which is why I don't take people's words very seriously. Why I try looking at their actions instead, because I grew up knowing what people say, and who people say things belong to, is bullshit. The only thing you really have is what you can put your hands on in five minutes, what you can do with your hands in a fight, and the things inside yourself that you don't let anyone touch.

In Montréal there's no middle school, so you go directly from elementary school to high school, so at the age of twelve and thirteen you're suddenly hanging out with sixteen-, seventeen-, eighteen-year-olds, obviously their lives are in a pretty different place, so I remember at the ages of twelve and thirteen the girls that I had grown up with started having sex with these sixteen-, seventeen-, eighteen-year-old guys. And they weren't having sex because they were ready for it, and they weren't having sex to understand their bodies, and they weren't having sex for pleasure. They were having sex to connect with power. They were having sex to connect to the people in our world who had some power.

My mom didn't really let me have a life outside of school, so I didn't go around having sex at the age of twelve and thirteen and fourteen. But my friends did.

My friend Allison is having sex with this seventeen-year-old guy named Curtis. And then Curtis breaks up with her, and that's when Allison starts cutting. At first it's small lines on the inside of her arm. And then it's larger lines on her upper thigh. And then at Allison's house one day on our lunch break, Meaghan's with us, we're in Allison's living room, and so calmly Allison picks up an X-Acto knife, slips it open, and starts writing in her arm "Andrew," like it's nothing. Andrew is some new boy in our school who maybe has a crush on Allison maybe, and Allison's not into him, the whole point of writing "Andrew" in her arm is to make Curtis jealous so he'll want her again.

I sit in the living room, not understanding when this became the world I live in. Not understanding how Meaghan is sitting there watching this so calmly. I sit there for a moment, and then I jump up, and I'm down the hall, out the door, out on the street. And no one's coming out after me, no one's saying,

"This is fucked up.
We should get help."

I'm just a girl standing on the street, looking at an open door.

KATIE sits on the circle of white vinyl, a fabric spotlight, on the floor. They build a box city out of origami boxes atop the circle.

We hear the following recording of KATIE while they build:

"There is a little girl who lives in an apartment in my head, and I look after her. The windows of the apartment are my eyes, so she sees what I see, and I keep her safe. So when someone looks at me funny on the street, I send her Schnauzer puppies, because she loves Schnauzer puppies. And when another girl calls me ugly, I hold up a mirror so she can see how pretty she really is. And when my lover hits me, I give her a hug, because she needs a lot of kindness.

But then I get mad.

Why should she get to be safe while I bear the world's bullshit? Why should she get to be whole while I crumble around her?

So I evict the little girl from the apartment in my head, I throw her and her tiny possessions out to the curb, and she doesn't fare well without me. I pass her on the street one night, begging for change. No one notices her because she's so small, but I see her right away.

And I feel bad, so I give her some change,
but then I take it back.

Because while I love her, I hate her, too. As I love and hate myself."

> *Owen Pallett's "I Am Not Afraid" starts playing.* KATIE *begins a series of repetitive gestures, slowly moving across the performance space. Then they turn around and, rooted in place, reach desperately to something always out of reach. This takes the length of the song.*

> *When the song ends* KATIE *gets their green jacket from behind the mirror and puts it on.*

I live just east of the Village
But I tell everyone I live in the Village
When I found the apartment I sold my male partner on it based on low rent and proximity to Ryerson

> KATIE *crouches next to the box city they've built and points to two different buildings in it: their apartment and Ryerson University, respectively.*

"If we're really low on money I can walk to school if I need to."

> KATIE *stands and walks around the box city.*

I really love living near the Village
And I tell everyone we live *in* the Village
Because I want to be close to that part of myself
And I think that if I'm surrounded by it, somehow it will seep into me, and my body will be flush and full and bright green with wholeness of it
And people will see me,
Hear where I live
And recognize my vibrance

But we live east of the Village
And he doesn't go out much
And he doesn't have a job

And then he doesn't go out at all without me
He knows everyone is looking at him on the bus
Seeing how ugly he is
How he sweats
How his hair is receding
I try to fill him up
To make him flush and full and bright green
Because I know
He isn't ugly
So I work
And he doesn't
And he resolves that if he was just in better shape that he'd feel better
So he gives me a list of workout gear and protein powder and nutritional supplements
And I buy them
Plant care

The sink is full of dishes
He says he's been busy burning his workout DVDs
All day
So I go to the Food Basics that's forty-five seconds from our front door to get
something that exists in its own receptacle and can be microwaved

I watch my reflection walk down the freezer aisle
And I don't like my long hair that waves out in the wrong places
I don't like the church clothes I'm wearing
Church clothes given to me by my grandparents so that *I'd* have something
they'd be comfortable being seen with me in
That kind of gift
But these church clothes are the only thing I have that's work appropriate
To the work I've left Ryerson to do
So that I can look after him
So that he can get better

In the check-out line
I see my stepfather's face
In the face of a stranger
And I am frozen with my frozen food

I take the microwave butter chicken home
We eat
He's horny
He reminds me we haven't had sex in three days

He says I'm not attracted to him anymore
I'm just like the people on the bus
I think he's ugly
If I were attracted to him I'd want to have sex with him
If I weren't bisexual, I'd want to have sex with him
So I make my body a receptacle
A nutrition supplement
I look up at the ceiling and wonder where I've gone

I'm slamming cupboards
I'm mad
I'm mad and he knows it
My birthday's coming,
"And you're not going to do anything, are you? Are you?"
"You want to see how much I love you, Katie? You wanna see? You wanna see?"

He pulls a book off the top shelf in the cupboard
Purchased with the last of buffer on his credit card
It's a collection of short stories by Alice Munro
Alice Munro, who I adore
The collection is called *Too Much Happiness*
I take the book with me to work in my backpack
The first story is about a woman recovering from losing everything

> KATIE *unzips the jacket and drops it on the floor. They sit on the floor and write on a Bristol board in black marker "*I AM READY.*" While they do this, we hear the following recording of* KATIE:

"*Like everyone's typical idea of wellness, and the fact that if there's something bothering you then that's something to like overcome, like . . . I don't think that you necessarily overcome everything . . . umm . . . or that you're capable of it.*

But . . . I also don't know what I would be without rage. And so, I'm perhaps very, very afraid to overcome . . . that, and actually feel peaceful, because I don't have any idea who I would be, like on a prag—like I don't even mean on like a meta-physical level, I mean like on a pragmatic level I'm like I don't know if I would make art.

I don't know if suddenly without that rage, going to my job, and filing those memos and all of that would be satisfactory, because then I'd go, and I'd buy the food I want, and I'd have like a lover, and we'd have a cat, and like, and that life that I witness around me all the time, like . . . that, that shit.

I look at my co-workers, they aren't exhausted all the time, they aren't fucking up at work because they're pushing themselves in other arenas, they aren't . . . there's nothing to hide.

Like they seem pretty fucking happy.

But like I can't bring myself to think that that's the goal. Because it's too banal. And it's too ordinary.

So maybe my goal isn't healing but my goal is to be extraordinary. In whatever means like is possible.

Which is why I want the whole world of people to be proud of me. 'Cause then I'll know I'm extraordinary."

> *A karaoke track of En Vogue's "Don't Let Go" begins to play.* KATIE *moves to the mic and grooves, then sings the first verse and chorus, about having the right to lose control.*

> *As the instrumental track fades, they grab the mic, again "stand-up comedian" style.*

So! Elementary school!

The boys in my school played soccer, and/or soccer baseball, and/or this game where they would take a weighted piece of fabric, hang that piece of fabric over a bar, and hit it over and over and over and over and over and *(hitting motion)*— I did not understand this game.

So the boys in my school did that, and girls in my school read teeny-bopper magazines and crushed on Jonathan Taylor Thomas, a.k.a. JTT from *Home Improvement.* Do you remember that? Do you remember when that was a big deal?

> KATIE *imitates an excerpt from the instrumental intro to* Home Improvement.

And the girls would trade the stickers that came in the Spice Girls bubblegum that we got at the dépanneur, and oh oh oh! We would get into these epic arguments over which one of us got to pretend to be Baby Spice in that day's schoolyard rendition of—

> KATIE *sings the first line of the chorus to "Stop" by the Spice Girls.*

So, occasionally, I was satisfied with these girl activities, but mostly I just wanted to play soccer. But like, can I be real with you?

> KATIE *addresses an audience member.*

Can I be really real with you?

I did not want to play soccer because I was some kind of tomboy. Like look at me, I'm dandy as fuck. I wanted to play soccer so that I'd have a valid cover for kicking people. I just really wanna kick people.

So in the reality of the fact that I was the only girl playing soccer, and in the far larger reality of the fact that I cannot play sports *at all*, there was no way I was not gonna be picked last.

And the kid who was always picked second to last was:

David Gaugin.

David was the only kid in school that like even *I* picked on—like his head was this giant balloon that was attached to the ribbons that were the rest of his body. And he had a very evident birthmark on his temple, and it was big, and red, so it wasn't really a birthmark at all, like it was just a bull's eye, you know? Like it was a bull's eye.

   KATIE hits their temple with the mic, like an arrow.

Bull's eye.

It was always me and David Gaugin waiting to find out what team we were on, de facto. Because of this we should have been allies, but oh no, we were enemies.

So the two team captains were named. One of them was always this big kid named Shawn O'Leary who had an inexplicably shaved head. Like it's a really aggressive thing, when a kid has a shaved head, like what does that mean—is he doing hard time after school?

So he was one captain, and the other team captain was always Jeff Bourgaise, and Jeff had pale, pale, porcelain skin, jet black dark hair, piercing blue eyes, and he was good at every sport, and I remember he had a toy Zamboni in his desk, and one day when he went away he gave it to me to babysit, and I was like, *(grinding against the mic stand)* "Oh my god, Jeff Bourgaise's Zamboni!"

So the picking goes as usual—a.k.a. I'm chosen last, but that's okay, 'cause I'm on Jeff Bourgaise's team—and we're playing, and then someone fouls me. And Jeff Bourgaise is screaming, "Foul! Foul!" And I'm like, Jeff, really, it's okay, I've been kicking people's ankles for like fifteen minutes, we can let this one go. But Jeff's insisting, "Foul! Foul!"

And he's insisting I take a penalty kick.

And the person facing me in the net is:
Birthmark bull's eye.

   KATIE whacks their temple with the mic again.

David Gaugin.

Jeff is setting up the kick, he's counting out the distance, toe-to-toe, one foot, two feet, three feet, he's serious with this shit, the category is Schoolyard Realness. Jeff sets down the ball, gives me a wink— Now, lover-boy, really? Now is when you choose to wink at me, now when I'm *already* about to have a heart attack? Okay, okay, okay. Fuck you! Fuck you and your perfect porcelain-ness!

I don't know what I intend, I don't even know what happens next—my soul decides to vacate my body for this situation. But I'm informed after the fact: I walked up to that ball with purpose, I took a kick, and I nailed that sucker into David Gaugin's net.

The intro to Mase's "Feel So Good" plays.

Oh, eat it, Gaugin! Eat it!

KATIE victory-shrieks. The song cuts out.

So the next day, lined up again waiting to be chosen, and . . .
I'm chosen ahead of David Gaugin.

Which is how I was upgraded from girl
To Worst Boy.

"Feel So Good" comes back on. KATIE dances and throws a kiss up to Jesus.

As the song begins a slow fade out, KATIE sits on the floor, slides open an X-Acto knife, and begins to carve out the "I AM READY" text from the Bristol board.

At the age of twelve I realized that the world my mom was describing to me was not the objective, real world. Like she would think that our local paper had coded messages to her in it, most often about how she was going to be the next prime minister. And she would write her responses to these coded messages on big pieces of Bristol board and tape them up, facing out, in our windows, in order to communicate with this vast power that not only believed in her, but *wanted* her. Which is why I am always asking very simple questions, like: Who am I? Where am I? What's real? Because I had that moment at the age of twelve of going, "Oh, oh, this person who is supposed to show me the world can't even see it." Can't see that she's not going to be the next prime minister, and can't see my stepdad for who he is.

My mom was always unemployed, and always devising these non-lucrative entrepreneurial ventures, like selling hand-decorated candles door to door or making jewellery, and I remember when my mom decided jewellery-making was *the answer*, she had me make hundreds of tiny boxes.

The area we lived in, in Montréal, it's this city of triplexes with balconies facing out onto the street, and my mom would sit out on our balcony, smoking. And then she noticed that there was this woman who lived across the street from us, who had all of these magnificent tattoos. And my mom would just watch her.

And then my mom wrote a song about all the things she'd been noticing about Tattoo. And she and my stepdad recorded the song. And when my mom decided she was going to meet Tattoo, she took me along, and I actually really liked when my mom took me along on these absurd adventures, because at least then I felt close to her.

So we go across the street and introduce ourselves to Tattoo, this woman who does not know that she's been observed, and Tattoo is actually a pretty good sport about it. She invites us into her home, introduces us to her three kids: Casper, Wednesday, and Freddie. And while these kids are named after scary movie characters, it's my stepdad who is the real face of horror. He's the real face of horror. And I need my mom to see that.

But instead, we sit at Tattoo's kitchen table and my mom plays this song, full of the details she's noticed about a stranger.

A recording of KATIE *singing "Tattoo" plays:*

Tattoo
Painted
Tattoo
Painted

No curtain
Just the flag
Drawn across her window
She's a patriot
With a monthly cheque
Living as high as she can
On the top floor
Inside the Union Jack
But it's far away
Oh, so far

Tattoo
Painted
Tattoo
Painted

She runs
Into the middle of the street
Stands there
Then she burns
The gasoline
Off the road
There's an engine
And it's running
Through her mind
Running through

Tattoo
Painted
Tattoo
Painted

> *While "Tattoo" plays,* KATIE *tapes up the cut-out "*I AM READY*" sign in the window, facing out.* KATIE *looks out the window, searching.*

> *When the recording ends* KATIE *moves around the outer perimeter of the audience seating.*

I'm at the Garrison, for a Mayworks poetry reading. No more than twenty others in attendance.

The MC, Tatianna, this small, slight, Black woman, takes the stage. She's wearing this yellow sundress in that way only Black women can wear yellow and have it be like—blam!

Tatianna, she's no bigger than me, but she has such . . . presence. Such fierceness. Such I-am-here-and-I-am-immovable-and-you-will-listen-to-me! And at some point it becomes apparent that she's gay, and she welcomes another woman to the stage, and they're also gay, and suddenly I realize I've never seen so many Black lesbians in one place in my life.

And Tatianna—there's nothing about her that's embarrassed, or apologetic. Poems about licking her wife's clit, poems about raising their son—I sit there, in dew, because powerful woman after powerful woman takes the stage and makes me feel like—yes. I can be someone other than the person I've been.

Weeks earlier I broke up with the man I'd been with for six years and lived with for four. I was pretty sure that if he called me a cunt again I'd kill him. Having been with him . . . basically my whole adult life . . . I'm terrified. But hearing these poets talk about being called cunts themselves, hearing their love and, more importantly, their respect for their partners . . . I don't want to go back to what I had.

I may be welfare white trash but it is hip hop, and spoken word, and Black women who feel like home and show me what's possible.

I loiter on the edge of a crowd after the show, waiting to talk to Tatianna, not knowing what I'm going to say but knowing I need to say something. I feel creepy, standing on the periphery of people she knows for *so long*, catching her eye every now and then.

Finally I get to her. I'm shaking. I say,

KATIE takes a step forward.

"Excuse me."

They take another step forward into the middle of the white vinyl spotlight.

"I'm sorry, I realize you're talking to your wife and I'm interrupting, and I don't meet people well, but—thank you. You give me courage."

KATIE steps forward again, then turns around.

(as Tatianna) "I saw you standing over there. Now you're here talking to me. I think you have your own courage."

And years of pain leap out of me, and Tatianna's holding me, and Tatianna's wife is holding me, and—

I walk out into the night on Dundas.

LCD Soundsystem's "All My Friends" instrumental plays as KATIE takes off their clothes. As they remove each item, they move around the room, making eye contact with an audience member per item of clothing, handing off the clothing to that audience member and then moving on to someone else.

KATIE, naked and fearless, walks by and looks each audience member in the eye, then goes to the microphone and strikes a series of rope-bondage poses, using the mic cord as rope with which to tie their body. While in a physically straining pose:

A festival of disassembly
"Can you photograph it?"
Rope burn
"Photograph it!"
Popped blood vessels concealed under hems at work
"Can you photograph it?"

Bruises are gifts and every session is Christmas
Muscles recover
Skin heals
Alchemy atrophies
And we need evidence
We need something to tide us over
Till the next holiday

> *While the song continues and increases in volume,* KATIE *runs to and tears apart the kraft paper drawings of the squirrel and robot, then rips off all the kraft paper on the free-standing mirror. As the music continues,* KATIE *yells over the volume at their reflection.*

I want a handsome doctor to say they're proud of me
I want a crazy bag lady to say they're proud of me
I want an oldest friend to say they're proud of me
I want a passport agent to say they're proud of me
I want a mother to say they're proud of me
I want a high school English teacher to say they're proud of me
I want a toddler set of twins to say they're proud of me
I want a Nubian princess barista to say they're proud of me
I want a foreign aid worker to say they're proud of me
I want a streetcar operator to say they're proud of me
I want the therapist I stopped seeing to say they're proud of me
I want a brother to say they're proud of me
I want a lover to say they're proud of me
I want a mother to say they're proud of me
I want all lovers to say they're proud of me
I want all artistic directors to say they're proud of me
I want a father to say they're proud of me
I want a voice teacher to say they're proud of me
I want a bondage specialist to say they're proud of me
I want the boy who crushed me into a fence and kneed me in the crotch in the schoolyard to say they're proud of me
I want Alice Munro to say they're proud of me
I want people who haven't been born yet to say they're proud of me
I want the people who have given up on their dreams to say they're proud of me
I want the people who have disintegrated to dust to say they're proud of me
I want my soulmate to say they're proud of me
I want the someday person I grow in my belly to say they're proud of me

I want you
I want you
I want you to say you're proud of me
You who I cannot trust

> *The music ends.* KATIE *yanks the vinyl spotlight out from under the city of boxes, which sends them flying, and wraps their naked body in it. The room is now a mess of microphone cable, ripped kraft paper, and scattered origami boxes.*

> *The lights in the room come down.* KATIE *sits on the floor, in the last remaining amount of light, leaning against the free-standing mirror.*

It's two o'clock in the morning, and I'm alone. And I've got this pocket map and this tiny, scrawled note that says West 30th Street, fifth floor, and with my pocket map and my scrawled note I get there. A really run-down lobby of an office building. As I'm waiting for the elevator, this really loud, bleach blond white woman, kind of sleaze, kind of scraggly, like I'm sure that when I'm thirty-five I'll look exactly like her 'cause I dye my hair all the time, she comes in with this guy, and they're being loud and really obnoxious, and they're like, "Is this the place? I don't think this is the place, is this, I don't know, is this the place?" And then she looks at me and says, "Are you going to a kinky thing?"

"Yep."

We get in the elevator, go up to the fifth floor. The elevator opens into what, at best, is a glorified walk-in closet, with like flower wallpaper, and this Black woman is standing there, next to a little table, and she's wearing full sweats and a toque, and the whole image is so strange that we just stand there. So the toque lady says, "Get off the elevator." So we get off the elevator. The bleach blond lady asks, "Is this a private party?" Toque lady says, "Yeah." Bleach blond lady asks, "So what does that mean, like are there rules, like what can happen, can like actual sex happen?" The toque lady looks at her and says, "Do what you want."

And we go in. The door opens into a dungeon. Into a dungeon on the fifth floor of an office building in the fashion district of New York City. And I am so far from anything I know it's not even funny.

And the first person I see, when I get in, is Amanda. She's the first person that my eyes meet. And I'm confused, and scared, and . . . she has the warmest smile I've ever seen, it just, it's like, it's like, sunshine, like our eyes meet and her face breaks into this grin and I'm just like:

Okay.

All right.

And I ask her, "Where can I drop my stuff, what do I do, can I get changed, I don't know like, what's happening, what do I, what do I do?" And she's like, "There's a bathroom, there's where coat check is, next to the whips and the other things, and uh, yeah, you know, you just walk around, do what you do." So I get changed. I put on so much antiperspirant. I check my bag, next to the whips and everything, and I realize I don't have any pockets and I'm not wearing a bra so I spend the entire night with my coat ticket clutched in my fist.

And I walk into a room and there's a man, I guess standing? But tied up like an "x," like his hands and feet are bound and there are two women working on him, and he's . . . being electrocuted.

And I sit down, 'cause I think I should sit down to watch this. Sitting across the room from me, watching it, is Amanda.

She comes over . . . I'm so taken by her . . . and I have a hard time talking to strangers at all, but at least I have *something* to talk about so I say, "I've never seen anything like this before." And she says, "I've never been to a party." And I'm like, "Really?" 'Cause she's dressed like she's been to a party before: black, leather boots with, you know, six-inch stiletto heels, a black thong, with mesh black booty shorts over it, but the mesh is fishnet so they're not really shorts at all. Anyone that tells you that classy is good is stupid—those mesh shorts were everything. Amanda says, "I've never been to a party because I don't normally stay after work."

"Oh, do you work here?"
"Yes, I've been a dominatrix here for the past three years."
"Do you like your work?"
"I love it."

She says, "I love it" in this way that makes me think of a gazelle. Like there are so many people around and there's so much happening and there's so much chatter, but she's wholly focused, like a gazelle in the middle of a meadow.

"I love it."

And then she tells me that she's never had her own slave, and she's looking for one, and I say, "Oh, okay, outside of the client thing, I guess, right?" And she's like, "Exactly."

And then she asks me if I sub or dom, and I say, "I have no idea."

So we're quiet for a bit, the electrocution's happening, Amanda says she's going to walk around for a while, she leaves, and . . . I'm an introvert, so it takes me time to put things together, but I start putting together: "I'm looking for my own slave," and, "Do you sub or dom?"

And I'm realizing that she's like, leagues, leagues, okay, it's not a real thing, people love who they love, but she's— I described the mesh shorts, I should also say that she's six feet tall and Dominican and . . . so much woman, like so much more woman than me. Next to her I'm a twelve-year-old boy picking my nose and throwing wads of paper at her and then running away laughing, that's how much woman she is compared to me.

Amanda comes back, and I tell her, "I've never done anything like this and I don't know how to do anything like this because I don't know if you ask for things and if you ask for things then I don't know what I'd ask for." And this is me going for it, as much as I'm capable of. Amanda says,

"Well, for a complete novice, I might do some spanking. Some scratching. Some hair pulling. There's a strap I like to use."

And I'm about to ask her if she'll do those things to me, but I don't have to because she looks at me, smiles *that smile*, and says,

"You wanna try?"

And in my head I scream YES! But out loud I say,

"I think I'd like that."

Amanda says, "Okay, I have to find somewhere to put you," and she's off, and I'm walking after her, and I'm following her through the party and I'm looking around at everyone, like, *everyone*, being like, "Do you see what's happening?! I'm following her, *her*, she's looking for a place to put *me*, this is happening!"

I ask her,
"How do I make it stop if I need to, is there a safe word, do we need one?"
Amanda says,
"If you want one. Or you can just say stop. I'll listen to you."
I ask her if I get to control who touches me.
Amanda says,
"Of course. But I think this is about you and me."

So I'm lying on my stomach. Amanda asks if she can pull my dress over my hips, I say, "Yes." She says, "Nice ass." Then she says, "Nice tan lines." And the first time she hits me I'm not ready for it and I'm really glad I'm not ready for it.

And she asks me if I'll kneel on this pommel horse thing, and I do, and people start to come in 'cause they see what's happening, and Amanda asks if she can lift my dress off, completely off. I say yes, she does, and I'm there in this ridiculously tiny black thong and my hair is a mess and I'm all self-conscious and I'm naked in front of a room full of strangers and I start fussing my hair and . . . and with that same—"I love it"—intensity, Amanda stands above me, takes my head in her hands, smooths my hair, and for a moment I'm five, and I'm looking up at someone who is going to take care of me and I know that everything is going to be all right. For that moment, *the rest of my life* was going to be totally fine, because it was in someone else's hands, and they were big, and they were strong, and they cared about me.

So I lean down into the pommel horse.

Amanda has long red manicured fingernails and she scratches me. She spanks me. She gets a strap and she straps me, and the next day I find that the corners of the strap leave tiny, tiny red marks, like bee stings.

And it's wonderful.

And she lays her whole body on top of mine and whispers in my ear, "Your ass belongs to me."

And I say, "Yes." And she says, "Yes, Mistress Amanda." And I say, "Yes, Mistress Amanda." And it's so fucking good to just be there. Like an animal. Not planning, not judging, not criticizing, just feeling.

I'm tied up for the first time. I see her smile again later when I'm tied, my arms above my head, and Amanda's thrashing me, and I'm wild, and *screaming*, and I can let that scream out, and I can let that *wild* out, because I'm tied up so I'm not going to hurt anybody, so I can *just fucking be* in this *intense fucking moment*, and I'm so fucking wild I bite my own shoulder, and I see her face next to my shoulder smiling that smile like, "Yes, Yes, YES! Just Be this Thing!"

Beat.

Afterwards, I lie on a torture bed, and look up at my reflection in a mirror on the ceiling. And the part of my mind that constructs narratives asks, "How does this connect to everything else that has ever happened in your life?" And another, more honest part of me answers, "Fuck connection."

A year later in Toronto, I sit in the basement of 196 Spadina Avenue with a dear friend, and I tell him stories. If you look up 196 Spadina Avenue on Google Street View, you'll see a shop called Charisma Furs.

Ginuwine's "Pony (Esta Remix)" fades in again, mounts, then fades out.

Thank you for being here.

The end.

GHOST LIGHT

SHAWN WRIGHT

For Regina, my mother.

ACKNOWLEDGEMENTS

Without the vision and gentle encouragement of my director and dramaturg, Thomas Morgan Jones, the events of this play would still be scattered
on random pieces of paper throughout my home or, worse still, locked in the
airless recesses of childhood memory. I am indebted to my sweet siblings,
in-laws, nieces, and nephews, whose support of me and this play is given so
freely and with such joy. I would be remiss not to mention that even though
this story revolves around my mother, I am so very proud to be the son of
Freelon Almroth Wright. I would also like to thank Tania Breen, Alison
Wearing, Matt Murray, David Hayes, and Christy Hughes. In very different
ways they have given me the courage to tell my story and, in doing so, have
helped me to live my life without shame.

REGINA'S PROFESSIONAL DEBUT

THOMAS MORGAN JONES

With *Ghost Light*, Shawn Wright wanted to give his mother, Regina, her professional theatre debut. He did that, and what's more, he did it in her home province of New Brunswick. First in the city of Fredericton, and then in Saint John, where she was born and where she now rests. His love, his courage, his artistry, and his vulnerability allowed for a dramaturgical, rehearsal, and production journey unlike anything I have ever experienced, and at the heart of it all was family and community. This play is an act of love.

It's also funny as hell. Theatre New Brunswick first met the piece because of the meeting of two old friends in Toronto: Shawn and Tania Breen, the director of TNB's Theatre School. They spoke about how Shawn had documented exchanges between himself and Regina during her stay at a nursing home while they watched *Murder, She Wrote*. During the show, the rule was that Shawn was to remain silent, and then during commercials he and his mother could talk about anything under the sun. Often, the episodes were re-runs, and Shawn would take to Facebook to share some of his mother's outrageously hilarious insights and perspectives. These Facebook posts soon had a following, and everyone under the sun encouraged Shawn to write a play or a book. As he wrote to me in his first introductory email, "These conversations were keeping us both alive on some level as she fought for her life and I fought with my grief. Vibrant stories in a sterile setting." And so, he took a writing course and started to try his hand at drafting something. He also received an Ontario Arts Council Theatre Creators' Reserve grant supported by Talk is Free Theatre to play with some theatrical form. He shared some of this writing with Tania in Toronto, and I will be forever grateful that her response was, "You should meet Thom."

And so we met. We talked for hours as he shared stories and some of the writing in progress, and I gave him some assignments and deadlines. What happened next is something I never could have expected. Shawn delivered a draft. And it was astonishing. When I sat down to read it, suddenly all of the power in the theatre turned off. I read in silence for ninety minutes. I laughed out loud, I marvelled at the breadth of the story, and during a final scene at the funeral parlour I paused to weep. When I set the script down, the power turned back on. This was the first of many, many, many visitations that we all believe Regina made on the process.

Not long after, Shawn and I met in person in Fredericton. We spoke about the draft. We spoke about where it would go. Shawn admitted he thought it could be a solo piece, but was concerned that was too narcissistic. I told him it wasn't. We came up with a new deadline. And then, because theatre is about leaps of faith, I asked him if he would honour us with premiering the play—the next season. And we jumped together.

The rehearsal process was deeply personal. One-person performance has particular demands on the performer, and in this case, on the writer as well. Shawn moved material, re-wrote, and would often break from rehearsing to share more stories of his family and his time with Regina. In many ways, the process became about family and community. At the first read, one of Shawn's first theatre mentors, Ilkay Silk, was present for the reading. He stayed with his sister while he was in Fredericton. All of us at the theatre came to know his family's stories and history throughout the process. When the staff was welcomed to an early run, Matt Carter, our director of communications and development (who is from New Brunswick) shared, "I know all of those places. I've been to that funeral parlour. This could have been my story or my family's story." And then our lighting designer Leigh Ann Vardy arrived, and more stories were shared. And then Alisa Palmer was coming through town and watched the first full run with all of the changes to the writing. And more stories, and more crying, and more gut-busting laughter.

And then we opened to an almost sold-out run in our intimate Open Space Theatre. At the top of the show, Shawn walks on stage with the house lights still on and lights a candle. A ghost light. And then he starts talking. And then he keeps talking to us, with us, for us, until he strolls off stage at the end. The next stop for Shawn after the curtain call was always the lobby, where he would greet every audience member as they left the theatre as though in a receiving line. The gathering of community in the lobby would last between thirty minutes and an hour as each audience member shared with Shawn stories of their own families, or memories of having seen his mother on stage or having been in a show with her. All of them were moved and inspired to have seen a New Brunswicker's story on stage—someone who knew this place and spoke to an experience they recognized. Many audience members also shared their own stories of coming out to their families with Shawn, myself, and also with Susan Ready, our general manager. Each performance was a community event and an event that built community. All this because of Regina, and because of Shawn.

At the top of the second week of performance, we (Shawn, Susan, myself, and stage manager Tammy Faulkner) toured the show to Saint John for two performances. Before each performance, Shawn was able to visit his mother at the cemetery, walk the streets named in the show, and breathe the same air as the story. I remember during the first evening, when describing the sea out the window of the funeral parlour, Shawn paused, and church bells from the church on the hill rang out and reverberated through the walls. Regina was there again (and this is not to mention all the times a candle would snuff out in rehearsal when Shawn would speak to his mother). As in Fredericton, Shawn greeted every member of the Saint John audience, tirelessly listening to their stories after ninety minutes of solo performance, thanking them, and hugging them. Always with a smile.

Many of Shawn's family members from New Brunswick and beyond travelled to the shows. They shared that the performances made them feel that Regina was alive again and in the room with them. They described their surprise at new angles to known family history, and their surprise at history about which they had no idea. One sibling shared with me, "I've always known Shawn was gay, but when he said, 'I'm gay' in the show, it was the first time I'd heard him say it."

All of us at Theatre New Brunswick were heartbroken to see the run end, when to our surprise, Shawn shared that he had been invited for a three-show run at the Storefront Theatre in Toronto. These three shows sold out so quickly that another show was added. And then another. And another. The production played eight times in total. As in New Brunswick, Shawn stayed to greet every audience member. Only this time, the audience was not from New Brunswick. Still, the universal humanity, the intense vulnerability, the specificity, and the goodwill of Shawn's story struck a chord in everyone. It's a story that is, like the process, deeply personal, and because of that we were all able to see ourselves, and our own families, through Shawn's experience.

I share this brief history because I feel that the story of how this project came to be—and how Shawn offered it to the world—is also the point of the play. Family. Community. A life in the theatre. The courage to honour the past, to honestly face the present, and to move courageously into the future carrying with a glad heart the weight, responsibility, lessons, and inspiration of the past.

Working on this production was one of the most humbling and inspiring artistic experiences I have ever had. And like every audience member who shared in Shawn's special story, I am grateful for it. And now, I am grateful to Dalbir, the editors, and everyone at Playwrights Canada Press for immortalizing a part of this gift by publishing it for others to encounter. It means that Regina's voice, Shawn's voice, can live on forever.

To give Regina the final words, "Every theatre has a ghost. A ghost who used to love being on the stage. And when all the mortals are asleep, that spirit follows the ghost light that's been left on for her. And she gets to recreate all the great roles she played in life. Doesn't that sound like a lovely place to end up?"

Ghost Light premiered at Theatre New Brunswick in Fredericton on November 17, 2016, with the following cast and creative team:

Shawn, Regina, and all other roles: Shawn Wright

Director/Dramaturg: Thomas Morgan Jones
Lighting Design: Leigh Ann Vardy
Stage Manager: Tammy Faulkner

The development of *Ghost Light* was supported by the Ontario Arts Council Theatre Creators' Reserve program.

CHARACTERS

Shawn
Regina
Bernadine
Female Employee
Donna

SHAWN enters from the wings, lights a candle centre stage, and speaks:

SHAWN: I have been making this walk from the wings to centre stage for almost forty years. Sometimes it's a few feet. Sometimes it's the length of a city block. I have been wheeled in on a throne, hobbled in on ten-foot stilts, hustled in on platform disco boots. I have made this entrance as a king, a murderer, a cater-pillar, a hubcap, Eleanor Roosevelt, Satan . . . Oh yes, in the 1980s I played both God and Satan in the same show . . . during Lent! I've even played a few parts twice . . . either because I've loved the character or needed the money.

But tonight, in what a costume designer would call "modern dress" (or my Mumma would call "modrin dress"), I stand as I have stood many times before—in front of folks who have made the precious effort to come hear a stranger's story and wonder how much of it (if any) will resonate with their own lives. In many ways tonight we are in the same boat: for although you have probably been to the theatre before, you have never heard this particular tale . . . and although I have been centre stage thousands of times, I am appearing in a role I have never played before . . . myself.

In 2008, my mother took a terrible fall in her kitchen, which led to full-time care. At that time I was travelling across the continent in a profession that both of us held dear . . . the theatre. My mother, Regina—or as she was christened in French, *Regina (pronounces it in French)*—had been an amateur actress of some renown, the belle of the St. Rose Parish Players in Saint John, New Brunswick. I got the bug from watching her onstage, and never looked back. Though her performances were contained to a tiny geographical area, folks back here still stop to tell me how mesmerizing she was in a host of different roles.

At eighty-six, when she moved into the nursing home, I would always visit at eight p.m., just in time to watch her favourite program, *Murder, She Wrote*. She would lie in her single bed and watch from the small rental TV. I would lie in the other bed. There was only one rule and it was a strict one: we could only talk during the commercials. So we'd have five minutes at a time to talk about everything under the sun. But when those five minutes were up I was instructed to be mute. Even coughing was frowned upon.

Often I wouldn't watch the tube; I'd watch *her* . . . humoured by how emotionally invested in the story she was, but saddened by how much I would miss her. Even though she would hang on for many months, I began some sort of private mourning process. I remember one evening falling asleep while her television blared and dreaming that an orderly had wheeled in a third bed to bear the weight of my grief.

Mumma couldn't care less whether the episode was a rerun or not. I, however, was not as enthusiastic. The first time the show was a repeat I opened my laptop to memorize some lines. But I found myself writing . . . about her . . . her time in the theatre . . . her trials . . . her life. Then I'd close the computer screen and feed her before the night nurse changed her. Then I'd return the next day for *Murder, She Wrote*. And if I'd seen the episode before, I wrote. I wrote to keep her alive. I wrote to keep myself alive.

> *Scene: The Nursing Home during commercials for* Murder, She Wrote. *My mother is bed-ridden at this stage in her life.*

REGINA: I don't know what they see in that Meryl Streep.

SHAWN: Is Meryl Streep on *Murder, She Wrote*?

REGINA: No, it's an advertisement for the movie afterwards. I just don't find her a bit good lookin'.

SHAWN: *(looks at the TV) Mum*, it's *Sophie's Choice*. She's in a concentration camp! Her head's shaved!

REGINA: Well, would it have killed her to put on a little bit of rouge?! It's still showbiz.

SHAWN: Well, she just had to give one of her kids to the Nazis. She's ain't gonna look that fresh!

REGINA: What other stories would I have seen her in?

SHAWN: Oh, I dunno. The one where the dingo ate her baby?

REGINA: What a mother! She gives one kid to Hitler and puts the other one in a dog dish.

SHAWN: What about *The Devil Wears Prada*?

REGINA: Now why would the Devil need an outfit?

SHAWN: No, Mum, She's the devil. The mean boss at the fashion magazine.

REGINA: Well, I can't afford no fancy outfits. No woman in New Brunswick can relate to that character. The only way you'd get me to pay good money to see that movie is if they changed it to *The Devil Wears Cotton Ginny*.

SHAWN: Have you seen her play Margaret Thatcher in *The Iron Lady*? If you were still on the stage I could see you in that part.

REGINA: Oh Lord, no. The only chance I'd have of gettin' that part these days is if they changed it to *The Iron Deficient Lady*.

★ ★ ★

SHAWN: My mother was born in the dirt. Well, more specifically, the sawdust. Anybody who was nobody in 1924 in Saint John, New Brunswick, lived beyond Melanson's Bridge on the aptly named Sawdust Road. The houses were not even numbered. My grandfather, Jean-Baptiste, earned his living burning garbage at a dump. My mother told me that she was thrilled when he would get home from his two-hour walk from the incinerator not just because she missed him but because he would often bring her a doll that someone had thrown out. Young Regina collected these dolls not to dress up or cuddle, but to use as audience when she practiced her plays.

She was kept home from school . . . a lot. Her mother, Sylvie, had been born sickly . . . which having eight kids did nothing to boost. By the time Regina was ten, she was the one taking care of little George and little Theresa, as well as her older sister, the troubled Mary Ann. Her mother had not the strength to even scrub a floor so Regina did that, too. But after chores were finished, Regina would corral little George, little Theresa, and Mary Ann alongside the charred dolls as audience for her self-written dramatizations. On Saturday afternoons, the weekly rehearsal period was declared officially over and Regina would cart George, Theresa, and Mary Ann up an extended ladder to the loft of the barn where, with pluck, Regina would offer a public performance. A happy and trusting child, Regina's one-girl shows would ironically revolve around a mature woman who was at the end of her emotional rope.

Her mama would save any chipped or broken plates so that Regina could smash them during her obligatory fit-of-rage monologue. A tragic death would round out the afternoon with little Regina silencing anyone who got in the way of her dreams. Though she'd always elicit the audience's sympathy by the last scene when, on bended knee, she'd plead to the heavens for forgiveness while throwing holy water in her face. I'm sure the sight of this diminutive child in pigtails begging the fates for redemption was an odd one indeed. Picture Pippi Longstocking as Lady Macbeth.

As far as I know, there has been only one occasion when my mother broke from her rule that her dramas be self-written. It was the week leading to her ninth birthday. During those few days, Regina found little time for the stage as most of her hours were spent entertaining a suitor . . . nay, two suitors. The first was Butchie Hebert—portly, but with the raven brow of a pre-pubescent Rudolph Valentino. Regina was smitten . . . right down to her basement. So much so that she turned a blind eye to his questionable intellect. She chose to think him ironic when he named his golden lab Blackie. She soon had to turn a deaf ear as well. One night under an autumn moon, sitting close together with feet dangling off Melanson's Bridge, she cooed, "Oh Butchie . . . there must be thousands of stars out tonight." to which our young scholar replied, "Thousands?! Oh, Regina, there must be hundreds!"

Bachelor Number Two was Nubby LeBlanc. I won't bother describing him since my mother's sole reason for liking him was that he was the only boy she knew who had read all of Lucy Maud Montgomery's books—and not just the ones about Anne. He actually read *Rilla of Ingleside* . . . on a camping trip! With a credential like that a girl could easily forgive a pronounced lateral lisp.

And so, from Sunday to Thursday, Regina was so busy being courted and sparked that by Friday she found herself with nary an idea for Saturday's spectacle. Panicked by a rare twinge of unprofessionalism, she raced barefoot through the filthy sawdust to the never-locked unpainted schoolhouse. She rifled through the cupboards of her beloved teacher, Mademoiselle Desjardins, also a lover of dramatic literature, but the texts were mostly in French. And though Regina could speak French she couldn't read it. For the past few years, English was only to be taught; it was decided in this community that French kept you impoverished. So she nixed the beautiful plays of Molière and Racine in favour of the sole English drama on that shelf. As Regina leafed through it, she knew she had found her heroine. After reading a few pages aloud, she felt connected to this character. Her heart raced as she sat on the empty school room floor, knowing that in less than twenty-four hours this eight-year-old would be digging deeper into her dramatic well than she ever had before . . . as she prepared to inhabit the fiery soul of a woman called Medea . . . For those not in the know, Medea was a Greek barbarian who revenged her lover's infidelity by killing her own children.

Medea went exceptionally well except for the temporary blindness. She had decided to enter in tears on her first big speech so she got Alcide Arsenault to blow smoke in her eyes. By all accounts this was a stunning effect, but on her way to centre stage her sight was so blurry that she stepped on the foot of old Widow Melanson, who let out a howl so loud that all the barnyard animals started a-squawkin' and a-brayin'. My mother said that she tried the smoke effect again in a few other plays, but it just never had the same magic.

* * *

SHAWN: When my mother started to work outside the home as a waitress at the Palms Restaurant in nearby Fairville she had little time for the stage. And even less time when my father, the charming baseball player Lefty Wright, started walking her home. It was now 1945. They married in '48 and proceeded to have a rapid succession of little ones.

Although she took leave of the stage for domesticity, she did have a weekly outlet for her soul . . . the Catholic mass. She sat alone and lived in spiritual reverie for one full hour every week. As I eventually would discover for myself, no one said the Lord's Prayer with more conviction and humility. Like the actress she was, she completely shed the skin of weekly Regina with every verse of scripture and welcomed a renewed Regina in. A Regina who could face yet another week of domestic heavy lifting.

Whenever possible, she would summon her sister, Mary Ann, to babysit so she could go to an afternoon movie by herself. She particularly loved the films of Susan Hayward. Her favourite was *I Want To Live!* in which Miss Hayward played a prostitute on trial for murder. My mother credited that film with reviving her own creative longings. With a household full of kids, she returned to the drama group and was given the leading role in *Food For Father*, which was taken to the competitive provincial drama festival. The year was 1958 . . . the year that Susan Hayward won the best actress trophy for *I Want To Live!* in Hollywood and Regina Robichaud Wright won the best actress trophy for *Food For Father* in Fredericton. And it wouldn't be her last. She won again the next year for playing a woman with two illegitimate kids who inexplicably did most of her scenes on roller skates. I didn't quite get the whole story when she explained it to me years later, but I do know that on opening night she skated right off the stage and into the lap of Monsignor Osbourne. She said the incident made Holy Confession with him from then on just a little bit awkward.

Scene: The Nursing Home during commercials.

You wanna watch the news after this or *Mary Poppins*?

REGINA: The news. I can't stand it when women sing right high. They say their lines right low like a normal person then start singin' right high and it doesn't even sound like the same woman. I lose the story.

SHAWN: What if she says her lines in the same high register that she sings the songs in?

REGINA: It's still high-class hollerin'.

SHAWN: Okay, who's your favourite female singer?

REGINA: Linda Ronstadt. She sings right low.

SHAWN: Well, I doubt that Mary Poppins would've won Best Actress with Linda Ronstadt in the title role!

After a contemplative pause.

REGINA: Hard to say.

* * *

SHAWN: My earliest childhood memory was watching my mother rehearse. Mumma always carried two things in her arms when she rushed into the St. Rose Parish Hall for play practise: her script and me. I wore an eye patch back then because my left eye was lazy. Dr. Baxter had me cover my good eye, the right one, so I wouldn't rely on it. I was five years old and strangers thought I was drunk. So I made my mother carry me to avoid public shaming. Also, I didn't want to scuff my new saddle shoes.

It was around this time that I met Bernadine Burns, resident second banana of the St. Rose Parish Players. It was hard to miss her. She was the only woman in town who went once a week to the barbershop for a buzz cut. My mother thought she was great. She was the Ethel to my mother's Lucy. Or, to be truer to the age, the Rhoda to her Mary. Speaking of Mary, a life-sized statue of the Blessed Virgin stood just inside the door. Bernadine exhaled a perfect smoke ring that landed right on my eye patch, then placed the still lit cigarette into the praying hands of the Virgin Mary. When she spoke she sounded a little like this:

BERNADINE: *(in a deep baritone)* Regina, give me the baby so you can take your coat off.

REGINA: He's not a baby, Bernadine. But he refuses to walk where it's not paved.

BERNADINE: I understand. Who would want to scuff those beautiful shoes?

SHAWN: *(to audience)* Finally, someone who gets me.

REGINA: I just love your new watch, Bernadine. What happened to the old one?

BERNADINE: Clare Graham threw it out of our dressing room window when I implied that she hadn't lost the baby weight. Is this little Tony?

REGINA: No, this is Shawn. He's the only one home now—he comes with me so Lefty can sleep between shifts.

SHAWN: Bernadine carries me to the corner of the room as if she is hauling a Hefty Bag to the curb on garbage day. She plops me down on a trunk filled with props.

BERNADINE: You might find a deck of cards in that trunk, Tony.

REGINA: Don't worry, Bernadine. He loves hearing us rehearse our lines.

BERNADINE: Help yourself to the Kit Kat in my purse. I haven't finished it all.

REGINA: He doesn't need treats, Bernadine. My kids have practically eaten their way through the Humpty Dumptys that I bought for the trick or treaters.

BERNADINE: Oh my God, Halloween. I was wondering about Tony's eye patch.

REGINA: Okay . . . Act 1, Scene 1: Marjorie barges into the Park Plaza powder room. "Delores, why did you call Gregory's office today and why did you tell me you did not?!"

BERNADINE: "Well . . . it's just" . . . Ah, shit, Regina, I forgot my first line!

SHAWN: I'm not sure if I'm allowed to laugh or not.

BERNADINE: A curse word and not a peep out of the boy. He belongs in the theatre.

REGINA: *(chuckling)* Oh Lord, the theatre is not for Shawn! My other kids scream like banshees day and night, you can't imagine the theatrics. Shawn rarely speaks.

BERNADINE: Regina, I need another smoke before we start again. Tony, honey, go to the seminarian's fridge and steal us each a Lime Rickey. I'll confess it on Saturday to Monsignor Osborne. Oh, and while you're at it, toss me my good bra.

★ ★ ★

SHAWN: My early theatrical instruction was not confined to merely watching from the wings. For example, every lunchtime my Mumma and I would sit at TV trays eating our Campbell's tomato soup and Wonder Bread, and watch *The Dick Van Dyke Show*. She would painstakingly explain the mechanics of the pratfall that Dick Van Dyke would do as he tripped over an ottoman during the opening credits. She would then make *me* do it with her instruction. Even if it did sometimes bruise, I was happy to have my first lesson in stage combat. To this day I rarely do a sword fight in a show without thinking of Dick Van Dyke.

The Oscars telecast was also a big training ground . . . all seven of us kids would watch the ten-second clips of all those nominated in each category and Mum would give us a precise review on who should win and why. And she was rarely wrong. The same went for the Miss Canada pageant. Oh, and lest I forget, bed-time rituals in our house were worthy of the ancient Greeks. If my siblings and I refused to go to bed after three warnings my mother would have a sudden and violent contortion . . . then with vacant eyes she would calmly pick up the biggest knife in the kitchen and start slowly toward us. We would scream up the stairs and put the covers over our heads. But even as I shook, I took mental notes of which knife angle was more effective for inducing terror.

When my brothers and I came of age to be altar boys in the highly dramatic Catholic mass, the four of them jumped at it. I, however, felt compelled to pass. I did the same when offered the school choir or band. I was waiting for my call to the legitimate stage. And it finally happened in Grade 3. I was to have a few lines in a skit called "The Safety First Train." I was honoured to have been given the role of "Caboose." Each grade would perform their skit in front of the whole school. I was beside myself with excitement. As the Grade 2's performed, we waited in the wings. Our leading lady got so excited that she peed through her leotard and our skit was cancelled. I would not get another chance on the boards until high school, when I was cast as the oldest boy in *The Sound of Music*. My mother helped me with my lines. She would play all the other characters as if her life depended on it. She was a powerhouse Mother Abbess, an adorable little Gretl, and a surprisingly unsympathetic Maria. Mum said that I needed to play the reality of the situation in Nazi Germany, that I needed to appear shell-shocked and terrified in every scene or the whole audience would think I was a phoney. So, unfortunately, I sang "Do-Re-Mi" as if I were in a Martin Scorsese film. On a side note, it was then that I had my first lesson in dealing with the scorn of theatre critics. Valerie Gregory of the *Evening Times*

Globe, obviously not taken with my penchant for ultra-realism, referred to me as Frederich Von Crapp.

Scene: The Nursing Home during commercials:

REGINA: Remember when I taught you to sing? I taught you the best kind of singin' on God's green earth . . . country western.

SHAWN: Mum, those songs were the worst! Five years old and you're teaching me harmonies to songs about drunks and adulterers.

REGINA: One of the great mysteries of showbiz is that the songs with the worst morals have the best melodies. I taught you to sing in the style of the artist I consider to be my mentor . . . Miss Tammy Wynette. Let's do the first one I ever taught ya . . . I'll sing it like Tammy and you add a harmony, but you gotta match my inflections twang by twang.

REGINA sings a few lines of "D-I-V-O-R-C-E" with her trademark heavy twang.

★ ★ ★

SHAWN: Ours was a religious home. A picture of a sorrowful Jesus dominated the living room. My mother said on more than one occasion that her two dearest wishes were: to have one of her boys become a priest, and to have a clean house. Neither of them came true.

Organized religion has been a constant struggle for me. My mother was such a devout Catholic that she once made a man change his religion. That man was my father. When my dad, born Presbyterian, asked for my mother's hand in marriage, she said she would only do so if he converted to Catholicism. His reply was "What? Are you saying you love Jesus more than me?" to which she replied, "Of course!"

I was not born with my mother's blind faith. It has been said that God is love. That I can get my head around, and even agree with. But it was not faith in God that chafed me. It was the Catholic Church into which I was born and from which I received all my early instruction. It was implied from the pulpit that God seemed to favour Catholics over everyone else.

Don't get me wrong. I have witnessed some beautiful acts of grace done by *the* most devout Catholic this side of St. Francis of Assisi: my Mumma. The tenderness with which she taught me to pray . . . both of us on our knees in the kitchen as I struggled to memorize the Lord's Prayer while being distracted by my older siblings playing ball outside the window. The sight of her at any given moment rushing to light a candle when someone in need crossed her mind. She kept a long list of people she knew who were struggling in some way or another. If any of us kids would mention a classmate who was having a rough time at home or at school, Mumma would add that child's name to the list. Same went for anyone in the community with an ailment (physical or emotional). I have even seen a few celebrities on the list. My mother, an entertainment junkie, was constantly hearing of the travails of the rich and famous on *Entertainment Tonight*. During her evening prayers, my mother would recite her usual litany of verses, then take out the list and read all the names out loud and ask God to help them carry their burdens. I always found that very moving. In her declining years she still did a list, but instead of reading each of the dozens and dozens of names out loud, she simply put her hand over the names and said, "Lord, bless all these people."

* * *

SHAWN: By 1973, the Parish Hall was torn down and the drama group disbanded. My mother's weight climbed and with it came a desire to be out of the spotlight. Still an avid churchgoer, she longed to read the scriptures at mass but now lost confidence to speak in front of people. Years later, when I was home one spring, I urged her to read at Easter mass . . . I stressed how all the parishioners (including me) would love to see her up front again. She took both my hands and said:

REGINA: When I was in a play I always wore the face of another woman. I could never speak as myself. You understand, Shawn. You're like me . . . people would kill for our confidence. But if they only knew. For two hours a night I see you grab the spotlight with such ferociousness . . . but at the curtain call . . . as yourself . . . you can barely look up.

When, Shawn . . .

When will you and I learn to star in our own lives?

* * *

SHAWN: When I turned sixteen, my father was given three months to live. We never did say much to each other. Mostly because we both had a certain shyness. But he was a good man. And he got a big kick out of my mother. While my mum was running around planning the approaching funeral, I spent a lot of time with him. We watched TV together every night until he moved to the cancer ward—watching TV, just the three of us . . . me, my dad, and Death.

Freelon Almroth Wright . . . Lefty . . . my dad

SHAWN lights a candle.

* * *

REGINA: Angela Lansbury uses her hands just right.

SHAWN: What are you talking about?

REGINA: So many actors don't know what to do with their hands. Like that dark-haired girl on *Three's Company.* When I was on the stage I kept my hands at my sides right natural . . . even if I said somethin' like "Oh, the phone's ringin'. I'd better run and get it before I go outside." But someone without my dramatic gifts like Bernadine Burns would be like *(REGINA uses broad gestures throughout the next lines)* "Oh, the phone's ringin'. I'd better run and get it before I go outside." That's the sign of an amateur.

SHAWN: As said by an amateur.

REGINA: And you should always say your lines loud, even in Toronto. And don't worry about spit. It's not a performance unless the front row is in danger of gettin' Hepatitis C. And for God's sake, do not overdo it with the makeup! Poor Bernadine . . . when she played the Whore of Babylon she drew a mole on her face the size of the Infant Jesus.

* * *

SHAWN: I remember sitting at my father's funeral wondering if any of my siblings were feeling conflicted about Catholicism as well. Without even asking the question, I got the answer with a resounding thud. When my middle brother Philip got married to the girl next door, he threw caution to Catholicism and married her in her Baptist Church. So it was even more shocking a year later when he announced that he had joined the Pentecostal Church. That was the biggest blow I ever saw my mother deal with. I daresay it appeared to immobilize her even more than my father's death had the year before. Philip's defection represented for her the ultimate rejection of the most important instruction she had imparted to us. A bit later, my eldest brother Peter became a Pentecostal, too. Then Philip became a Pentecostal minister! My mother was devastated and confused. The irony was not lost on me that one of her boys became a clergyman after all . . . but be careful what you wish for, Regina. As a closeted gay teenager with so many of my own confusions, the introduction of the Religious Right into my own home set fear into my heart. I had to get out of there.

I paid my way through university by singing at coffee houses and weddings, along with odd stints as a runway model for bridal shows. Yes, there was a time when I could wear my shirt tucked in with confidence. I joined a university drama group where I had two amazing mentors: one in musical comedy and one in heavy drama. My big break came when I competed at the provincial drama festival where my mother had won her two trophies thirty years earlier. I got lucky, too. The adjudicator was from New York City and offered me two acting jobs in a row.

I returned briefly to New Brunswick to pick up my degree in English Literature from UNB then drove straight to Toronto to start a career. I knew no one in this big city, but I was disciplined, I was hungry, and I figured what I didn't know I could learn. I knocked on a lot of doors and within two weeks I was cast as a servant to an actor I recognized from the TV show *Fraggle Rock*.

It has now been thirty years since I took that drive to find my life. I never did get to sing with Tammy Wynette and to my mother's horror I wound up in a movie with Meryl Streep. Her hair had grown in.

⋆ ⋆ ⋆

SHAWN: Mum, did you always get the leading part?

REGINA: Every time except once. Oh, how I longed to play Our Blessed Virgin in *The Lady of Fátima*. You know that story, dontcha, Shawn? In 1917, Mary appeared as a vision to the peasants of Fátima, Portugal. If I do say so myself, my audition was legendary. I came out of the wings with my hands held up to Our Lord. In order to look right mysterious I wrapped my whole head in cheesecloth. And they gave the part to Bernadine Burns! I got the part of a peasant woman with no name. But I knew the audience did not want to see me in the background, so I put a big gardenia in my hair and everywhere Bernadine went onstage I went, too. Also, I had a great idea to make the show right supernatural. Every time Bernadine said a line I said it, too . . . but just a little bit before Bernadine said it. I ended up really enjoying that show.

* * *

SHAWN: From the time I was in grade school people would say "Shawn, you need to put those stories about your mother in a book." And I thought, "Who would read a book about a four-foot-eleven Acadian woman teaching her son life lessons while chasing him with a knife?!" And how would it be marketed? As a white trash *Tuesdays With Morrie*? But as I listened to my mother telling me her stories in her final months, I thought, "A book . . . hmm . . . What about a play?" I'd never written a book before. Well, I'd never written a play before either . . . but I do know that the stage is my turf . . . and it was her turf, too. And, ironically, it is the place where we both played other people to feel most like ourselves. And I did want to get her back on the stage . . . in a big part . . . for one last time . . . I wanted her to make her professional theatre debut.

But as I continued writing, I discovered a more private reason. My brothers and sisters all have children. I do not. My siblings all had something tangible and beautiful to offer my mother—something with the DNA of both of them. Well, I am offering my mother this play—a grandchild of sorts—measured not by pounds and ounces but by scenes. It has both our DNA, and to be fair I gestated these ideas for at least nine months. And let me tell ya, it's true what they say about that first trimester.

* * *

SHAWN: When my two brothers left the Catholic Church in favour of Pentecostalism and it broke my mother's heart, I vowed I would never give her any grief about her faith again.

Philip said, "Mum, Peter and I don't pray to Mary anymore. She was just a woman. She had no glorious ascension into heaven." I saw Mum cry over that one. She told me when I moved out of her house that the Virgin Mary would be my mother now in the dangerous big city. I may have scoffed silently, but truth be told, in moments of crisis, I *have* prayed to the Virgin Mary . . . as recently as . . . well, I might have even prayed to her at 7:59 tonight.

I really did cast my Pentecostal brothers as villains during that period, but the truth is they were always very sweet men and continued to be so. It's just that they believed as fervently as my mother did . . . but in the opposite direction. She eventually let go of the arguing and the sadness . . . they were her babies . . . she even went to Phil's induction as a minister. I had a harder time shaking it. Although I was not a big fan of Catholicism, I was so afraid of right-wing fanaticism, which I perceived their religion to be. I was probably too ignorant to be so high and mighty, and, really, what was *I* doing to save the world? Avoiding organized religion?

The last thing I'll say on this subject is that I find it hard to believe that God has an individual plan for us. If our entire lives from cradle to tomb are predestined then why are we even trying? It's like *Murder, She Wrote*. Why do the writers bother to put Angela Lansbury in peril each week? The audience knows that no one is going to kill Angela Lansbury. It's been predestined. It's CBS's divine plan. Kidding aside, I sat at my mother's deathbed asking myself, "*This* is God's plan for this wonderful woman? To suffer depressed in a lonely bed?"

There appeared a great irony at the end of my mother's life. She had always spoken of the glorious reward that follows a physical death. But in her final months she seemed so afraid to die. She began speaking more and more about her early life and those she loved on Sawdust Road: her father Jean-Baptiste, her mother Sylvie . . . deceased.

SHAWN *lights two candles.*

Her siblings:

Bertha: the eldest, champion speed skater, physically powerful. My mother, a worrier, would rely on her for no-nonsense advice. Deceased.

Lights candle.

Christine: a strong advocate for union rights in the workplace, but wound up in an abusive marriage. As a child I was taught to help her hide, and how to lie to her husband when he came looking for her. My mother adored her and they spent much of their time together splitting their sides laughing. Deceased.

Lights candle.

Art: a sweet man who suffered from a then-unknown PTSD from WWII. His wife left and took his kids. After his divorce Mum happily did his laundry. As she ironed his shirts, I'd sit beside him as he ranted about his disappointment in most everything. But he was always tender with us kids. Deceased.

Lights candle.

Mary Ann: caring and troubled. Like her brother, Art, she was anguished. Phobic of most everything. Never married. Often wore black. Always covered up head to toe, even in summer. Not only our favourite aunt, she was also our beloved babysitter. She's still living.

George: the playboy. Jolly and easy to be around. Lured by the pace of Montréal as a teen. Dated glamorous women with names like Veronica. Married late in life but no kids. Developed Lou Gehrig's disease. My mother was heartbroken that her own condition prohibited her from travelling to the deathbed of her baby brother. Deceased.

Lights candle.

Theresa: Pretty and cosmopolitan. Appeared onstage for a time, no doubt inspired by sitting with the charred dolls in the barn. Moved to Toronto, changed her name to Terri, and married well. Visited often, but Mary Ann felt that Terri could "put on airs." Was lovely to my mother, but was viciously critical of my siblings and I concerning our mother's care. She's still living.

Benoit: The eighth and often forgotten sibling. He smiled for the first time when he was eight months old. My grandmother exclaimed, "He's getting better!" But her friend Dora, who read energies, said, "No, Sylvie, it means the end is near." He died that night.

Lights candle.

* * *

SHAWN: Mum, I went to see Mary Ann tonight.

REGINA: My sister? Dear Lord, I haven't seen her in over a year. Since she had to leave her home, too. Is she still very forgetful? Maybe it's a blessing we weren't put in the same place.

SHAWN: You know, Mumma, the dementia seems to actually be helping her out. It's like she's forgotten to be afraid.

REGINA: Has she stopped walking like me? She loved to walk. She'd walk all the way to Zellers and back.

SHAWN: I don't know. She was in her chair.

REGINA: Did you give her a Christmas card from me?

SHAWN: Yes.

REGINA: Did you put twenty dollars in it?

SHAWN: Yes.

REGINA: Did she really seem okay?

Pause. Sadness starts to take her.

When's *It's A Wonderful Life* on?

SHAWN: At ten.

REGINA: Could you leave it on that station when you go?

SHAWN: I'm staying late tonight . . . I have to make sure you're asleep when Santa comes.

★ ★ ★

SHAWN: I had zero birds and bees talks with my parents. I'm not sure if this was indicative of most parents of my generation or just the Catholics. I honestly do not know where they thought we'd learn. I guess from the biblical readings in church? I was determined to find out so I went to the Encyclopaedia Britannica for answers. This did more harm than good. For when I looked up the sex page, I happened to see a picture of a skin rash that looked like something I had on my knee (probably acquired from a change in laundry detergent). I thought I had syphilis. I was ten . . . the closest contact I had with anyone or anything was my onesie pyjamas.

Relatives and neighbours would ask if I had a girlfriend. So I kissed a girl named Rhonda Springer on the playground. Everyone thought that was so cute and would tease me. Although I don't remember the kiss being unpleasant, I can't recall if I liked *her* or the attention it rendered *me*. I mostly had girls for playmates but harboured no ulterior motives. I remember my own mother saying, "Shawn, all those girls will have boyfriends soon and they won't want to hang around with you anymore." Though her motive was kind, I felt shamed to hear from my mother that something wasn't right with the company I was keeping. I did know that I had crushes on some of the male TV stars. There was a big debate at that time as to which *Gilligan's Island* star you had the biggest fancy for: Ginger or Mary Ann? I stayed silent 'cause I chose the Professor.

I eventually did have a sexual experience with a male classmate in my teens. Though enjoyable, it terrified me on some level, so I immediately found a steady girlfriend . . . That relationship was chaste, but that was common enough in those days not to warrant her suspicions.

But things really came to a head when I started working professionally. Creative professions have always been havens for individuality, and I was very uncomfortable and often dismissive of those who were "out." But internalized homophobia can be cruel.

I eventually got my act together and settled down for a few years at a time with a couple of wonderful gentlemen. But I kept it from my family because I didn't want to hurt my mother. Isn't that stupid? I hid a crucial part of my heart from her. I felt troubled about that. I felt troubled about that for a long time. And cowardly. When would I learn to star in my own life?

Things definitely got better when I came out to my wonderful sister, Paula. She was coming to stay with me in Toronto and, well, it was just time. I knew she'd be great about it, but there are still traces of that self-hating nag in the back of my skull. Nowadays kids come out in high school or earlier, but I wore the shackles of a different generation. My mother was well into middle age when homosexuality was decriminalized. Decriminalized! I wonder what she thought in 1968 when that happened . . . especially since it was decriminalized by her idol, Pierre Trudeau.

But, as I would find out, my mother had a secret of her own. She revealed it to us when she was seventy-two years old. In 1969, she overheard a conversation between my then eighteen-year-old brother, Peter, and his girlfriend. The girlfriend was pregnant and decided the baby would be put up for adoption. My mother told no one, not even her own husband about his first grandchild, even on his deathbed.

Well, that baby, Maryse, eventually found my brother and asked him to come to her wedding, and we all met and it was lovely. But I realized during that time that I was like my mother on yet another level. She was frozen by a shaming secret like I was . . . afraid of what someone might think of her and her son . . . afraid of what her loving husband might think of her and her son.

Ironically, my newfound niece, Maryse, was my only family member to bring up my being gay before I said anything first. She said, "Hey, Uncle Shawn, my man and I are in Toronto and heading out for dinner. Why don't you and your boyfriend join us? At least I think that sweet-faced guy I see you with on Facebook is your boyfriend?" I had to work that night but I thought, "Good on ya, girl. Good on you and your generation."

★ ★ ★

SHAWN: Ed Maloney, director of the St. Rose Parish Players, always told my mother that she would eventually make it to Hollywood. And she did. But it was me who got her there. She was well into her seventies. For Christmas I gave her a return flight to Los Angeles to come see me in a musical that I was appearing in at the Ahmanson Theatre, just down the street from the Dorothy Chandler Pavilion, where the Oscars we watched together every year were held. My two sisters came with her. This was before 9/11, which was good because my mother never owned a passport. My sisters said that at US Customs Mum showed them her birth certificate and her Club Z points card from Zellers. I put the gals up in an apartment hotel on Hollywood Boulevard. When the concierge told Regina that staying in the next room was the actress Rue McClanahan, Regina exclaimed, "Oh, I am honoured to share the same floor with one of TV's *Golden Girls* . . . I wonder if she really *is* a slut?"

Knowing my mum was an insomniac, I picked her up at the crack of dawn the next morning for her first full day in Tinseltown. I took her to breakfast while my sisters slept off jet lag. We were seated beside my company manager, Arnie Gershowitz. My mother's eyes lit up. "Oh, I am just thrilled to meet you, Mr. Gershowitz. As a showbiz personality myself, I am indebted to the Jews. They made show business."

"Well actually, Mrs. Wright, I believe modern drama began with the ancient Greeks."

"Oh, but the Jews made Hollywood!"

"Well, Mrs. Wright, I cannot disagree with that."

"Nor should you, Mr. Gershowitz. From the loins of Israel (I thought what the fuck is this woman going to say now?!) From the loins of Israel came the great American movie studio heads of the golden age . . . Harry Cohn, David O. Selznick, and the grandpappy of them all, Louis B. Mayer, who incidentally was born in my hometown of Saint John, New Brunswick, Canada."

Arnie seemed impressed. He paid the cheque though Mum insisted on leaving the tip. I think she must've brought her old eyeglasses with her because although she did indeed leave a generous amount it was all Canadian Tire money. When I alerted her to this she blushed. "Oh, where is my head! I only use them bills on Mondays."

"Mondays?"

"Yeah, that's the only day when Pizza Delight by the Legion takes Canadian Tire money at par."

"Oh, how charming."

"Yeah, jeez, on Mondays I've been known to hand the pizza guy a Sobeys bag filled with Canadian Tire money."

"What's a Sobeys bag?"

"A Maritimer's briefcase."

Donna, Paula, and I had a great week with Mum in LA. She said it was a dream come true to see a real live palm tree and movie stars' homes, and to see me, her baby, perform on a stage even more glamorous than the ones she fell asleep dreaming about on Sawdust Road. But on her last day there, she sadly confessed that we did not do the one thing she wanted to experience most while on California soil.

"What's that, Mumma? Anything you want. The plane doesn't leave until tonight"

"I want to trace the steps that O. J. Simpson made the night of the murders."

Remember, this was a woman addicted to *Murder, She Wrote*. Our first stop was O. J.'s mansion at North Rockingham Avenue. We parked at the curb.

"Mum, I hope to the Risen Lord that you are not planning on getting out of this car."

"No, I just want to sit here in the way that O. J. sat surrounded by the SWAT team. I wanna see if I can channel his frame of mind, his hopes, his fears."

I stepped on the gas and sped to South Bundy Drive.

"OK, Mum, here's Nicole Brown Simpson's house, the scene of the crime. You've seen it. Let's get out of here."

As I looked down to check the GPS on my phone, I heard the passenger door quickly open and close. Imagine the sight of my nearly eighty-year-old mother planting herself on the doorstep of the crime of the century.

"Paula, go get her!"

Both my sisters bolted to fetch this deranged Acadian pipsqueak from making a mockery on sacred ground. I saw Mum give some sort of instructions and then Donna ran back to the car, rifled through Mum's purse, and took out the little plastic knife from the McDonald's we ate at earlier. I was then temporarily distracted by a group of passersby pointing in horror as Donna took photos of my elderly mother placing Paula in a headlock and pretending to slash her throat! Oy!

* * *

SHAWN: I have now officially lived longer than my father. I am grateful for this, but I can't deny that I have been feeling my mortality clock ticking since his death. When I became fatherless at sixteen it freaked me out that there was no longer a buffer generation between me and the great beyond. Added to my mortality fixation is my acute hypochondria. My doctor chides that I can self-diagnose an upset stomach as full-blown diphtheria. I once demanded a colonoscopy and endoscopy on the same day. I felt like a rotisserie chicken.

But I learned to stop my navel gazing once my mother's health declined. She found it hard to keep her spirits up. I no longer wanted her to have a prayer list where other folks reaped the benefits. I needed her to use all her energy on prayers for herself. So *I* took on her "list." She'd tell me who needed prayers and I'd pray for them. *Me*, the doubting Thomas! But, in truth, my siblings did more for her than I did since they lived there. And they were going through their own trials. My sister, Paula, was going through a terrible time. Her son's wife, Leah, was diagnosed with a rare cancer well into her pregnancy. Sweet baby Dylan miraculously survived and continues to thrive. His mother, Leah, was not so lucky. Then, of course, my eldest brother, Peter, was waging a battle with his own cancer. Mumma wondered why he didn't visit as much. When Peter finally did pass, Donna broke the news to Mum in the gentlest of ways. It took a while for grief to find Mum's tongue, but she finally whispered, "Donna, do you mean I only have four boys now"?

   SHAWN lights a candle for Peter.

My mother had not been outside for months but insisted on going to the funeral. I sat next to her wheelchair in the front pew. To bear witness to the particular grief of a mother burying a child, especially when she's your mother, too, is as sorrowful an image as I ever hope to regard. We were now more protective of her than ever. We were six cubs protecting a wounded matriarch in the middle of the woods.

* * *

REGINA: I want you to buzz the nurse?

SHAWN: Okay. Can I help you out at all?

REGINA: I want you to go home. I need her to change me. I don't want you here.

SHAWN: I'll just go to the lounge for a while.

REGINA: I want you to go home!!

Pause.

It's awful being like this. Unable to move. My hands don't work anymore. I can't even use a spoon. I pretend I'm sick almost every afternoon so I don't have to be wheeled into the cafeteria while all the other women walk in on their own. Women older than me! And I drop that spoon over and over and over until a nurse I don't know has to feed me. And she makes no bones she'd rather be anywhere else. I am humiliated. And I'm so frightened. Where's Jesus? Why can't Jesus find me?

A long pause.

Are you gonna be okay?

Without me, I mean?

SHAWN: *(with sincere conviction)* How could I *not* be? With everything you've given me?

REGINA: Shawn, did I know you as well as I could have?

SHAWN: *(meaning it)* You know me.

REGINA: My wish for you, my precious boy, is that you are as good to yourself as you were to me.

SHAWN: I'm gonna go out while you get changed.

He's almost out the door.

REGINA: Shawn . . . do you think there'll be a good show on TV for us tonight?

SHAWN: *(a half smile)* You're the show.

* * *

SHAWN: I was away when she died. I was in a musical in Toronto with no understudy so the producer would not let me fly home. Where others would turn to God, I turned to the other source my mother said would never fail me: my theatre family. I announced to the cast when I arrived for Tuesday night's performance that my mother had been given the last rites. After I put my costume on and approached the stage, I saw that they had lit a candle for me in the green room. They had turned to God for me.

The next morning she was dead. I still had seven more shows to do before the funeral. I happened upon a podcast that week that gave me great solace. It was from the CBC Radio show *Tapestry*. The program was about burial rites and coming to terms with mortality. The host's name was Mary Hynes. I had no idea what she looked like but her voice in my headphones kept me from going crazy that week.

When the final curtain descended on Sunday's matinee and the show closed for good, I got on the subway to go to the airport. My thoughts were consumed with the funeral in the morning half a country away. As I sat waiting for the northbound train, a woman approached me and said:

"Were you one of the actors in the play this afternoon?"

"Yes"

"I felt profoundly moved by your performance. Thank you for sharing your gift with me, with all of us."

As I turned around to thank her, something dawned on me. I stood up, looked her straight in the eye and asked, "Are you Mary Hynes?"

She said, "Yes."

* * *

SHAWN: How many times had I taken this ten p.m. flight from Toronto to Saint John? The one where despite the fact that immediately upon finding my seat and pulling my hoodie down over my face, pretending to be asleep, I am still *always* the one the stewardess chooses to break the window in case of emergency. The one where the aircraft is so small that the smell of asparagus is as likely to come from the woman slurping soup two rows ahead of me as it is from the man peeing at the urinal two rows behind. The flight that, once landed, is so small I can peer out of the still-intact emergency window to see the lady closing the Avis Rent-A-Car kiosk. Avis closes at twelve midnight at the Saint john Airport. The flight from Toronto gets in at 12:10. Seems logical to everyone there. Makes me want to throw a shoe at someone.

So I take a cab. Despite it being February, the driver wears only a T-shirt. Though shy on height, he has an extraordinarily large belly. This makes it easy to read the words on his T-shirt: WORLD'S GREATEST DAD . . . RUNNER-UP. It's quite something to see him squeeze behind the wheel. He is mercifully quiet during the twenty-minute ride save for one yawn that is so expansive it makes the horn blow.

I remember opening the window a crack in the backseat and marvelling at how fog fights for supremacy here, even in the winter. Many a night as a child, with my bedroom window raised just a sliver, I would lie in the dark while the mist seduced the closed curtain for entry . . . then ultimately enveloped the room and myself as if my very existence was being conjured by one of the Brontë sisters.

I thought of my father's death, the knock on the classroom door, "Your brother is waiting for you in the office," the hollow stares from teenage eyes that have not yet mastered emotional grace, the acne-scarred pity as I walked the gang-plank of black and white tiles to the principal's room . . . "Dad's gone," Philip explained with the voice of a grown-up, a matter-of-factness that did its best to veil his innate tenderness for his baby brother, which rang that day as clear as the recess bell.

Although Philip was the first to offer me the cold truth, the initial painful stab was felt one week before. My mother and I were sitting at my dad's bedside when she turned and asked me: "Do you have a clean suit?" All of a sudden it dawned on me what she meant—clean enough for a funeral. I could feel an immediate something as yet unnamed start to shoot through my veins like black ink, while at the same time something just as ferocious started to shoot the other way to numb it. The numbing won. That year, anyway. And the next year. And the next year. And the next year. It did ease up gradually. Very gradually.

The cabbie turned the radio on. Not loudly enough to shake my reverie though CFBC Classic Country does try awfully hard. He dropped me off at Peter's place. Well, Peter's widow's place.

As I drifted off to sleep, I remembered a scenario I hadn't thought of in years. It was a humid summer night, near midnight. I couldn't sleep so I went down-stairs where Mum was at the kitchen table hemming a pair of pants for Jamie. She was in her thirties then. I was maybe six.

REGINA: Oh, I am just in a lather of sweat! Do you want to go out for a walk?

SHAWN: *(to audience)* I was in my pyjamas. She was in a thin housedress. The street was deserted. I could smell a bonfire wafting from Sawdust Road. I held her hand as we went through the dark hollow past the Parish Hall. "Mumma, look! The light's on. Someone's rehearsing in there."

REGINA: No one's rehearsing. It's the ghost light.

SHAWN: What?

REGINA: The last person to leave the theatre every night must leave a lamp on in the centre of the stage.

SHAWN: Why?

REGINA: Every theatre has a ghost. A ghost who used to love being on the stage. And when all the mortals are asleep, that spirit follows the ghost light that's been left on for her. And she gets to recreate all the great roles she played while she was living. Doesn't that sound like a lovely place to end up? . . . Oh, these mosquitos. Let's go home Shawn. C'mon.

★ ★ ★

SHAWN: At nine a.m. sharp, my dead brother told me the weather report and which roads to avoid due to construction. My consciousness finally caught up to my eardrums, and I realized that I had been dreaming of him when my iPhone kicked in to my desired wake-up sound: CBC *Information Morning*. I didn't really want to ruminate on what this day held for me so I jumped immediately into the shower. I put on my suit, said a quick hello to Kathy, and jumped into a borrowed Toyota Corolla. The only quibble I have with Saint John other than Avis's premature closing is that the east side Starbucks opens at ten a.m. For a neurotic Torontonian this is akin to an apocalypse. Well, not a huge apocalypse. Maybe a Grande as opposed to a Venti. I waited for my espresso, "me nerves right jangled" . . . all the while trying not to use the steering wheel as a teething ring.

Once my coffee came, I turned on my cell phone, which started an incessant series of beeps heralding love and support. So many of the texts were variations of "I never knew her, but from your stories I wish I had." I thought how much she'd love that then I changed my tune.

REGINA: What stories are you tellin' bout me? Hopefully not that I used to get you to take my teeth in a Ziploc bag to the Denture Repair.

SHAWN: I had been feeling so sorry that I missed the two-day viewing of the body, but was that a blessing in disguise?

Could I have managed to say even one word to those visitors?

My mother had exhibited so much grace at my father's wake. All those people in a gloomy receiving line, shuffling their feet, trying to come up with some fresh variation on "Sorry for your loss." Then I saw the most beautiful thing happen. With each person in line *she* comforted *them*. The perfect hostess. She told each of them what *they* meant to my father. She was so specific in her reassurances to them . . . even in her grief. *She* took care of *them*. She carried them. I wonder whom she asked to carry her? As if I don't know. I was given instructions to go to Castle Funeral Home for the closing of the casket at 11:45 and then the funeral would start at noon. But I found myself arriving there an hour early.

The door was open. There seemed to be no one around though I could hear the faint sound of a vacuum cleaner upstairs. On the wall room assignments were listed for Bessie Briggs, Ralph Tippett, and Regina Wright. My mother had been on so many exciting lists in her day (cast lists, awards lists) and yet this sterile assemblage of strangers would be the last. Ironically, earlier that morning her best friend, Deanna Gerrior, also died but would only be arriving tomorrow . . . so, Deanna would share a cold list of strangers as well. As it turned out, Bessie Briggs and Ralph Tippett were allotted the smaller rooms, meaning that my Mumma, the belle of the St. Rose Parish Players, would occupy the deluxe suite overlooking the Atlantic Ocean. Outside her room was a guest book. The last person to sign was Bernadine Burns. I wondered if when she picked up the pen she got the Blessed Virgin to hold her smoke?

As I took a deep breath and was about to finally enter the room, a female employee stuck her head around the corner:

FEMALE EMPLOYEE: You must be Regina's boy from Toronto. There's an hour before we have to move her to St. Rose's. Spend as much time as you want. My family and I have known Regina since we were kids. Such a character. So sweet. You'll see we done her up real nice. She never looked better.

SHAWN: As she shuffled back to her office I thought "*Never?!* She's *never* looked better??* Not even on her wedding day? An opening night? Are embalmers that vain that they seriously believe that a lifeless corpse looks better than she did on prom night?" I strode into that room, went up to that coffin, stared right into my mother's face and thought, "Jesus, she *does* look good!"

I joke, of course, but she did look like her sweet self. I was so happy to see her. The first thing I said was: "Mumma, I made it." You know when you realize how significant a moment was in your life but you didn't realize it at the time? This was not one of those moments. I knelt down in silence . . . just staring . . . just loving her and staring. I thought of how this room had been packed and buzzing for two days with family and old friends. I was just gutted not to be with them all. But maybe this was the way it was supposed to be. I'm her last born. She was there for the miracle of my first moments on Earth and I am here for the mystery of her last. It all felt very sacred to me. I felt like some sort of sentinel . . . a soldier guarding a queen.

I ended up having a full hour with her . . . just me and my Mumma. I spoke right to her face but I wasn't sure where she was hearing me from now. Above me? Beside me? From my own heart? I walked to the window and looked at the majesty of the Atlantic waters . . . strong, constant, and rushing away from me . . . just like her. I started to cry. So I just pulled up a chair beside her and spent the whole time revealing what was in my heart. I spoke about everything and nothing. I'd be silent for a while, and then I'd sing stuff that she liked or that used to make her laugh.

I spent a lot of time just looking at her hands . . . her palms were clasped together and her rosary was loosely placed between her fingers as if she were praying that I'd be okay. They did a beautiful job with her hands. And . . . I actually mustered up some courage and looked her right in the face and said, "I'm gay." It's strange. It's the new millennium, I have passed fifty years old, and the person listening to me is dead . . . but I found those words almost impossible to say.

That is how much of a life-long albatross this has been for me. My lips would hardly let the words past. But I said it. I said it to her face. I said it.

* * *

SHAWN: I have been blessed with a lot, but in cases like this, as a childless person, it's hard not to think: "When my time comes, who will be there for me? Who will take care of me? An hour before my casket is closed, who will be the sentinel for me? My circle of friends assures me we will all take care of each other, but really what shape will we all be in? I just have to have faith . . . like I was taught.

My siblings, nephews and nieces, and their spouses all eventually made their way into the room. I hadn't seen most of them since Peter's funeral. They spoke of all the people who had paid their respects this week . . . many of whom, to my delight, would be at the post-funeral gathering in the auditorium at the community centre. I know that room well. It's the perfect place for a send off for Regina. It has a stage.

Sweet old Father Riley poked his head in and said, "It's time." He helped my sister place a blanket inside the casket over sweet Regina. Because it was February; Paula couldn't bear the notion of Mum going into that cold ground wearing only her good dress. That's how grief makes you think. That's how love makes you think.

The funeral director slowly closed the lid of the coffin. It's quite surreal to see the last strain of light ever to hit your mother's face, but I felt honoured to bear witness to it. As riveting as it was, I kept sneaking glances at my siblings. Like my mother and myself, it was clear that each of them had learned how to play a part. For these were not the faces of my childhood playmates . . . they were now the faces of battle-scarred warriors.

But with the gentle drop of that coffin lid, the warrior façades began to melt into a look I can only describe as "orphaned." I was proud of their strength. I was proud of their fragility. My nephews lifted the casket and we all followed it to the awaiting hearse. Single file. The children of Regina Wright: Donna, Jamie, Philip, Paula, Tony . . . and, in spirit, Peter.

In the parking lot, Donna asked if I wanted to drive with her to St. Rose. But I wanted to be with my own thoughts. I took the keys out of my pocket. My sister walked me to my car.

DONNA: I'm so glad that you had that hour alone with Mum.

SHAWN: Me too.

DONNA: What was it like?

SHAWN: I just talked and talked.

DONNA: For the entire time?

SHAWN: I think so.

DONNA: What did you say in a one-sided conversation for that long?

SHAWN: You'd be surprised how many ways there are to say thank you.

The end.

GA TING (FAMILY)
家庭

MINH LY
李明海

I dedicate this play to my parents.

They came to this country with nothing, but somehow managed to give me everything, including their unwavering love and support.

Ly Nguu Tu and Ly Thi Mai, I thank you . . . and I love you.

ACKNOWLEDGEMENTS

I would like to give a huge thank you to Chris Gatchalian at **the frank theatre company** and Donna Yamamoto at Vancouver Asian Canadian Theatre for seeing something in my play that led to two impactful productions, and it being included in this anthology. *Ga Ting* wouldn't have had the success it did without the artists who were involved in the workshops and productions; from the bottom of my heart, I thank you all. Special mention to BC Lee, who assisted greatly with the Cantonese translation in this publication of *Ga Ting*.

EMBODIED VALIDATION IN
GA TING
C.E. GATCHALIAN

As the show's producer, I have sometimes described *Ga Ting* as "*Guess Who's Coming to Dinner* with a dark, queer Asian twist." This reductive précis may work for promotional purposes, but fails to do justice to the play's nuanced, generous humanity.

The story of *Ga Ting* is simple. Matthew, a young white accountant from Vancouver, flies to Toronto to meet Hong and Mai, the parents of his Chinese-Vietnamese ex-boyfriend Kevin, who has recently died. The discussion that ensues over dinner reveals not only the order of events that led to Kevin's death, but the intercultural and intergenerational tensions at the heart of contemporary Canadian society.

When **the frank theatre company** decided to produce the play's world premiere in 2014, we knew we had a play the likes of which Vancouver—and perhaps even Canada—had never truly seen before. While the play's "coming out" aspect may have been familiar, its specific cultural context, and especially its bilingualism—the play, as you will see, is performed in both English and Cantonese—was not. While strides have certainly been made the last two decades vis-à-vis culturally diversifying our stages, Canadian theatre, on the whole, remains sharply disconnected from the country's current and ever-evolving demographic realities.

Along with our co-producers, Vancouver Asian Canadian Theatre, we decided to present the play at the Richmond Cultural Centre in Richmond, a politically conservative, heavily Chinese suburb south of Vancouver. I was both excited and nervous about the choice. Excited because it was evidence of our thinking outside the box and creating an opportunity to reach out to new, diverse audiences; nervous because of my own assumptions about how an ostensibly socially conservative community might respond to the play's subject matter.

The show played to capacity houses over its two-week run. The audience for the show was the most diverse I had seen in my entire life, with respect to race, age, ability, and sexual orientation. Audience members of Chinese descent talked not only about how it was the first time they had gone to live theatre and heard their language included as an integral, dynamic, non-negotiable part of the play; more fundamentally, they said it was the first time they had seen *a reflection of themselves*. If you believe, as I do, that one of the primary duties of theatre is to offer concrete, embodied validation of an audience's experiences and existence, then *Ga Ting* did exactly that. In this sense, *Ga Ting* is a revolutionary piece of theatre.

I must add that if novelty is all this play has going for it, it would not have affected and impacted as many people as it has. The play's strength is its refusal to succumb to dualism. There are no good guys or bad guys—the traditional Chinese parents may be uninformed about queerness, but they are well-meaning, hard-working folks who genuinely loved their child. The white lover, as expected, holds mainstream liberal Canadian values, but, like most white Canadians, is co-opted by structural racism in ways he himself is not fully aware.

Ga Ting's success can be attributed in part to the precise time in which it premiered—near the end of the right-wing Harper era, when there was pushback against the past decade's cultural homogenization and a yen to confront and celebrate difference. But because it is, at its core, a compassionate yet honest representation of the human experiment that is Canada, *Ga Ting*, I believe, will be produced for many years to come.

Ga Ting premiered at the Richmond Cultural Centre in Richmond, BC, on March 22, 2014, co-produced by **the frank theatre company** and Vancouver Asian Canadian Theatre, with the following cast and creative team:

Hong Lee: BC Lee
Mai Lee: Alannah Ong
Matthew: Michael Antonakos

Director: Rick Tae
Set and Costume Design: Christopher David Gauthier
Lighting Design: Gerald King
Sound Design: Heath Whitelock
Projections Design: Ian Chan
Stage Management: Shannon Macelli

Ga Ting had a second mounting presented by the Cultch in Vancouver, BC, produced by **the frank theatre company**, which opened on March 8, 2016, with the following cast and creative team:

Hong Lee: BC Lee
Mai Lee: Alannah Ong
Matthew: Brian J. Sutton

Directed: Rick Tae
Set and Costume Design: Christopher David Gauthier
Lighting Design: Gerald King
Sound Design: Heath Whitelock
Projections Design: Ian Chan
Stage Management: Shannon Macelli

Ga Ting also had support from the Canada Council for the Arts.

CHARACTERS

Hong Lee: the father, Chinese, late fifties
Mai Lee: the mother, Chinese, fifties
Matthew: the boyfriend, white, late twenties/early thirties

PRODUCTION NOTES

Bold text represents dialogue spoken in Cantonese.

Surtitles are projected to translate English into Cantonese, and Cantonese into English.

"Flashbacks" are initiated with an ocean wave sound effect; these scenes from the past begin at the "fall of the ocean wave." An ocean wave also brings the play back to the "present." Perhaps projections can help support the setting of the flashbacks.

Lights up to reveal MAI *and* HONG's *home. A living room leads into an open kitchen with a dining table. The floors are hardwood. Chinese calligraphy adorns the walls, as do a couple of Chinese paintings. The space is very full of items collected throughout the years. Perhaps a Chinese shrine cabinet is in the living room, with a couple of Chinese god statues.*

MATTHEW *is wandering around the living area, shamelessly touching and looking at items.* MAI *is in the kitchen, cooking dinner. She is wearing an apron. There is definitely a rice cooker in the kitchen.*

MATTHEW *arrived from the airport only a few minutes earlier. He is dressed well, with a fitted T-shirt, perhaps, and a blazer. His carry-on is in the living room, and so is a wrapped canvas. There is a vase with bamboo in it on the coffee table. After nosing around for a few minutes,* MATTHEW *picks up a picture frame with a younger* MAI *and* HONG *at a beach in Vietnam.* MAI *approaches.*

MAI: That was long time ago. We very young.

MATTHEW: I can see that, you looked good! I mean, you still look good now, for your age . . .

MAI: Is okay, I know I am old. Sit, dinner almost ready.

MATTHEW: You really didn't have to go to all the trouble. I could have ordered something in, or taken you both out. Do you like steak? There's always the Keg.

MAI: Oh no. Don't be silly. We prefer eat in. This is no trouble. You go to trouble.

MAI gestures to the bamboo.

No need bring present.

MATTHEW: The bamboo? It's nothing. Thought you would like it . . . and by the looks of things, I think it fits right in.

MAI: I like, thank you.

MATTHEW: So . . . dinner's almost ready?

MAI: Ah yes!

   MAI *continues to put dinner together.*

I cook much better before. Now not so good, cook not so much. Only two people live here, easy to get food at restaurant before we come home. We eat very little now. When you get old, you worry about everything. Too much cholesterol, too much fat, too much . . . uh, so-dium, too much sugar, eat too much. So we eat not so much. So, I cook very little.

MATTHEW: I'm sure everything will be delicious. It smells great.

MAI: Hope you like. Better than the Keg.

MATTHEW: Does Mr. Lee need any help?

MAI: No, he is okay.

MATTHEW: You sure? I'm not much of a handyman, but I can try to help. Kevin usually fixed things around the house.

MAI: Yes?

MATTHEW: Well, more like, design things and choose the wall colours.

MAI: Yes, he always very creative. Since Kevin young boy he love drawing. Start with crayons. Ah . . . anyway, Mr. Lee is fine. All day he have time to fix washroom sink. But no, he have to wait for you to come before fixing sink. He will come down soon. Relax, Matthew, sit down.

MATTHEW: Okay.

   MATTHEW *sits.*

MAI: Oh no!

MATTHEW: What's wrong?

MAI: I give you nothing to drink.

MATTHEW: I'm fine. Don't worry about me.

MAI: We have apple juice . . . water . . . and milk—we have milk. I say to Mr. Lee, buy some beer, but he forget.

MATTHEW: Really, Mrs. Lee, I'm fine. I prefer wine anyways. I'm really into Malbecs lately.

MAI: Mao-bec.

MATTHEW: It's a purple grape variety—a type of red wine.

MAI: I'm sorry, I have no Mao-bec.

MATTHEW: That's okay, I was just saying, I didn't mean I wanted any.

MAI: Mr. Lee does this all the time. Wait and wait last minute, then forget what I ask him to do.

MATTHEW: You know what? I would love a glass of water.

MAI: Water?

MATTHEW: Yes.

MAI: I get you water.

MAI gets MATTHEW a glass of water; she pours it from a Brita pitcher.

Your flight was good?

MATTHEW: Yes.

MAI: I tell you call us when you get to Toronto airport, Mr. Lee can go get you. Raining all day. But you did not call . . .

MATTHEW: It stopped raining, and I just ended up calling an Uber. It was fine.

MAI: Uber?

MATTHEW: It's an app on your phone, you put in your location and—

MAI: I know Uber. I use all the time when Mr. Lee is too busy to drive me. I have very good smartphone, touch screen. Like magic.

MATTHEW: Haha . . . I know, it's crazy what things phones can do these days.

MAI: I worry, Matthew. I think you get lost.

MATTHEW: Just a delayed flight.

MAI: It's okay, you here now . . . plane delay all the time. Good weather, bad weather. All the same. They always delay.

MATTHEW: Sorry about that.

MAI: Not your fault. You not fly the plane. Food not ready, so I am the one who is sorry.

MATTHEW: It's no big deal, Mrs. Lee, I'm not even hungry yet.

MAI: Call me Mai.

MATTHEW: Okay . . . well, you can call me Matt.

MAI: Matt.

MATTHEW: Yes.

MAI: Matt.

MATTHEW: Yes, that's it.

MAI: Matt.

MATTHEW: Yup, that's my name.

MAI: I like that name. Matt. Good name. Matt mean something?

MATTHEW: Yes, I googled it once . . . it actually came from the Hebrew name "Matityahu," and means "gift from God." No surprise there, right?

Short beat.

Just kidding. The Greek version of Matthew is Mattathias, which means "divine."

Beat.

MAI: Very nice. I don't know what "Kevin" mean, but his Chinese name mean ocean. More simple. It's—

MATTHEW: "Hoi."

MAI: Yes! Yes! Hoi. He tell you?

MATTHEW: Yeah, he told me. My name isn't quite as . . . beautifully simple.

MAI: No. I like.

MATTHEW: Thank you.

HONG enters. MATTHEW leaps to his feet to be polite.

HONG: **The food is not ready yet?**
還沒有飯吃呀?

MAI: **Almost.**
差不多啦.

HONG: **I'm starving.**
餓啦.

MAI: **Wait a little.**
快啦.

HONG looks at MATTHEW. MATTHEW looks at HONG. Beat.

MATTHEW: Hi, I'm Matthew . . . or Matt for short.

HONG leans in to shake MATTHEW's hand.

HONG: Yes. Hong . . . Hong for short.

MATTHEW: Haha . . . yeah, that's funny . . .

HONG: Yes, I am funny man. All the time my friends say to me, "Hong, you so funny!"

Beat. HONG gets himself something to drink.

MATTHEW: Faucet's all fixed . . .

About to say "Hong" but thinks better of it.

. . . Mr. Lee?

HONG: Yes.

MAI: Matt bring us present.

MATTHEW: It's nothing, really.

MATTHEW offers the bamboo to HONG.

MAI: Bamboo.

HONG: Mm. Very . . . original.

MATTHEW: I thought you would like it.

HONG: Yes, of course.

MATTHEW: How's your weekend been?

HONG: Good.

Beat.

MATTHEW: Excuse me, can I use your washroom for a sec?

MAI: Yes, yes, door there, turn right.

MATTHEW: Thanks, wash my hands before dinner. Germs on a flight, you know?

MATTHEW exits.

MAI: **Why are you being so weird?**
你古里古怪的做什麼?

HONG: **I am trying to make conversation.**
我在沒話找話說.

MAI: **Don't be mean.**
你給我老實點.

HONG: **I don't know what you're talking about.**
你甚麼意思.

MAI: **Please be nice to him.**
對人家客氣點.

HONG: **Okay, okay . . . hurry up, I'm hungry.**
得了得了, 快點開飯吧, 我餓死了.

MAI: **I'm serious.**
我可是認真的.

HONG: **I know.**
知道了.

MAI: **Help me get the rice.**
去盛飯!

HONG grabs some bowls of rice and brings them to the dinner table. MATTHEW enters.

Almost ready, Matt.

MATTHEW: Can I help?

MAI: No. You sit.

MATTHEW: Okay.

MATTHEW sits. MAI and HONG finish getting the table ready. MAI lights candles.

You have a nice home.

MAI: Thank you. When you get old, all you have is home. So have to take care.

MATTHEW: It shows. Love the hardwood.

HONG: Hm.

MAI: One more candle.

HONG: Candles. She love candles.

MAI: Good after cooking. Get rid of frying smell.

MATTHEW: I like the smell of a kitchen after some cooking.

HONG: Candle just cover it up.

MATTHEW: Well . . . I like candles, too. Ginger peach?

MAI: Ginger peach?

MATTHEW: That candle, the scent, it smells like ginger peach.

MAI: I don't know . . .

MAI pick up the "ginger peach" candle and reads the label on the bottom of it.

Yes, yes, "ginger peach." Wah, you have very good nose.

MATTHEW: I used to work part time at a home decor store when I was in school. We had candles aplenty.

MAI: Candles of plenty?

MATTHEW: Plenty of candles . . . lots . . .

MAI: A lot—

MATTHEW: Yes . . . scented candles . . . lots . . . of candles.

HONG and MAI blank-face stare at him.

I like the smell of a well-used kitchen and candles . . . together, it's great.

MAI is now seated as well.

MAI: Yes . . . great, very great. Enough candle talk. Start eating . . . eat!

HONG is already eating. Beat.

You need fork?

MATTHEW: I can use chopsticks just fine.

MAI: Eat!

MATTHEW hesitates.

Something wrong? You not like the food?

MATTHEW: No, it's just . . . I imagined this moment. Meeting you both over dinner, and believe it or not, this is kind of how I pictured it. This setting, the plates . . . everything. It just feels surreal that this is finally happening. I was taking it all in. Everything looks fantastic.

MAI: Thank you. Eat a lot. I don't want leftover.

MATTHEW delves into the food. Beat.

We cannot wait for you to come. Right, Hong?

HONG: Hmhmm. I could not sleep last night. So excited.

MAI: **What are you saying?**
你在講什麼?

HONG: **I said I couldn't sleep last night, because I was so excited.**
我就說我興奮的一夜難面.

MAI slaps HONG on the shoulder.

MAI: Anyway . . . we meet at last.

MATTHEW: Yes . . . at last.

Beat. HONG is scarfing down a lot of food.

MAI: **Don't eat so fast.**
做什麼吃這麼快?

HONG: **I told you I'm hungry.**
我說過我餓啦.

Beat.

MATTHEW: You made a lot of food.

HONG: Because you are here.

MAI: **It's because he's here that there's so much food. You should be happy.**
你是託他的福才有那麼多好菜吃. 你才該高興.

HONG: **I am happy, very happy.**
高興, 當然高興.

MATTHEW: Did I say something?

MAI: What you mean?

MATTHEW: Is something wrong?

MAI: No, no. Nothing wrong.

MAI eyes HONG.

HONG: Nothing wrong.

MAI: **Thank him for the gift.**
謝謝人家的禮物呀.

HONG: **What gift?**
什麼禮物?

MAI: **The bamboo!**
竹子呀!

HONG: **I thanked him already.**
不是謝過了嗎.

MAI: **No you didn't.**
沒有.

MATTHEW: Woah, there's a lot of talking going on!

HONG: Ah . . . thank you for bamboo.

MATTHEW: You're welcome. I was told bamboo brings good fortune.

HONG: Hmhmm.

> *Beat. Everyone eats.*

MATTHEW: How long have you lived in Toronto?

MAI: Long time . . . we move here from Vietnam and stay here.

MATTHEW: You might have loved Vancouver. You get the ocean, mountains, and a ton of beaches.

HONG: Beaches in Toronto, too.

MATTHEW: I'm sure there are, I was just—

MAI: Yes, when Kevin a little kid, we take him all the time to . . . Wasaga Beach. It was his favourite . . . so much energy, always run around the sand. But one time . . .

> *Flashback to when Kevin was a child.* MAI *and* HONG *are watching Kevin at the beach shore.*

HONG: **Mai, where is Kevin?**
阿美，凱文呢?

MAI: **He is just over there, in the water with the other kids.**
他跟其他小朋友在那邊玩水.

HONG: **You let him go by himself?**
你就讓他一個人去玩?

MAI: **He's fine.**
沒問題的啦.

HONG: **Mai, I think something's wrong, he's not moving.**
有點不妥. 他沒在動.

MAI: **What? Let's go down there. Kevin! Kevin!!**
什麼, 下去看看, 凱文! 凱文!!

HONG: **Oh, wait . . . he's moving again, he's fine. Scared me to death.**
等一等, 他在動了, 沒事, 嚇死我了.

MAI: **That's not funny, Kevin. Don't you ever scare your father and I like that again.**
凱文, 這不能開玩笑, 以後不可以這樣嚇我和你爸.

HONG: **Did you teach him how to float in the water?**
是你教他浮水的?

MAI: **No, I can't even float.**
沒有, 我自己都不會.

HONG: **Kevin, you're still laughing? Stop laughing this instant. Never do that again, it scared us to death. Stop it!**
凱文, 你還笑. 不准笑. 以後不可以這樣, 把我們都嚇到了.還笑!

Present.

MAI: To this day, we still don't know who teach him to float.

MATTHEW: Maybe he taught himself when you weren't looking.

HONG: I always looking.

MATTHEW: Really? Always? That's impossible.

HONG: Possible.

MATTHEW: You can't always have your eyes on someone.

HONG: Possible.

MATTHEW: Impossible.

HONG: Possible.

MATTHEW: Okay, how many pieces of bok choy has Mai eaten so far?

HONG: Stupid question, I not looking.

MATTHEW: See?

HONG: I watch Kevin closely before, he was baby and my son. Mai my wife. After we marry, no need to watch so closely. She is grown-up woman. Will not choke on bok choy.

MATTHEW: I don't know what we're talking about anymore.

MAI: We talking about how Kevin surprise us all the time. He do things when we not looking.

HONG: I always looking.

MAI: **Enough.**
夠了.

Kevin always know what he want.

MATTHEW: Yes he did.

Beat. More eating.

How are you two doing . . . with everything? I mean . . .

HONG: Good. Fine.

MATTHEW: You sure?

HONG: You expect another answer?

MATTHEW: No. It's just . . . it can't be—

MAI: We are his parents. We do our best. It is hard . . . but we try. How are you . . . with everything?

MATTHEW: It hasn't been easy, but of course we all . . . have to move on eventually.

Beat.

I'm sorry . . . I didn't mean it that way.

MAI: It is okay.

Beat.

MATTHEW: How was the funeral? Everything went smoothly?

MAI: Yes.

MATTHEW: So . . . I really wanted to be there.

HONG: The food is very good today.

MATTHEW: I can't help but wonder why I wasn't invited.

HONG: We forget.

MATTHEW: You . . . forgot?

HONG: You are not family.

MATTHEW: But I am—I mean . . . I was.

HONG: No.

MAI: What Mr. Lee mean is—

MATTHEW: I was very much a part of Kevin's family. So were his friends.

HONG: Not blood.

MATTHEW: Just because I'm not blood, doesn't mean I didn't love him. I called and called . . . left messages . . . sent you a letter about Kevin I wanted to share at the funeral. I tried to find out what was going on, but no one got back to me.

MAI: Too soon, we did not know what to do with . . . you and Kevin and . . .

MATTHEW: Kevin's funeral was my chance to say goodbye to him. I just wish you could've given me that.

HONG: What you want now? Us to say we sorry? It happen.

MATTHEW: I want to understand why you couldn't have included me?

HONG: You have no idea what we go through. You only think what you want. What you think is right. You give money for funeral? You organize everything? You raise Kevin from baby to big man? You know him two, three years. That is all.

(to MAI) **The soup is also very good tonight.**
今晚的湯很好.

MATTHEW: What did you just say?

HONG: I said the soup is very good tonight. Have some and shut up.

MAI: **Hong!**
阿鴻!

MATTHEW: I should have been at the funeral.

HONG: You come to mine! And it happen very soon if you keep talking like this.

MAI: **Choy, choy, choy . . . don't say things like that!**
呸!呸!呸! 講這什麼呀. 阿修, 我了解你的傷痛!

I understand why you upset, Matt.

HONG: **We owe him nothing. He didn't need to be there.**
我們可沒欠他的. 沒必要讓他在那場合出現.

MAI: **We should have invited him.**
我們應給讓他來的.

Beat.

Matthew, when Kevin died, it was all too much, we cannot handle. Too much family visit already. But tomorrow . . . if you want, we can take you to cemetery.

Beat.

MATTHEW: I would like that.

HONG: **I don't have time.**
我沒空.

MAI: **Then I will go by myself.**
那我自己去.

HONG: **It's too far to bus.**
坐巴士太遠.

MAI: **Then I will ask my sister to drive us.**
我叫我姊帶我們去.

MATTHEW: All I'm saying is what happened, how you dealt with everything, I don't think Kevin would have wanted it like that.

MAI: I know . . .

MATTHEW: I want you to understand . . . that it—

MAI: We understand. I am sorry that you not there.

MATTHEW: Thank you, Mai.

HONG: You get apology. Happy now?

MATTHEW: We'll visit the cemetery tomorrow then?

MAI: Yes . . .

Hong?
好的, 阿鴻?

HONG: **It's your problem, do whatever you want.**
你的事, 跟我無關.

HONG gets up to scoop himself some more rice from the rice cooker.

MATTHEW: I understand that this is hard for you, Mr. Lee. It's just . . . I miss him, too.

Beat.

MAI: How long you stay in Toronto?

MATTHEW: A couple days, meetings with a few clients.

MAI: What do you do?

MATTHEW: For work?

MAI: Yes.

MATTHEW: I'm an accountant.

HONG: You do tax?

MATTHEW: Not exactly. I work for KPMG, a big accounting firm.

MAI: Oh.

MATTHEW: I know, you probably would have expected me to be in something more . . . creative, design-oriented. Something with more pizzazz!

MAI: No.

MATTHEW: Truth is, I like stability. I started off as a clerk, now I'm an auditor. We got a few new accounts in Toronto, that's why I'm here. Basically my job's to analyze numbers to help maximize profits.

MAI: You enjoy?

MATTHEW: It's a job. Not everyone's lucky enough to love what they do for work.

HONG: A job should be like that. You don't need to love it.

MATTHEW: But it—

HONG: Work is just work. Do you make good money?

MAI whacks HONG.

MATTHEW: I do well enough, but I'm definitely not rich.

HONG: Good. I not open restaurant because I love it. I open restaurant because I need it. And after twenty years I still do not love it.

MATTHEW: You must love it a little . . .

HONG: Need. Not love.

MAI: **Enough, enough.**
夠了,夠了.

(to MATTHEW) Try this, you did not have any yet.

MAI puts some food in MATTHEW's bowl.

MATTHEW: Sure . . . hmmm, yummy.

MAI: Yummy?

MATTHEW: I meant . . . tasty.

MAI: Please, tell us more . . . about yourself.

MATTHEW: Sure, but I really don't know what else to say.

MAI: Anything.

MATTHEW: Um . . . I was born and raised in Vancouver. You don't find many of those there. Trust me, everyone seems to be flying in from everywhere else.

MAI: Yes . . .

MATTHEW: And I got my undergrad at UBC. I eventually landed myself a corporate job . . . lucky me.

MAI: What else?

MATTHEW: Well . . . my favourite colour's blue, this is my third time in Toronto . . . and . . . I really loved your son, and have always wanted to meet his parents. I wish this happened earlier, when he was—

HONG: Why?

MATTHEW: Because you're his family.

HONG: No need.

MATTHEW: Mr. Lee, we were boyfriends. All of us should have gotten together a long time ago.

HONG: For what? To talk about what? No need before for you to come.

MATTHEW: But enough of a reason for us to meet now?

HONG: Mai think so.

MAI: If we know what we know now, we maybe meet before. But we not know you then, Matt. Kevin not say much about you. And when he pass, we so busy with funeral, family visit, no time to answer your messages. When you call again a few weeks ago, everything settle down, so . . . we are here. Please understand.

MATTHEW: Yes, here we are.

MAI: You meet us now.

  Beat.

Kevin meet your parents?

MATTHEW: He did, a couple months in. They adored him.

HONG: Of course.

MATTHEW: What do you mean, "of course"?

HONG: You people always so open-minded. Accepting everyone, and you—

MATTHEW: —"You people"?

HONG: Caucasian, white, Greek, French, English, you all look the same . . .

MATTHEW: You're generalizing.

HONG: Generalizing?

MATTHEW: To talk about a large group being the—

HONG: I know what it mean.

MATTHEW: So?

HONG: So, I should not "generalize"?

MATTHEW: I wouldn't do that to you.

HONG: Oh no? What about bamboo?

MATTHEW: Do you not like it?

MAI: No, Matt, we love it.

HONG: Why bamboo? Why not lilac?

MAI: Some more soup!

MATTHEW: I just thought—

HONG: You just thought that all Asian people—do you even know what background we are?

MATTHEW: Yes, of course, you're Chinese.

HONG: We are Korean.

MATTHEW: What? Weren't you just speaking Cantonese? Oh my God, I'm—

HONG: Of course we are Chinese! Do you see any kimchi on the table?

MATTHEW: No—

HONG: And we have a Chinese restaurant, not a convenience store.

MATTHEW: Now you are generalizing.

HONG: Joking.

MATTHEW: Funny.

HONG: Yes, all Chinese families can use bamboo in the house. We all need good fortune.

MAI: **What are you saying?**
你在說什麼呀?

MATTHEW: It's okay . . . I'm sorry if I offended you with my gift.

HONG: I am not offended. But you should not be upset with me for "generalizing" your family if you are that way yourself.

MATTHEW: Okay, lilacs next time . . . if there is a next time.

HONG: I prefer sunflower.

MATTHEW: Sure.

Beat.

MAI: Kevin talk to you about us?

MATTHEW: Of course he did.

MAI: What he say?

MATTHEW: That you are closed-minded, controlling, and unaffectionate.

MAI: What?

MATTHEW: But he also said that you're generous, hard-working, protective, and he wouldn't trade you for the world.

MAI: Unaffectionate? He did not think we love him?

MATTHEW: He knew that you loved him. He just never heard it. Sometimes hearing it helps.

HONG: Why you need to hear if you know?

MATTHEW: Because he's human and not a robot. Is saying "I love you" to your own son so hard?

HONG: It is not what we say, but what we do. We work hard to give him everything. That is our way.

MATTHEW: Your way might not have been enough is all.

HONG: That is you. That does not mean it is us. We are not that kind of family.

MATTHEW: You were the kind that didn't communicate.

MAI: We talk to him.

HONG: Enough! You are not here to teach us how to be a better family.

MATTHEW: You're right, I'm not here to teach you anything. But you could have asked your son more questions. Kevin wanted to talk to you more.

HONG: Are you blaming us for what happen?

MATTHEW: I'm just saying things could have been different if you were more involved in his life. He tried to tell you that his bipolar was getting worse. You knew he was unstable.

MAI: Kevin bipolar is very hard for us to understand.

MATTHEW: You mean it was hard for you to accept?

MAI: We try . . . we think he just moody.

MATTHEW: There was nothing to think about. He was diagnosed by a doctor. He told you it was something that needed medication. But what, you thought it was just mood swings? It was a disease.

MAI: He was emotional about everything.

HONG: We do not believe happy sometime then sad sometime so wrong.

MATTHEW: Well it was. He was often depressed. You both could have pressured him to open up to you more . . .

MAI: *(to HONG)* How come we not know?

MATTHEW: How did he seem when he visited?

MAI: Fine.

MATTHEW: Happy?

MAI: Yes.

MATTHEW: Glad to be home?

MAI: I think so.

MATTHEW: Healthy?

HONG: What are you doing?

MATTHEW: She said you didn't know, so I'm just wondering how you could have missed all the hints.

MAI: Maybe we not ask enough questions.

HONG: He have mouth, too. If he want to talk more, he can talk more.

MATTHEW: How often did you call him?

MAI: I call him every week.

MATTHEW: I meant you, Mr. Lee.

HONG: Enough. I know my son.

MATTHEW: Then why are you trying to learn more about him through some stranger?

MAI: You close to Kevin—

HONG: **Enough! I don't want to hear anymore!**
夠了, 我不要再聽下去!

MAI: **Relax, Hong. He is just trying to explain some things to us.**
別這樣了, 阿鴻, 他只是想跟我們解釋一些事情.

HONG: I talk to him like my parents talk to me.

Beat.

I ask him how he is. How is school? He always say, "fine." Everything is always "fine." Why I think something is wrong?

MATTHEW: It can't be "fine" when everything is always "fine."

MATTHEW and MAI attempt to interject during HONG's following passage.

HONG: Again, you think you know what is right. Just because I do not tell my son I love him, or hug him, or ask him a lot of question does not mean I do not know how to be a father. I teach him how to be in society. To have manners, to be polite. To respect his elder. I raise him to understand what hard work mean, that money has to be earn. There is a lot more to being a father than saying "I love you." You do not have a child and maybe never will. You have no right to tell me what to do!

MATTHEW: Okay . . . I hear you, and I understand. All I'm saying is . . . Kevin didn't feel that you ever really talked to him, or cared to know who he really was. You never truly liked the fact that he was an artist, did you?

MAI: We did not mind.

MATTHEW: But you were never really happy about that, right?

Flashback to when Kevin was a teenager.

HONG: **A painter? How will you make money?**
做畫家? 你能賺多少錢呀?

MAI: **Let him be.**
由得他吧.

HONG: **Kevin, think this through. Painting? How would you pay for rent and food? You have to eat, you know?!**
凱文, 你想清楚. 畫畫? 要不要交房租, 要不要買菜? 你要不要吃飯?!

MAI: **Son, we are just worried about your future.**
兒子呀, 我們是擔心你呀.

HONG: **You don't know how hard the real world is. You think not being afraid is enough? Huh? How will you raise a family?**
你知不知道這世界艱難, 你以為膽子夠就行, 你怎麼養家活口?

Beat.

Well, it is something you need to think about!
你要好好想想呀!

MAI: **It's very risky. Your dad would not have been able to give you the life you have if he continued to only paint.**
你這太冒險了. 如果你爸也只靠畫畫, 你以為他有辦法一手把你養大.

HONG: **No, I couldn't just do what I wanted to. I had responsibilities. I had you!**
不可能. 我不能想做什麼就做什麼. 我有責任. 我有你!

MAI: **He's not blaming you for anything. Your father is simply saying—**
他不是什麼都怪你, 你爸爸是說—

HONG: **I don't want to argue with you anymore!**
我不跟你吵了!

Beat.

That's right, when things don't sound good to you, you run up to your room and hide.
好吧, 一講你不愛聽的, 你就躲到房間裡.

Beat.

MAI: **He is talented and stubborn.**
他有天份, 也很牛脾氣.

HONG: **You really think he is talented?**
你真的認為他有天份?

MAI: **You've seen his drawings since he was a kid, what do you think?**
你也看過他從小畫的畫, 你怎麼說?

HONG: **I think talent is not enough.**
光有天份是不夠的.

MAI: **You don't need to be your father, you know?**
你不需要跟你爸一樣.

HONG: **I'm not.**
我沒有.

MAI: **Then maybe we should let him be.**
那或許我們應該跟他說.

HONG: **I just don't want him to . . . do I have a choice?**
我只是真的不希望他 . . . 有我說話的份\嗎?

Present.

MAI: But we never stop him after that.

MATTHEW: You never encouraged him either. Kevin wasn't making hundreds of thousands of dollars, but he was making it work. Yeah, he also worked at a Second Cup. At least it wasn't Starbucks, and every artist has a day job.

HONG: Why you say all this? We could do this, we could do that.

MATTHEW: He could have used more support.

HONG: Something wrong with you! I lose my son. And now you want me to say sorry for everything? That what you want?

MATTHEW: No . . . I want you to understand . . . Kevin would want you to—

HONG: No! You want. You don't know—you have no way to know for sure what Kevin want.

MATTHEW: I know he would've wanted me to be at his funeral. I know he wanted us all to get together. I know he wanted you to understand—

HONG: I understand! I know what I want to do for him. I give him the best funeral I can afford. The best cemetery, not too crowded. The best tombstone. The best . . . everything. I want the best for him. When he alive, and now! All you have are ideas. You think I should listen to my son more, talk to him more, understand his feelings. I set up good life for him. I make sure his path is good. All he has to do is walk on it!

HONG is clenching his heart as though he might fall over. He sits down, possibly away from the dinner table, in the living room area.

MATTHEW: Are you okay? I'm sorry, I didn't mean to . . .

HONG: What you mean not matter. What you do matter.

MATTHEW: I'll get you some water.

HONG: No, I don't need you to—

MAI: **Stop it!**
夠了!

It's okay, Matt. Let me.

MAI brings HONG a glass of water.

Calm down, don't get so frustrated. Here, drink this.
冷靜點, 幹什麼氣成這樣. 來, 喝點水.

HONG drinks some of the water. Beat.

MATTHEW: I'm sorry for upsetting you.

MAI: Mr. Lee also very passionate. Kevin get his temper from his father.

(to HONG) **Do you want more water?**
你還要水嗎?

HONG: **I have enough.**
夠了.

MAI: Matt, we help him go to Vancouver. We give money for him to go. We support him the way we know how.

HONG: **You don't have to explain things to him.**
你不用跟他解釋.

MATTHEW: He would have loved for you to show up to one of his art openings.

MAI: Too far away.

MATTHEW: Maybe you could have taken some time off and gone there?

MAI: Not easy to take time off, Matt. We always have to be around to look after restaurant.

MATTHEW: He thought you weren't all that interested, so he didn't push you. But he really wanted you to come.

MAI: He always say he was—

MATTHEW: Fine?

MAI: Yes.

MATTHEW: The way he looked at the world around him was . . . special. He'd make me stop and observe things I'd usually just walk by. He was able to see colours in the mundane I would never notice, and brought them out in his work. Kevin wanted you to know how good he was. There was this abstract piece of Toronto and Vancouver he did a few months after we met. His heart really was in both cities. It was the first time I realized how talented he was. Kevin's love for his work was contagious . . . he inspired me to do more of what I loved.

Beat.

MAI: What?

HONG: **Why are you still talking to him? Tell him to go.**
你還在跟他談什麼, 叫他走吧.

MAI: **Don't be like that.**
別這樣.

What, Matt? What did Kevin make you do?

Beat.

MATTHEW: Sing. I loved singing when I was a kid. You know, did the whole choir thing and took music throughout high school. But to pursue it any further wasn't realistic. I just kept telling myself there is a huge commonality between music and math. What I love about both is the specificity. With math, it's about being exact, precise, calculated. With music, you need to be just as precise but with rhythm, beat, and keys.

MAI: Wah.

HONG: *(sarcastically)* Good for you.

MAI: Kevin painting make you want to sing?

MATTHEW: He reminded me of how it felt to be on stage.

MAI: You on stage before?

MATTHEW: Actually, last year Kevin pushed me to compete in an *American Idol*-like competition.

MAI: *American Idol*, Hong. You love to watch *American Idol*.

HONG: Hm.

MATTHEW: Well, it wasn't "the" *American Idol*. It was a competition in our neighbourhood called *Westend Idol*.

HONG: *Westend Idol*, Mai. Not same thing.

MAI: **It doesn't matter, he sang in a competition.**
總也是歌唱比賽呀.

HONG: **So what? Big deal.**
又怎樣, 了不起啊?

MAI: You win?

MATTHEW: Not exactly.

HONG: See?

MATTHEW: I placed second. It was for fun anyways.

MAI: Oh, wah, second place. You must be very good.

MATTHEW: I'm not bad.

MAI: Sing something for us.

MATTHEW: Uh . . . no, really, I can't.

MAI: Please.

MATTHEW: Not now.

MAI: Hong, you want to hear Matt sing?

Beat.

HONG: I love to. Please, go ahead.

Beat.

MATTHEW: Well . . . okay. Um . . .

Flashback to Westend Idol.

(to Kevin) This is for you, babe.

> MATTHEW *starts to sing. "Over The Rainbow." He sings it beautifully flowing into . . .*

> *Flashback to* MAI *and* HONG *at home when Kevin was a baby.* MAI *is holding Kevin, and* HONG *is by her.* MAI *is putting Kevin to sleep humming the same song* MATTHEW *is singing ("Over The Rainbow"), and slowly flows into singing it herself. After a while, she sets Kevin down into his crib.*

HONG: **What are you singing?**
你在唱什麼?

MAI: **"Over the Rainbow."**

HONG: **Where did you learn that song?**
那裡學來的?

MAI: **They taught it to us in night school. Singing a song is teaching me English.**
英文夜校. 唱歌學英文.

HONG: **Sing Cantonese to him, Mai. You don't want him to not know his mother tongue.**
唱中文歌給他聽, 別讓他以後連自己的母語都不會聽.

MAI: **I know, I know, relax, it's just one song.**
我知道, 別緊張, 一首歌, 沒那麼嚴重.

HONG: Listen to me sing.
聽我來唱.

> HONG *starts to sing a Chinese ballad.* MAI *continues to sing "Over The Rainbow" to toy with him. Both melodies blend together, flowing into* MATTHEW's *singing in the present. Transition to . . .*

> *Present.* MATTHEW *finishes singing. Awkward silence.*

MATTHEW: It was that bad?

MAI: No, no. Very good. You have beautiful voice.

HONG: Not bad.

MATTHEW: It was one of Kevin's favourite songs.

MAI: We know.

> *Beat.*

MATTHEW: Anyways, I played it safe . . . but not Kevin. He pursued his passions wholeheartedly. He was always shamelessly himself, didn't care what people thought of him. I just wish he could have been more of who he was around both of you when he visited. I mean . . . be out . . . openly gay at home, here.

MAI: If he say something before . . . maybe I understand.

MATTHEW: He didn't think you would.

> *Flashback to* MATTHEW *talking to Kevin in their apartment.*

What are you so afraid of? You don't even live with them anymore, it's not like they can kick you out. Christmas is as good as any other time to come out. It'll be like . . . an extra Christmas gift. Will you put that paintbrush down for a sec and listen to me?

I love you. I want you to be happy. And no matter how happy you might seem in Vancouver living your life with me, our friends, and pursuing your art . . . I think you're still missing something. When you go to that . . . dark place, it scares me because I can't do anything.

I think telling your parents will help. I know, I know . . . you come from a traditional Chinese family, but they've got to deal with it. Being gay is almost trendy nowadays. So please just do it this time when you get home . . . for me . . . for us . . .

You don't want to disappoint them . . . right.

> *Beat.*

Present.

MAI: We did not know for sure . . . but sometimes, before . . . I think maybe he was . . .

HONG: **Mai, what are you saying?**
阿美, 你在說什麼?

MAI: I sometimes feel he like boys.

Don't say you didn't know.
不要說你不知道.

He have no girlfriend in high school. Not play hockey, not play baseball, not play—

MATTHEW: Whether someone plays a sport or not doesn't tell you if they're gay. I'm in a curling league.

MAI: Matt, you not help.

MATTHEW: Dodgeball?

Beat.

Nevermind.

MAI: I am his mother. Deep down, I know.

(to HONG) You know, too.

MATTHEW: What were you so afraid of?

MAI: That he will be hurt. That the world see him as not normal.

MATTHEW: That didn't happen. He had a lot of friends.

MAI: Yes, I think he maybe . . . queer, but not for sure.

MATTHEW: Why do you say "queer"?

MAI: Pride Festival, I see "queer" everywhere.

MATTHEW: Gay . . . gay! He was gay.

HONG: "Queer" sound less gay.

Awkward beat.

MAI: Tell me . . . when you first meet Kevin?

MATTHEW: It was a little over three years ago.

MAI: He just finish school.

MATTHEW: That's right.

MAI: We think he will come back home after he graduate. But no, he say he want to stay in Vancouver.

MATTHEW: It's a beautiful city.

MAI: So where you meet?

Flashback to a gay dance club. Club music fades in. MATTHEW *is at the club with Kevin.*

MATTHEW: Hi. Kevin, you said? I'm Matthew, or Matt, whatever.

Beat.

Well, you said Kevin, or Kev whatever, so I thought I'd—nevermind.

Beat.

Yeah, I'm here with friends or at least I was. You?

Beat.

Oh come on, the fact that they're all coupled up is . . . cute.

Beat.

Cute like me? Haha yeah . . . anyways . . . I like your piercing, the hole's a bit higher than the norm, it's . . . unique.

Beat.

Wait . . . where are you taking me?

Beat.

Nah, my friends might come back, let's just stay here.

Beat.

No, that's not true. I am into Asians. I mean it's not my preference, but you're . . .

Present for MAI *and* HONG. MATTHEW *remains in the flashback at the dance club.*

HONG: You are racist.

MAI: HONG!

HONG: He just say he not like Asian. What is wrong with Asian? Hm?

MAI: Let him explain.

MATTHEW: . . . different. I'm sorry that came out wrong. I like all sorts of guys, just not typically Asian ones.

MAI: Just like how you only like Asian ladies when you young, Hong.

HONG: We meet in Vietnam, not much choice.

MATTHEW: The point is . . . you got my attention, I didn't expect it.

HONG: Why?

MATTHEW: Well . . . you're not typically Asian.

MAI: Typical?

MATTHEW: Yeah, come on, you know Asian men in the gay community have certain . . . connotations . . .

MAI: Connotations?

MATTHEW: Things we think Asians are like.

MAI: What kind of thing?

MATTHEW: Well . . . um . . . honestly? Okay . . . Asian men are thought to be effeminate, not very athletic, submissive, all bottoms—I mean, God, you're really putting me on the spot here . . .

HONG: That is stupid.

MATTHEW: I know, you're right, I admit it, I'm a bit prejudiced. Anyways, prove me wrong.

Transition to a few moments later at the dance club.

A Long Island for me? Thanks. Budweiser . . . interesting choice. I didn't see you as a beer drinker.

MATTHEW has a sip of his drink.

Yummy. Hey, there's nothing wrong with saying yummy. Tasty . . . better?

MATTHEW now also shifts back into the present.

From that night on we were inseparable. We ended up going to Denny's after the club. Boy, your son could eat! He had a sampler, a milkshake, and a piece of apple pie at two in the morning. I just went for my usual Grand Slam—love my pancakes!

HONG: He still always look so skinny when he come home. He never eat enough.

MATTHEW: Oh, trust me, he ate . . . a lot. And he looked good. Like . . . reeeally good. I just wanted to . . .

Beat.

MAI: How you remember all this?

MATTHEW: It was our first meal together. I guess you remember things like that with someone you love.

MAI: So what happen after you eat? At Denny's? . . .

MATTHEW: Well . . . um . . . I think we went our separate ways that night after we ate. Yeah . . . or probably we went back to my place . . . and . . . um . . . we took a Grand Slam to go.

MAI: You can do takeout at Denny's in Vancouver?

MATTHEW: Yes, yes you can . . . and Kevin licked the second Grand Slam clean. It was incredible.

Beat.

Chemistry is a weird thing. It's like this invisible string that ties you to someone, and you just want to be around each other all the time.

Flashback to MATTHEW with Kevin at an apartment viewing.

Sorry I'm late! Oh wow . . . big windows.

Beat.

An art studio, really? I think that room's better off as my office. Hardwood floors, nice, nice. Wow, the bedroom's huge. Yes, and of course even better, the closet's huge. Something you still need to get out of.

Beat.

Okay, okay, not now.

Beat.

All right, the big closet's yours, I'm not the one who's hiding.

Beat.

All right, I'm sorry, I'll stop. Stainless steel appliances are great, but it's not like you cook.

Beat.

Eight hundred dollars each . . . let me think about it . . . I'm kidding.

Beat.

I mean this place is pretty amazing. I don't need to commute all the way from Commercial Drive anymore. English Bay is at our doorstep. I'm game.

Beat.

Whoa, calm down. What's this?

MATTHEW has a jade pendant on a necklace in his hands.

Oh wow . . . yeah, I know it's jade. "Beauty, grace, and purity"? Everything I am! I'm kidding!!

Beat.

I love it, babe. Thank you.

Present.

MAI: We believe jade is invaluable.

HONG: You live together? Two men . . .

MATTHEW: We did.

HONG: You do not care what people think?

MATTHEW: No, I didn't . . . and you shouldn't either.

HONG: Do not tell me that until you bring up a family with nothing but your bare hands. When I first come to this country, before I open restaurant, I work in a window factory.

MAI: **Don't talk about that now.**
現在提這幹嘛.

HONG: One break time, there was a water station. All the workers line up to fill cups with water. They keep pushing me back.

MAI: **That was a long time ago, Hong, why are you bringing it up?**
老掉牙的事還提來幹嗎?

HONG: So I push one back. Then they gang up on me, start fight. They big group. I am one person. Boss not believe what I say. Back then, I do not know English. Boss look at me, think I start trouble, so he fire me. So . . . how you look, "What people think," does matter.

MAI: **Enough, enough.**
夠了, 夠啦.

Beat.

MATTHEW: I see . . . but we didn't get together to piss off the world . . . or you. We met and fell in love, we didn't know any other way. Kevin never cared what people thought. He only cared about what you thought.

Beat.

If that wasn't the case you might have gotten this sooner.

MATTHEW moves to the wrapped canvas that is in the living room area and picks it up.

This is what Kevin was going to give you.

MATTHEW hands MAI the wrapped canvas.

I found it in the closet. It was labelled "To Mom and Dad." That's when I called you. I thought you should have it.

Beat.

Go on, open it.

MAI begins unwrapping the canvas. The canvas is unwrapped. Silence. MAI takes some time to turn the painting right-side up. It is of Kevin's attempt to write the Chinese character "FAMILY," with the backdrop a painting of Toronto and Vancouver melded together (perhaps two well-known landmarks from each city flowing into each other). MAI turns the canvas around to show HONG.

MAI: **Look, Hong.**
阿鴻, 你看.

HONG: **"Family."**
家.

MATTHEW: What does it say?

MAI: Family.

MATTHEW: Family.

MATTHEW chuckles.

Of course . . . and that's the painting I told you about. Toronto and Vancouver in one. They were both his home.

MAI: It is beautiful. Sometimes I think he forget about us.

MATTHEW: He never did.

HONG has approached the canvas by now.

HONG: It's very good. Very good. He remember where he come from.

MATTHEW: Yeah, he did. Who knows, maybe your ways can get him to the same place.

MAI: What place is that?

MATTHEW: His true self.

MAI: Thank you for bringing this to us, Matt.

MATTHEW: You're welcome.

Beat.

I was hoping you could share something with me.

MAI: What you mean?

MATTHEW: I'm planning to have a memorial for Kevin when I get back to Vancouver.

HONG: A memorial?

MATTHEW: We didn't really get a chance to say goodbye. It's an opportunity for everyone to say their farewells . . . have a bit of closure.

MAI: Oh.

MATTHEW: Nothing big, at a local art studio. Just a bunch of his friends. Everyone would love to hear a bit about Kevin from his parents. I was hoping you could write a few words for me to share.

Beat.

MAI: Yes.

HONG: No.

MATTHEW: Why not?

HONG: I do not have time to write anything.

MAI: **Don't be like that—**
别這樣—

MATTHEW: It's a celebration of your son's life, with his friends.

HONG: We do not know them. They do not know us.

MAI: What do you want me to write?

HONG: I say no.

MATTHEW: Anything . . . anything about Kevin at all. Doesn't have to be long, a few sentences will do.

HONG: The people that go . . . they all . . .

MATTHEW: Gay?

HONG: Yes.

MATTHEW: Some.

HONG: **Mai, we don't know the kinds of people that will be at this event.**
阿美. 我們不認識那種人.

MAI: **It doesn't matter.**
沒關係.

MATTHEW: You don't have to worry, Mr. Lee, we won't be there celebrating his sexuality. He did enough of that when he was alive, trust me.

HONG: If we are part of memorial, it will look like we are okay with Kevin being gay.

MATTHEW: Is that a bad thing? It'll be about time.

MAI: I will give you something tomorrow . . .

MATTHEW: Thank you, Mai.

HONG: I want no part of this.

MATTHEW: It's for Kevin.

HONG: It is for you. You want my son to be someone not normal.

MATTHEW: That's not true.

HONG: You want to make sure everyone know who he is in your eyes.

MATTHEW: You're totally twisting things around.

HONG: You make him into something he is not in front of all the people!

MATTHEW: I want to make him out to be who he was for everyone. I want people to know how special he was to me. Is that so wrong? I want people to know that he used to have this goofy smile, which was this cute, slanted grin he had when he was excited about something.

MAI: You really love him.

MATTHEW: Yeah.

HONG: Two men should not be together like that.

(to MAI) **That song make him gay.**
都是你那首歌惹的禍.

MAI: **What are you talking about?**
你在講什麼?

HONG: **That rainbow song, that gay song you sing all the time is what made him gay.**
就你那首gay 歌, 天天唱,天天唱, 不是gay 都給你唱成gay.

MAI: Don't listen to him.

MATTHEW: I don't know what he's saying.

MAI: **How can you say that I made our son gay?**
你怎麼可以說是我把他變成gay 的?

MATTHEW: What are you saying? What's happening?

MAI: He say I sing "Over The Rainbow," make Kevin queer.

MATTHEW processing what he just heard.

MATTHEW: He said you singing "Over The Rainbow" to Kevin made him queer . . . what?

HONG: You lead him down wrong path, too.

MAI whacks HONG.

MATTHEW: What path do you think I led your son down?

HONG: If not for you, he will still be here. He will still be normal.

MATTHEW: Normal, gee . . . I wonder what you mean by that?

HONG: You know what I mean.

MATTHEW: Yes, I made your son gay. I admit it. It's all because of me.

HONG: He not like that before you.

MATTHEW: You mean he wasn't gay.

HONG: Yes, call it what you want.

MATTHEW: You sure he didn't "like boys" before he met me?

HONG: Why else he become that way? He not like that before Vancouver. If I know for sure he was learning bad ways . . .

MATTHEW: Bad ways?

HONG: I would have . . .

MATTHEW: You would have what? Tried to change him?

HONG: I would have help him . . . there are doctors . . .

MATTHEW: Your son didn't need to be fixed!

HONG: If you could like girls, would you? If you can choose?

MATTHEW: We can't choose.

HONG: But . . . if you can?

Beat.

MATTHEW: I don't know . . . maybe. Life might be easier.

HONG: So, can you blame me to want to give my son an easier life?

MATTHEW: No . . . but you can't make a gay man straight.

HONG: You make my son gay.

MATTHEW: How?!

HONG: How I know? I not gay.

MATTHEW: This is ridiculous. I can't—wow.

MAI: Mr. Lee need time.

MATTHEW: I'm sorry . . . I need a smoke.

MATTHEW heads to the door.

HONG: Go!

MAI: You smoke? Kevin smoke, too?

MATTHEW: He was an artist, of course he smoked. He thought it made him look hip.

MAI: Hip?

MATTHEW: Cool. It just rained again . . . maybe I'll get more gay by catching a rainbow.

HONG: Smoking give you cancer!

MATTHEW has exited out the porch door. Beat.

Good job on the Kung Pao chicken tonight.
今晚的宮保雞丁很好.

Beat.

Very good. Everything is very good.
樣樣都很好.

Beat.

I'll take care of cleaning up when he leaves. You just rest.
他走了, 我來洗碗, 你早點休息.

MAI cleans up giving HONG the silent treatment.

Hey, stop . . . stop while you're ahead. I'm your husband. Why are you being like this to me over that kid? Mai, I'm talking to you.

你見好就收啦. 好歹我是你老公. 為了那傢伙, 犯得著跟我這樣? 我在跟你說話.

MAI: You promised me that you would keep it together tonight.

你答應我今天晚上好自為之的.

HONG: I don't want to know him. You think he will bring us closer to Kevin, not me.

我不想認識他, 是你認為他可以幫我們多瞭解凱文. 我可沒說.

MAI: Then why did you agree to have him come?

那你幹什麼答應讓他來?

HONG: Because he had something of our son's.

因為他說他有我兒子的東西.

MAI: He could have mailed it. But you finally agreed to have him visit.

他可以用寄的. 可你還是答應讓他來.

HONG: Because you wanted it . . . because he kept calling and wouldn't give up. Because I wanted to see if he was to blame for what happened.

因為你天天吵呀, 因為他天天打電話來呀, 因為我要看看到底他和凱文的私有甚麼關係.

MAI: You already decided he is to blame because he is gay. Give him a chance. I want to know my son, Hong, everything about him. Don't ruin it.

你早就因為他是gay 就甚麼都怪他. 你就給人家一次機會嘛. 我要知道我兒子的一切. 你不要把事情搞砸.

HONG: What else is there to know?

還要知道些什麼?

MAI: We've talked about this! That last time we talked to Kevin on the phone . . .

我們講過呀. 凱文最後打電話來的那次 . . .

    Flashback. Phone rings, and MAI *picks up. It's Kevin on the other line.*

Are you okay? Work is good?

好嗎? 工作順利嗎?

    Beat.

Are you not well? You're with Matthew again? No?

不舒服? 你跟馬修在一起? 沒有?

    Beat.

Here, you should talk to him. Just a moment ... Hong!
你來跟他講 ... 等一會.阿鴻!

   HONG gets on the phone.

HONG: **Hello. How are things?**
喂 ... 怎麼樣?

   Beat.

Do you want me to send you some money? You eating enough?
要不要寄錢給你? 吃飽了嗎?

   Beat.

Here, talk to your mom.
來, 你媽跟你說.

   MAI takes the phone.

MAI: *(to HONG)* **You finished talking so quickly.**
這麼快.

(into phone) **If you ever need to talk to us about something, just say it.**
你有什麼想講的你就說吧.

   Beat.

Okay, take care of yourself. Okay?
自己照顧自己. 好.

   Beat.

Okay, I—
我一

   Kevin's hung up.

(to HONG) **He said he loves me.**
他說他愛我.

   Present.

HONG: **So what?**
那又怎樣?

MAI: **Matt wasn't there with him. He was always there.**
馬修沒跟他在一起, 平時都有.

HONG: **So what if he wasn't there?**
那又怎樣?

MAI: Kevin was my son. I know when something is wrong. I heard it in his voice . . . and he said he loved me.

凱文是我兒子, 我知道不對路, 我聽得出來. 而且他會說他愛我.

HONG: Maybe he finally missed us and wanted to come home. You're reading too much into it.

也許他終於想家想回來. 你想太多了.

MAI: No, Hong. I want to talk to Matt some more. I need to know exactly what happened that night.

不, 我要再跟馬修談談, 我要知道那天晚上到底發生什麼事.

HONG: Why don't we just ask him if that's what you want? I'll go out there right now and ask him.

既然這樣那就直接了當跟他說嘛. 我現在就出去問他.

MAI: What are you going to ask him? "Excuse me, did you do something that night that caused Kevin to drown?" Do you think he will admit it if he was at all responsible?

你要怎麼問? "對不起, 你那天晚上幹了甚麼事, 害他淹死的?" 你想他會承認什麼嗎?

Beat.

I can see he loved Kevin, so I don't get it. We just have to keep listening to everything.

我看得出來他愛凱文, 所以我才弄不懂? 我們就繼續聽下去吧?

HONG: He thinks he knows our son better than we do. How can I listen to that garbage and not say anything back?

他就是認為他比我們更了解我兒子. 他這樣胡說八道,我不罵回去才怪!

MAI: For me, Hong. Please, go out there and talk to him. Tell him you want him to stay.

就算為了我吧. 阿鴻. 你就出去跟他說你要他留下來.

HONG: I . . . really can't—

我, 我辦不到—

MAI: Please, do this one thing for me, will you? All I'm asking is for one night you do what I ask,

我就求你這一次吧. 就一個晚上你聽我的. 行嗎?

HONG: But—

可是—

MAI: **Don't you want to know the truth?**
難道你不想知道真相？

Beat. HONG *heads out to the porch.* MAI *continues to clean up the dishes.*

Outside at the porch, HONG *approaches* MATTHEW. *Beat.*

HONG: You not smoking.

MATTHEW: Forgot my light.

Beat. HONG *hands* MATTHEW *a light from his pants pocket.*

Thanks.

Beat.

I also left my cigarettes in my jacket pocket inside.

Long beat. HONG *takes out a pack of cigarettes, opens it, and offers it to* MAT-THEW. MATTHEW *accepts the offer and takes a cigarette from the pack.* MATTHEW *lights his cigarette and hands back the light. He smokes. Beat.* HONG *looks at the pack of cigarettes for a moment. He takes out a cigarette, lights it, and smokes.*

Cancer?

Beat.

HONG: My son look hip like me?

MATTHEW: Your friends were right, you are funny.

HONG: Mai not know I smoke again, but I need something. Smoking . . . help me.

MATTHEW: Helps you how?

Beat.

HONG: It help me remember . . .

MATTHEW: Kevin?

Beat.

He wanted to live the dream you had for him. Become a businessman, dentist, doctor . . . straight. He wanted that so badly. But it just wasn't who he was.

HONG: Enough . . . what happen that night?

MATTHEW: What night?

HONG: The night Kevin died.

MATTHEW: What do you mean?

HONG: Mai think you . . . nothing. We do not have to talk.

MATTHEW: Mai thinks what?

HONG: She think you . . . know everything. You can get us closer to Kevin.

MATTHEW: I can try.

HONG: No more talk. We can just stand here . . . go back in few minute.

MATTHEW: Aren't you tired of it?

HONG: What?

MATTHEW: Pretending. When Kevin was alive you were pretending everything was fine. Him being bipolar, your relationship with him, his sexuality. And now . . . with me, you're just trying to fake it to make Mai happy. Why can't you just talk to me?

HONG: We have nothing to talk about! You are here because Mai think you have all the answers. Not me. I let you stay for Mai, that is it.

MATTHEW: Oh, I thought you had me here so you can have someone to blame. So you won't feel guilty for what happened.

HONG: Why I need to feel guilty?! I did nothing wrong.

MATTHEW: You don't know your own son!

    HONG *raises his hand about to strike* MATTHEW. *He holds back . . .*

HONG: He died because of you!

MATTHEW: How?!

HONG: If you never met Kevin . . . everything will be different.

MATTHEW: You're right, things would be. He might've met someone else . . . some other man for you to blame. I am more than just some guy Kevin met at a dance club one night, Mr. Lee. Stop looking at me as though I'm the monster that wrecked your son's life.

HONG: You did!

MATTHEW: He grew up, he changed, he grew into who he was meant to be. You need to stop blaming me, or anyone else for what happened.

HONG: You keep him in Vancouver. We tell him to come home, but you keep him there.

MATTHEW: He chose to live there. I didn't force him to stay. And how was him staying in Vancouver a reason for what happened?

HONG: Because we cannot protect him!

MATTHEW: He didn't need your protection.

HONG: He drown!

Beat.

MATTHEW: Really? You truly believe everything that led to Kevin dying was because he turned out gay, because of me?

HONG: I know you not help!

MATTHEW: I'm outta here.

HONG: Good!

MATTHEW puts out his cigarette and enters the house.

Inside, MATTHEW sees MAI with a large platter of mango pudding.

MATTHEW: I have to go—

MAI: No, no, sit. We have dessert. Mango pudding. Why Mr. Lee not come in?

MATTHEW: He's just finishing . . . uh . . . getting some fresh air.

MAI: Matt.

MATTHEW: Yes?

MAI: I know he smoke.

MATTHEW: Oh, sorry, I didn't mean to— Why don't you just tell him you know?

MAI: He try to hide it from me. So I let him hide it. He feel better.

MATTHEW: But what if he doesn't really want to hide it from you? Maybe he's just afraid you'll be upset.

MAI: Then I hope he will tell me. Up to him.

Beat.

Sit down, we have dessert!

MATTHEW: I'm sorry, I can't, I really gotta run.

MAI: Why, what happen? You do not like mango pudding?

MATTHEW: No, I love it. But you know this isn't working. Mr. Lee doesn't want me here. He's not listening to anything I have to say, it's pointless. I'm sorry I can't help you clean up.

MAI: We not finish. Mr. Lee need some time to open up. I go get him, you stay.

MATTHEW: He's not going to listen.

MAI: I make sure he listen.

MATTHEW: You can't—

HONG enters.

MAI: Matt, sit down!

(to HONG) **What did you say to him? He wants to leave now.**
你跟他說了什麼? 他這就要走.

HONG: **Good.**
很好.

MAI: **I'm not done hearing about my son.**
我還有很多事情要知道.

MATTHEW: Excuse me . . .

MAI: Matt, wait.

HONG: **Let him go.**
讓他走.

MAI: **I want to know more.**
我還要知道更多.

HONG: **We don't need his stories, Mai.**
我們不需要聽他編故事.

MAI: **My son is already dead. Please!**
我兒子已經死了. 我求求你!

HONG: **He's my son, too!**
他也是我的兒子!

MATTHEW: Please stop arguing.

MAI: We not arguing. We just talking. Right, Hong?

HONG: We talking.

MATTHEW: It sounded . . . never mind. It really was good to meet you, Mai.

MAI: Kevin love mango pudding.

MATTHEW: I know. He introduced me to it.

MAI: Eat some before you go.

MATTHEW: I can't.

MAI: Matt, why you like this?

MATTHEW: I'm not like anything. This was a mistake.

MAI: Not mistake. Sit down.

HONG: **Let him go.**
讓他走.

MATTHEW: Good night, Mai. Good night, Mr. Lee.

MAI walks to block the door. She still has the mango pudding in her hands.

MAI: Sit.

MATTHEW: Mai, please.

HONG: **He should have left already.**
他早該走了.

MAI: **Be quiet.**
閉嘴.

Matt, stop.

MATTHEW: Let's not make this any harder. Please move out of the way.

HONG: **You're being crazy, Mai.**
你瘋了. 阿美.

MAI: **Then let me be crazy. I don't care.**
我就發瘋給你看. 我不管了.

MATTHEW walks toward the door.

Ahhhhhh!

MAI intentionally smashes the platter of mango pudding on the ground. Beat.

HONG: **Mai.**
阿美.

MATTHEW: You okay? Let me help you—

HONG: You help enough. Look what happen now.

Mai, what are you doing?
阿美, 你在幹什麼呀?

MAI: Big mess I make.

MATTHEW: Big mess we all made.

MAI: I clean.

HONG: **What are you doing? Sit.**
你這是幹什麼? 坐下吧.

HONG grabs a broom and dustpan to sweep up the mess. MAI goes to the fridge.

MAI: **Let me be.**
我來.

MATTHEW: Mai, why don't you sit down for a bit?

MAI takes out another platter of mango pudding from the fridge.

You have another one?

MAI: We run Chinese restaurant.

MATTHEW: Right.

MAI also brings bowls and spoons to the dinner table. She scoops mango pudding into the bowls. She sits, scoops a spoonful, and eats the mango pudding. HONG and MATTHEW simply watch MAI. Beat.

MAI: Matt . . . please sit.

Hong, sit down and eat.
阿鴻. 來坐. 吃.

HONG puts down the broom.

Tea?

Beat.

Matt, tea? Please, sit. I make tea.

MATTHEW: No. I've been here for too long already.

HONG: He take away our son, Mai. He kill Kevin.

Are you blind?
你是瞎了眼嗎?

MATTHEW: There! You hear that, Mai? He finally said it out in the open. That's what you wanted to say all along, isn't it?

HONG: Yes!

MAI: No, stop!

MATTHEW: That's not fair. I've had enough of this. I tried, Mai.

MAI: Mr. Lee need—

MATTHEW: No, no more time. No more talking. He's not listening, so what's the point?

MAI: I listen.

HONG: I listen, too, but what you say . . . is garbage!

HONG and MAI's following lines are delivered on top of what MATTHEW is saying.

MATTHEW: Mr. Lee, I'm in your house, and I want to give you the respect you deserve, but you're not making it easy. Your son is dead! And he never got to have the family he wanted because he thought he wasn't good enough for you. Because you made him believe he wasn't normal.

(HONG: I not make him believe anything. He think what he want.)

MATTHEW: His bipolar was nothing to worry about. Him being gay is just a phase. It wasn't. He was a fucking fag.

(HONG: Get out! Get out now!)

(MAI: Stop! Both of you, stop!)

MATTHEW: I am, too . . . and we were in love, and made love. If that's too much for you to handle, too bad. Don't try to find out who your son really was. I just feel sad for you.

HONG throws one of the small bowls of mango pudding toward MATTHEW. He misses.

HONG: Get out! You said you leaving, so go! How dare you talk to me like that? Who you think you are?!

MATTHEW goes for his jacket, puts it on, then heads for his carry-on during the following.

That's it, Mai. Get him out!!
把他打出去!!

Get out!

MAI: **He's leaving. Now what?**
他要走, 現在呢?

HONG: **So what? Good!**
怎樣? 很好呀!

MAI: **You promised!**
你答應的!

HONG: I did my best!
我盡力了!

MAI: Did you?
你有嗎?

HONG: Did I not?
我沒有嗎?

MAI: Aahhhhhgg! You still don't understand!
哎呀, 你怎麼總不明白!

HONG: Mai, stop being crazy!
阿美你不要再發神經!

MAI: I need more—
我需要知道更多—

HONG: More what?
更多什麼?

MAI: Truth!
真相!

MATTHEW has everything he needs and is about to exit through the porch door.

Matt . . . stop. Please stay!

HONG: You need to let him—
你就讓他—

MAI: Matt, stay.

MATTHEW: We don't need to do this anymore. You got what Kevin left for you. I met you. You met me. It's enough.

MAI: Where you go the night Kevin died?!

MATTHEW stops in his tracks.

MATTHEW: Excuse me?

MAI: You not with him. Where you go?

MATTHEW: Um . . . uh, I was out, I guess.

MAI: Out?

MATTHEW: Yes.

MAI: Why you not with Kevin?

MATTHEW: We had our own lives, too.

MAI: But he not well that night, and you not there.

MATTHEW: I'm sorry, um . . . how do you know this?

MAI: He call me. He told me he was by himself that night.

MATTHEW: But you didn't even know who I was.

MAI: I not know who you are with Kevin, but I hear your name many times. Kevin always talk about going out with his "good friend," Matthew. He say you at the movies that night.

MATTHEW: Okay, yeah, I was at the movies. Why did you ask if you already knew?

MAI: I want you tell me . . .

MATTHEW: Tell you what?

MAI: Who you go with?

MATTHEW: When?

MAI: To see movie.

MATTHEW: A friend . . . why are you asking me all this?

MAI: I don't understand why you at movies! That night Kevin not feeling good. You say you love him. Why you not there?!

MATTHEW: I was!

MAI: You were not!

Beat.

MATTHEW: A few days before . . . we got into a big fight.

MAI: What?

Flashback to MATTHEW *and Kevin in their apartment.* MAI *and* HONG *engage in dialogue but they remain in the present.*

MATTHEW: Of course you feel sick, after all the partying you did last night.

MAI: Partying?

MATTHEW: Drugs! Tell me what letter of the alphabet you're on right now, I have a hard time keeping track.

HONG: You say you know him!

MATTHEW: No, I don't know, that's why I'm asking. If you're going to throw up, do it in the washroom, I'm not cleaning up your mess.

MAI: And then what?

MATTHEW: You know what? Screw this . . . I'm done. I can't do this anymore. Did you hear me? I said I can't do this anymore.

MAI: What you mean?

MATTHEW: This . . . us . . . this way . . . I can't. You always say you'll tone it down, but when?! After Doug's birthday party this weekend—Jesus! Are you listening to yourself? Really? The fact that you even had to ask.

MAI: He say he will try.

MATTHEW: I don't want you to tone things down, and I don't think you can. I want you . . . to be . . . you, whoever that is. I just think . . . maybe this is you growing up, and I'm not where you are right now. I can't be where you are right now . . . I'm sorry.

HONG: What you saying?

MATTHEW: I don't know what I'm saying—I mean, I do know. We should probably take some time off. Yeah, I need to clear my mind, think some stuff through.

MAI: You leave him?

MATTHEW: I didn't say I want to break up with you, stop!

MAI: Then what you saying?

MATTHEW: Why are you forcing me to say it? For once in your life can you just let things be and stop trying to control everything? I did love that part of you, but it's getting out of hand. Okay, fine, no! I don't love your controlling, obsessive ways anymore!

MAI: You say you love him.

MATTHEW: All right, then I don't love you!

MAI: Say again.

MATTHEW: You want me to say it? Really?! I'll say it. I think we should break up! I want to break up with you!

HONG: You end it.

MATTHEW: It's over! We're over!!

Beat.

Happy now?

Everyone shifts back to present.

MAI: No.

MATTHEW: We weren't together anymore, okay?!

Beat.

I thought he would be okay. I didn't think . . . I'm sorry, maybe I should have told you sooner.

MAI: Yes.

MATTHEW: The breakup might have hit him harder than I thought it would . . . which might have caused him to go overboard with all the drugs. I don't know if it did, I just—

HONG: My son is gone because you leave him?

MATTHEW: I don't know. I wish I knew he was taking it that hard.

MAI: You the only one who can help him then.

MATTHEW: I couldn't—I did, for a really long time. But it was scary, and I couldn't bear seeing him go down that road anymore.

MAI: If you really love him, you push forward. You not give up.

MATTHEW: It felt like I had no choice. It was as though he pushed me out of love.

HONG: Love is not here only when it is easy for you.

MATTHEW: I've been through hard times with Kevin. But you don't know how much it hurts to love someone who doesn't seem to be there, even when they're standing right in front of you.

MAI: What you mean?

MATTHEW: His bipolar . . . he was moody, never satisfied, would flip out all the time over little things. When he was depressed, I'd look into his eyes but not see him.

HONG: If you know he is sad a lot, why you not check on him?

MATTHEW: Now you wish I was with your son all the time.

HONG: I wish you never meet him. But you already meet, so if you able to help . . .

MATTHEW: No one knew what was going to happen. Not me, not you, not Kevin. It could have easily been like any other night. He'd go out, and when he came back, I'd end up getting him Gatorade or whatever else he needed. I didn't know he was going to party again and go down to the beach by himself.

HONG: Not like any night . . . he died!

MATTHEW: I know that.

MAI: I told you something wrong that night, Hong.

HONG: It was late. What we do? Fly over there?

MATTHEW: You knew.

MAI: No, we not know he was going to . . .

MATTHEW: After the phone call, why didn't you call me to check in?

MAI: We not have your number.

MATTHEW: We could have done something . . . together . . .

MAI: If we know each other then . . .

HONG: We would say more . . . on the phone . . .

MATTHEW: You had twenty-five years to say more.

HONG: And you should be there for him, not go see movie! Why you not stay with him a few night longer?!

MATTHEW: I wish I was there for him, too!

Beat.

MAI: You want our forgiveness? That why you come?

MATTHEW: No . . . maybe—I don't know . . . I told you, I wanted to give one last thing to Kevin, to share what I knew about him . . . with you. It was the least I could do for him.

MAI: I wish we share earlier, we could maybe help him together.

Beat.

You really . . . love my son?

MATTHEW: Yes.

MAI: More than anything in the world? Will you give your life for him?

Beat.

MATTHEW: I don't know if I'd give my life for anyone.

Beat.

MAI: Maybe Hong is right.

MATTHEW: Mai—

MAI: Maybe we blame you, but not because you are gay. Not because you are in relationship with our son. But because you did not love him . . . enough. He did not have anyone else in Vancouver. He think he have you . . . but no.

MATTHEW: He did . . . for a while.

MAI: You choose bad time to end your love. Hong, if we only accept him . . . for everything . . .

MATTHEW: I'm sorry . . . I wish I could have changed things.

MAI: Me too.

MATTHEW: So . . . can you forgive me . . . for not being there . . . for—

MAI: —not loving my son enough?

MATTHEW: I guess.

Beat.

MAI: No, I cannot.

Beat.

MATTHEW: This isn't right.

HONG: My son die is not right.

MAI: Matthew. You should go.

MATTHEW: This is it, huh?

Beat.

What if I want to stay for a while longer?

MAI: No reason for that.

MATTHEW: I want to sit here for a bit.

MAI: Why?

MATTHEW: Just sit and remember Kevin.

MAI: Matthew. No.

Beat.

MATTHEW: I see. You got what you wanted . . . an explanation for the unexplainable—your son's death. Now that you can pin it on me, you have no use for me anymore.

MAI: Go now.

MATTHEW: You're all I have left to remember him by, too.

MAI: You choose to live by memory. You choose to leave our son when he needed you!

MATTHEW: I know that! Do you think I don't feel any guilt? But you can't just blame me and move on. We're all at fault, including Kevin. He wasn't perfect. I wasn't perfect. We didn't have the perfect relationship. We tried to make it work, and it just didn't. That's what happened. If you were hoping for a sweet, fairytale-like story with no problems about your son, and us together, I don't have it. Our lives were not that story, and that's the truth.

MAI: Please . . . go.

Beat.

MATTHEW: I loved him as much as I knew how.

MATTHEW takes off the jade necklace and offers it to HONG. HONG accepts it.

Thanks for dinner.

MATTHEW exits. Beat.

MAI: **I need some time to myself. I think I want to stay at my sister's tonight.**
我需要一個人冷靜一下, 今天晚上我到我妹家.

HONG: **He's gone now . . . everything's okay.**
他走了 . . . 沒事了.

MAI: **No, it's not. We lost our son, and only now we know everything.**
不是沒事了, 我失去我兒子, 可到現在才明白真相.

HONG: **So you're just going to walk away from me?**
你就這樣丟下我?

MAI: **I just need to think things through.**
我只是要把事情想清楚.

HONG: **What is there to think through? I'm your husband.**
還有什麼要想清楚? 我是你老公.

MAI: **I don't know, I just want to run away from everything.**
我不知道, 我只是想一個人躲起來.

HONG: **Like how Matthew ran away from Kevin? You want to be just like him?**
就像馬修拋棄凱文一樣? 你也有樣學樣?

MAI: **I'm not being—**
我沒有一

HONG: **If you leave me now you will be like him.**
你要現在離開我, 你就會跟他一樣.

MAI: **Just give me a few minutes.**
你等我一下.

MAI exits. HONG picks up the painting and embraces it. Long beat. HONG notices something stuck on the back of the frame. It is a folded up piece of paper. He unfolds it, and discovers it is a letter from Kevin. HONG reads it. Beat. MAI enters.

I can clean up, you— What is that?
我來收一下 . . . 這是什麼?

HONG: **A letter from Kevin.**
兒子的信.

HONG hands MAI the letter. She reads it.

MAI: "Dear Mom and Dad . . . "

Flashback. The letter from Kevin turns into a letter of acceptance from an art school in Vancouver.

He got accepted.
他申請到學校了.

HONG: **Got accepted to what?**
哪個學校?

MAI: **The art school in Vancouver.**
溫哥華的藝術學校.

HONG: **My father left him money to go to school wherever he wants. Now he's leaving us and going to Vancouver to study art. How is he going to make a living?**
我爸留給他的錢說讓他去自己想念的學校, 現在可好, 跑到溫哥華去搞藝術.
真不知道他以後怎麼生活?

Lights up on MATTHEW in present day, at the cemetery, intercutting flashback scene with MAI and HONG.

MATTHEW: Hey, what's up? Been a while, huh?

MAI: **Hong, relax.**
阿鴻, 別擔心啦.

HONG: **He's changed, Mai.**
阿美, 他變了.

MATTHEW: So much has changed since you've been gone.

MAI: **He's growing up.**
他長大了.

HONG: **He's a different person.**
變了個人似的.

MATTHEW: I think your dad is changing into a different kinda person.

MAI: **He's still your son.**
他還是你兒子.

HONG: **He has an earring.**
他還戴耳環.

MATTHEW: He called this morning, and told me where I'd find you . . .

MAI: **It's a phase.**
過一陣就沒事的.

HONG: **And his behaviour is so erratic lately.**
他最近的情緒很不穩定.

MATTHEW: . . . then he hung up. Well, baby steps, I guess.

MAI: **That's what kids do nowadays.**
現在的小孩就這樣.

HONG: **They get piercings and piss off their parents?**
鑽個耳洞來氣我們?

MATTHEW: I really pissed him off last night.

MAI: **What are you so afraid of?**
你怕什麼?

HONG: **Nothing. I just . . . he's different.**
沒有, 只覺得他 . . . 變了個人似的.

MATTHEW: We had our differences . . . but they clearly love you.

MAI: **We went through this already—**
我們談過的—

HONG: **No, I mean different from everyone else.**
我的意思是他跟別人都不一樣.

MATTHEW: They're trying to show it now.

MAI: **What do you mean different?**
你說有什麼不一樣?

HONG: **He's not like other boys.**
他跟其他男孩子不一樣.

MATTHEW: I hope you can see it.

MAI: **You really don't see it, do you?**
你真看不出來?

MATTHEW: I hope you're goofy smiling.

HONG: **See what?**
看出什麼?

Lights snap out.

DEAR ARMEN

LEE WILLIAMS BOUDAKIAN AND
KAMEE ABRAHAMIAN

ADDITIONAL EDITS AND COLLABORATION WITH
ANOUSHKA RATNARAJAH

This work is dedicated to mothers, grandmothers, aunties, and all the caregivers who carry the feminized and emotional labour of raising our communities. To Armen Ohanian and our ancestors, who have always been with us. To the queer and gender bending that have always been part of our cultural legacies. To the artists, historians, and whisperers of our unspoken herstories. And, especially, this is for us queer and trans SWANA beauties who have been yearning to find more of our stories—everywhere.

ACKNOWLEDGEMENTS

Thank you to all of the funding support we received to make this work possible. Beginning with an acknowledgement of funding and assistance from the Canada Council for the Arts, the BC Arts Council, and the Province of British Columbia. Thanks also to all of our Indiegogo funders, our sponsors, and the many people who helped us raise funds in all the ways.

Beyond funding, this work involved the time, labour, and love of many incredible people. Thank you to each and every one. To Tiffany Golarz, who was with us in the beginning. To Zabelle Berberian for translating the first version of our script into Armenian. To Nigol Abrahamian for hosting us and our work in Armenia. To Anoushka Ratnarajah, for breathing new life into this piece as director. To Haig Ashod Beylerian for creating and performing a beautiful score for this work. To all our guest performers, for their contributions to the play and to the zine. To our colleagues and friends who puzzled over this piece with us and offered us time and guidance. To all the folks who let us crash on their couches and beds while we were on tour. To all those who helped us make stunning merch over the years. To our volunteers for their vital support and work. To the venues/spaces and organizers who hosted our work. To the writers who covered us in the press. To our partners and furry creatures who supported us on so many levels throughout the life of this piece. To our endlessly generous audiences and communities, for all the feedback, engagement, and support.

"THE UNREAL SELF" IN
DEAR ARMEN
ART BABAYANTS

*The dancer is more than a woman, she is a dream, and that to preserve
she should show the world only her unreal self.*
—Armen Ohanian

Having been performed in Canada and Armenia, *Dear Armen* presents a
complex, multi-faceted performance piece (rather than a play), which is rich
in references to Armenian history, queer history, and feminist philosophy, as
well as a number of contemporary Canadian-Armenian diasporic experiences.
Dear Armen, created by lee williams boudakian and Kamee Abrahamian in
collaboration with Anoushka Ratnarajah, gives centre stage to women, *queer*
characters, and performers by weaving together stories of a historical figure—
Armen[1] Ohanian (born Sophia Pirboudaghian, 1887–1976)—and a number of
women characters of Armenian descent living in modern Canada.

Written in English, with only a few token lines in Western Armenian[2] spoken
by some characters, *Dear Armen* seems created with a Western anglophone
audience in mind. Another indicator of such a target is the Herculean effort the

---

1   "Armen" is a male name in Armenian. The play also mentions Ohanian's transitional
name, "Armenuhi," where *uhi* is a suffix indicating the feminine gender.

2   The Armenian language has many regional dialects that are not always mutu-
ally understandable. All Armenian dialects fall under two major categories: Western
Armenian and Eastern Armenian. Western Armenian dialects are spoken in the present-
day Turkey, Syria, Lebanon, and most of the Middle East. Their grammar, pronunciation,
vocabulary, and spelling are vastly different from Eastern Armenian dialects, which are
spoken in the Republic of Armenia, the Russian Federation, and Iran. The diasporic
characters of *Dear Armen* use Western Armenian—a subtle reference to their country
of origin (Lebanon). Conversely, Armen Ohanian being born in the Russian Empire

piece makes to explain the complexity of the sociopolitical and personal contexts experienced by its characters to a reader (or audience member) unlikely
to be familiar with the lost or little-known histories of Armenia, the Middle
East—stories outside of the Western historical canon. More importantly, *Dear
Armen* also makes an effort to illuminate *her*stories—Armenian women's stories that tend to fall outside of the traditional Armenian historical canon, and
that remain unknown to most Armenians. It is not surprising that the creators
of *Dear Armen* put to the fore their fight against "memoricide"—a derivative of
genocide—a full or partial erasure of records, archives, or any kind of oral history
and memories related to a certain person, people, or event. Given that Armenian
diasporic discourses are often dominated by the Genocide of 1915—an ethnic
cleansing organized by the Young Turks government[3] (Akçam)—addressing
stories beyond the Genocide, as well as their significance for the understanding
of Armenian history and identity, can be seen an act of *queering*.

The queering effect of *Dear Armen,* though, goes far beyond its thematic
content and comes through a number of other features, such as the character
presentation, role allocation, and the performance genre and structure. The
image, or rather the spirit of Armen Ohanian permeates the piece poetically,
musically, textually, choreographically, metaphorically, and even philosophically.
Ohanian was an Armenian dancer and writer born in Shamakha (present-day
Azerbaijan), who lived in the Russian and Persian Empires, France, and Mexico,
and who developed an artistic gender-bending persona under whose name s/
he performed and s/he published a number of books. The play assumes a play-
ful take on Armen's persona, presenting it through four character entities: the
Writer typing up his/her texts on an old typewriter, the voice of Armen reading
excerpts of Ohanian's memoirs *The Dancer of Shamakha*, the Armenian Dancer
reflecting a critical take on the traditional veiled Armenian female dance, and
a Masked Performer—"a contemporary of version of Armen (. . .), pushing
boundaries of Armenian female artistic identities and possibilities." The contemporary characters of the performance are: Garineh, an angsty teenager; her
adult self Garo, a scholar investigating the life of Armen Ohanian; and Garineh's
conservative aunt Morkoor, a Lebanese Armenian and first-generation Canadian
who raised Garineh as her own child, and who now refuses to accept Garineh's
queer identity as well as her use of the pronoun "they." Among other characters,
there is a Musician providing live music (as it would be in traditional Armenian

(present-day Azerbaijan) was mostly likely a speaker of an Eastern Armenian dialect.
However, in *Dear Armen*, the Armen's lines are in English only.

3   T. Akçam, *The Young Turks' Crime against Humanity. The Armenian Genocide and
Ethnic Cleansing in the Ottoman Empire* (Oxford: Oxford University Press, 2012).

dancing) and a Local Artist, for whom the performance allocates space and time to present their work disrupting the assumptions of naturalism and pushing the audience toward the ideas of "mask," "image," "persona," and "constructedness." Following Ohanian's legacy, the authors subvert any attempt to see *Dear Armen* as a purely biographical or autobiographical piece, reminding the audience that the theatre is an artifice, and *queering* a need for one single coherent narrative.

This type of queering is also supported by the fact that *Dear Armen's* actors are required to take on different characters throughout the course of the play. At different points—sometimes in the middle of a scene—an actor transforms from one character to another: Morkoor becomes Garineh, who then becomes Armen the Writer, who then becomes the Dancer, and so on. While this technique hints at obvious parallels between the historical figure and the contemporary characters at the centre of the performance, it once again speaks to the desire of its creators to queer the genre of narrative-heavy plays steeped in identity politics, presenting an unproblematic view of the characters' ethnic, linguistic, or cultural identity. Additionally, this role switching and the continuous insertion of various performance genres into the fabric of *Dear Armen,* combined with the use of live music and the embodied presence of a musician in the show, reminds the audience about the constructedness of the "real," the "images," the "identities," the "personas" one can take on throughout the course of one's life. It also makes us empathize with the struggle to accept and embrace other people's personas or identities, especially those that *challenge* established societal norms or categories.

Dear Armen was conceived during a three-week artist residency in September 2013 at the Abrahamian Arts Centre in Yerevan, Armenia. Since its inception, *Dear Armen* has morphed from staged reading to interdisciplinary production, featuring two distinct versions and five incarnations. In addition to a staged production, *Dear Armen* has lived as a short film, a zine, and a site-specific immersive performance installation. As part of the project's lifespan, the production toured to major North American cities between 2014 and 2016, including New York, Toronto, Montréal, Boston, Detroit, Los Angeles, San Francisco, Portland, Seattle, and Vancouver, and participated in two residency/creation periods in Yerevan (2013 and 2015). The short film is still playing at festivals (2015–2017). Our core creative team includes:

Co-creators and Lead Performers: Kamee Abrahamian and lee williams boudakian

Director: Anoushka Ratnarajah
Musician and Composer: Haig Ashod Beylerian
Additional Support: Tiffany Golarz

Dear Armen was developed with assistance from the Canada Council for the Arts, the Province of British Columbia, the BC Arts Council, and BC Supplemental Touring for various parts of the creation, production, and touring of this work.

CHARACTERS

Garineh: Sixteen years. Angsty teenager. An abundance of internalized oppressions playing out about race and ethnicity, against the budding aware- ness of a queer identity. She rebels hard against her Morkoor (aunt). She does not see herself as conforming to the gender expectations played out by Morkoor. Garineh has a kind of depth and darkness juxtaposed to an anxious naïveté. Element: fire. Props: bedsheets, drawing materials, dress, strewn clothes.

Garo: Thirty years. The grown-up version of Garineh. Writer and researcher of Armenian descent. Gender-variant and queer. Uses "they" pronouns. Has been separated from family and Armenian community for many years. Very much still working through identity issues. Has a partner named Ty. Element: air. Props: computer, books, cellphone, papers, face makeup.

Morkoor: Garo/Garineh's aunt. Traditional overbearing Armenian woman. Wears a headscarf and an apron. Often stressed out, worrying, and bossy, but deeply loving and caring. Took in Garineh when her mother left and raised her as her own daughter. Element: earth. Props: cloth/towels, headscarf, apron, baby blanket, towel-as-baby, tablecloth, flour, two bowls, knife and chopping board, onion, garlic, dustpan and brush, oil, rolling pin, dough.

Armen: An embodiment of the voice of Armen from the memoirs. Sitting at a small table in the middle of the audience, a writing studio. When the audience hears the recordings of excerpts from Armen's memoirs (accompa- nied by the live musician), her area is lit up—she is typing away. At times she looks disgruntled and emotional, at others she is focused on the task at hand. Elements: air and fire. Props: old typewriter, scattered papers, envelopes, glass of liquor, makeup, red scarves.

The Voice Of Armen: Disembodied voice recording of Armen Ohanian reading excerpts from her memoir *The Dancer of Shamakha*. Element: water.

Armenian Dancer: An embodiment of Armen as the "Armenian Dancer." Wears a veil and traditional dress. Element: water. Props: red veil, red ribbon.

Masked Performer: An interpretation, a contemporary version of Armen. Exposing skin and pushing boundaries of Armenian female artistic identities and possibilities. Element: fire. Props: mask, rose petals, pantyhose.

Audience/Local Artist(s): A local artist/activist. Elements: air and fire.

Musician: A live musician (cellist, guitarist, or other).

PRE-SHOW

Some audience members are given family photos when they enter the space. Audience enters as MUSICIAN *plays. On stage,* MORKOOR *soothes a baby in her arms. Both* MUSICIAN *and* MORKOOR *are in in their own world. They do not acknowledge the audience. The sounds are haunting and nostalgic. The general tone for audience members is one of uncertainty and subtle confusion, as folks try to figure out what they are supposed to do. The music plays steadily.*

GARO *enters about five minutes into this and sits at their desk. Then addresses the* MUSICIAN.

GARO: Hey, can we play something a little more upbeat . . .

The music changes. This whole scene upsets MORKOOR; *she puts the baby down in* GARINEH's/GARO's *room, and exits in a huff.*

Audience is left to watch as GARO *works through some of their research.*

INTRO

MORKOOR *re-enters distracted with cleaning. She bustles about, seeming flustered. She has a gravely serious look on her face as she cleans every surface she can reach with a kitchen towel.*

She looks around the space as though she has misplaced something important, and then begins to notice audience members. She looks at people with a disgruntled look, making eye contact and prolonging the sense of confusion that people may be feeling.

With a sigh, as though just remembering what she is supposed to be doing, she begins rushing people to their seats. She's hasty and pushy. Barking orders. Reprimanding them for wearing shoes in her house and making her floor dirty.

She sees someone with a photo and takes it from them, then searches through the audience and demands that they give her back her photos.

MORKOOR, *with her stack of photos, heads to* GARO's *desk, putting them on their desk and arranging them neatly. She takes off the apron and headscarf and leaves them at* ARMEN's *desk.* MORKOOR *exits.*

SCENE 1

GARO: *mid-stage right, desk placed closer to centre and almost touching up against* ARMEN. *Desk has computer, books, papers strewn about, and a cellphone.* ARMEN: *mid-stage left, a second desk facing Garo, and on it are a typewriter, books, and papers.* MORKOOR: *downstage left, broom and chair off to side, cloth on the floor.* GARINEH: *downstage right, bedsheet, clothes strewn, and drawing materials on floor.*

Throughout the play, actors switch in and out of characters. In Scene 1, the actor playing GARO *also plays* MORKOOR *and* GARINEH. THE VOICE OF ARMEN *is heard as a recording accompanied by the* MUSICIAN.

Lights up MUSICIAN.

Cue MUSICIAN *and cue sound for* THE VOICE OF ARMEN.

THE VOICE OF ARMEN: Everything loses its contours . . . Where am I? What am I? . . . An imperceptible melody touches my ears. Is it the song of the stars dancing around the moon? Is it my body singing with happiness? Is it my soul reaching the unattainable? It is the mystic rapture of being one with the night and the moon. It exists, then . . . The sun appears and restores form and outline to the Earth. The desert is the desert, a floor of sand reflecting the heat of the solid sky. I am I, weary in a weary body.

Music fading.

My soul is sobered; no longer lost in immensities, it takes up the burden of today. Has it lost forever the way to that mystic happiness?

Lights up on GARO.

Lights down on MUSICIAN.

GARO & THE VOICE OF ARMEN: No. Someday, somewhere, I shall find again that incommunicable happiness.

GARO is sitting at the desk, flipping through pages, talking with their partner, TY, on phone/Skype.

GARO: Isn't that just the most beautiful? There are these passages in her book that just . . .

I mean, are you gonna be jealous if I tell you, I'm falling in love with her?

Laughs.

Shall we go into poly-relationship processing mode?

Laughs again. Sighs.

No, but really. This is taking a really long time to come together. It's coming, but it's not coming fast enough.

Yeah. I talked with my advisor, Ms., er, Dr. Schneider. She read what I have and had little nice to say about it. She said . . . the research is *thin*. That I need more *citations*. That this piece is *young*, and *in need of a lot of work*.

I mean obviously it needs work. That's what I'm doing. I'm working on this thing . . .

TY: *(discouraged)* Oh, hun. You're carrying a lot right now.

GARO: Yeah, it's definitely something. I mean, it's weird to be here *and* trying to work on this thing. I haven't really been sleeping and I feel haunted. By the work. By this house. Old memories. It's . . .

TY: What can I do?

Do you want to share some of what you're working on right now? I could listen while you read some of it to me?

GARO: Aww, yeah, thanks.

Actually, I wouldn't mind reading you a bit of this presentation. It's the one I'm doing next week.

You really want to hear it? You've heard this stuff over and over the last while.

TY: Yeah. I sure do! But really, go for it, I have some time now.

GARO: Okay. Okay. Like I said, it's still super rough. So, go easy on me, okay?

TY: No way. I never go easy.

GARO laughs a little. Becomes momentarily shy.

They flip through notes a bit more. Stands up and faces the audience. Begins speaking, with purpose and intent.

GARO: Thank you so much for joining me here. My name is Garo Berberian, and for my thesis, I've been researching Armen Ohanian's life and creative works. In particular I've been focusing on Ohanian's first published memoir, *The Dancer of Shamakha*.

Pause.

As I share with you my research, I would like to acknowledge myself as a visitor to these lands. I am here to share with you work that intersects with herstories of genocide and displacement.

Pause.

It is significant to be doing this work while also living on and visiting lands that have been so painfully colonized.

Pause.

My hope is that through this work, we can invite the complexities of our shared and different struggles, and to highlight the significance of naming.

Pause.

A few words about myself, and what brought me to Armen.

As a researcher and writer, I'm interested in the stories of women and queers who are not often or not at all represented in literature or history books. I'm interested in remembering. Especially my ancestors.

Pause.

I'm a Southwest Asian Armenian, with members of my family more recently coming from Beirut, Lebanon, and Aleppo, Syria. My family consists of genocide survivors, refugees, and now immigrants to this continent.

Pause.

In my family, silence between women has been a common sound. Don't get me wrong: it's not that the women in my family don't speak. They speak. And often loudly.

It's a different kind of silence. The women in my family did not speak of their experiences . . .

And me, I'm interested in how I can write or speak into that silence.

Lights down on GARO. *Lights up on* MORKOOR.

GARO *moves to* MORKOOR's *area, transforming into her, picks up blue cloth, and gets on all fours and starts wiping down the floors.*

MORKOOR: What do you mean the women in our family don't speak of experiences?

What kind of things is this to say? Pshhht. Go upstairs and get your dirty laundry and put it in the washings. Inch amot.

To an audience member.

Family is the most important thing in the world, you know? The most important. It must always comes first.

Wiping intently.

You know, there are families who they don't talk to each other? They don't never call or speak with each other. They are like strangers. I know of one family like this. And that auntie, she is such a sad womens. She sacrifice everything, and now she is alone.

Looks at audience member.

But not this family. This family, we are not like this. This family is the most important family.

Responding to GARINEH, *whom we don't hear.*

The mop? Garineh, I know what I'm doing. The mop doesn't clean everything the way I like it. Look at these corners . . . you think the mop can get in there? Go from here, I just wiped down the floor under your feet. Go take the sheets from your bed and put them in the washings, I said already.

Lights down on MORKOOR, *who drops cloth and walks over to* GARINEH's *area, picks up a corner of the bedsheet, and transforms into* GARINEH. *Lights up on* GARINEH.

GARINEH: Yup. That's what she's like. She compares us with other people and guilts us into not being like them. You've got to love ethnic guilt. That cultural post-genocidal guilt that gets you just where it counts.

Oh, she'll talk to you about the neighbours, and she'll talk to you about those other families, most of whom she invents, but she won't actually talk about this one.

But, try asking her a question about herself. Try. Try asking her what it was like before.

Shhhhhhhhhhhhhhhhhhh! They might hear you.

Yeah, no. We bury things. Time. Stories. Bodies. Bones. We bury them in our yards, sometimes in our closets. It's a whole thing. Then we disinfect. We begin with the sheets on the bed. Always the sheets on the bed. They need to be bleached. Preferably washed the first time by bare hands dipped into the corrosive liquid. Kill two birds with one. Make. Sure. To. Remove. Any. Trace.

And me, I'm not interested in hiding or burying. I'm not interested in keeping the silence, in removing the blood and guts.

As far as I'm concerned, if it means staining all the white, then so be it.

> *Lights down on* GARINEH, *who drops sheets and moves across the stage, into* GARO. *Lights up on* GARO.

GARO: I'm interested in writing about the women and queers that came before me who did not have documents, or whose documents were lost because of displacement, deportation, migration, genocide.

Because I am . . .

> *Changes tactics, clears throat.*

Having limited understanding of the women I am a direct descendent of, I began more broadly researching historical Armenian women. Trying to piece together the missing links in my understanding and knowledge.

I found Armen by chance. A friend of mine, Naiyri, asked me one day if I'd heard of Armen Ohanian. I hadn't.

Like any good diasporic ethnic person who wants to know about their history because, sadly, they don't already know it: I googled.

My whole thesis began with Google.

I mean no wonder Schneider thinks this research is weak, right? What original sources do I have?

In the months I've been reading about and chasing after Armen, she has become . . . a kind of mentor. A kind of obsession. Reading her memoir and hunting down biographical information on her has been, for me, a way of engaging with an Armenian woman's voice that I've . . . felt . . .

> *Pause.*

You see . . . Armen left trails to follow, even if those trails don't always lead to the "truth." And somehow in finding some of Armen, I am finding something of myself.

Lights down on GARO. *Lights up on* MUSICIAN. *Cue* MUSICIAN.

Cue sound for THE VOICE OF ARMEN.

THE VOICE OF ARMEN: I expressed, with a poetry of movement as cool and chaste as the dawn, the awakening of the human soul to the beauty of love.

ARMENIAN DANCER enters through back of venue.

Beyond the curtains the musicians touched the strings of their instruments. Music softer than the light of the candles and sweet as their perfume stole through the golden draperies. I rise, spreading my veils like transparent wings, and advancing into the open space begin my dance.

Lights down on MUSICIAN.

Lights up on ARMENIAN DANCER.

Cue sound for ARMENIAN DANCER.

SCENE 2

ARMENIAN DANCER enters into the space from behind the audience, wearing a red veil and wrists tied with a red ribbon; she approaches an audience member and has them take the ribbon off. She performs a traditional Armenian dance, slowly moving through and weaving between the audience members.

Music fades. Lights up on ARMEN.

ARMENIAN DANCER takes off the crown and puts it on ARMEN'S *desk. She asks an audience member to help unzip her dress, and walks back to the desk becoming* ARMEN.

Lights down on ARMENIAN DANCER.

ARMEN: The dancer is more than a woman; she is a dream, and that to preserve it she should show the world only her unreal self.

Lights soft-wash on ARMEN. *Lights up on* GARO.

SCENE 3

ARMEN is sitting at her desk typing her memoirs.

GARO is at a desk, flipping through pages of their thesis.

GARO: Armen Ohanian was born in 1887 as Sophia Pirboudaghian. She was born to an upper class Armenian family in Shamakha, which is part of what is current day Azerbaijan. Having lost much of their possessions and wealth due to an earthquake in 1902, Sophia and her family moved to Baku.

They arrived shortly before escalation of Azeri-Armenian conflicts. The anti-Armenian pogroms, which reached their height in 1905, meant attacks on Armenian communities, raids of people's houses . . .

Pause.

Lights soft-wash on GARO. Lights up on MUSICIAN. Cue MUSICIAN.

Lights up on ARMEN.

ARMEN pauses her typing and removes the page she has been working on. She begins reading, getting lost in the memories.

ARMEN: There was no laughter in our dreams, filled with vague apprehensions and terrors, and awakening seemed a part of nightmare when at midnight we sat up in our beds, aroused by shouts and the pounding of sabre hilts on our gates.

Places a page on GARO's desk.

Then, half-stupefied with sleep and fear, we ran to our mother in our nightgowns, while the tramp of heavy boots and the light of torches went from room to room. The most hidden corners of our house were searched, even to unclean laundry, kitchen utensils, beds. Amid the wails of the servants and the harsh orders of officers, our rooms were reduced to a chaos of overturned tables, emptied chests, heaps of rugs and blankets, while hurriedly we covered ourselves with any garment we could find, in order to pass the inspection of the searchers.

Grumbling, they went away at last, leaving us trembling, weeping, divided by fear and anger.

Lights soft-wash on ARMEN. Lights down on MUSICIAN. Lights up on GARO.

GARO is sitting at a desk going through different pages.

GARO: I've been cross-referencing what I know of my family's dates and places of origin with those of Armen's. Just to see. The monolith of the 1915 genocide, which directly impacted my family, has overshadowed my understanding of Armenian history in surrounding regions over the last century.

Armen was born in Shamakha around the same time my great-grandma was born in Moush.

Lights soft-wash on ARMEN. *Lights up on* GARO.

GARO moves downstage right and speaks into an invisible map.

ARMEN simultaneously moves downstage-left and sits on the ground, starts drawing her own map.

Shamakah. Baku. Tehran. Moush. Kilis. Beirut.

Our ancestral homelands versus nation borders. Our families that escaped and didn't escape war. Wars that on the surface seem to be about land, ethnicity, and religion. But then, the glaring impact and implications of empire and imperialism.

Azeri-Armenian "conflicts." The anti-Armenian pogroms.

While Armenians and Azeris fight along ethnic, cultural, and religious lines, and competing land claims, who was/did/is this fighting really benefiting? As I zoom out, I see contested pieces of land with other empires fighting to control them. If we look at where Russia played a role. Where Ottomans did. Who armed who.

Flash to a different region. Similar time frame. The Ottoman Empire. Late 1800s. The "Armenian Question." Kurds and Armenians pitted against each other. Time and again. Sassoun. Zeitun. Then World War I. The mass deportation and extermination of 1.5 million Armenians from our ancestral homelands.

Refugees. Again, different region. Moving forward through time now. Lebanese-Syrian conflicts. Lebanese Civil War. Syrian occupation of Lebanon. Israeli attacks on Lebanon.

Shifting national borders.

And there's the French. The Ottomans. The British. The US. Russia. Israel. "Conflicting narratives."

Repeating histories. Repetition with a pattern . . .

Lights down on GARO, *who crosses behind* ARMEN *into* MORKOOR. *Lights full/ up on* MORKOOR. ARMEN *listens to* MORKOOR, *feeling moved.*

MORKOOR: What truth you want to hear?

Always questions you are asking. Why you are asking questions? You have no shame?

You can't write my stories.

I don't have stories, I am not a book.

I have life. And this one, it is mine life.

How you can speak about a life you don't know? If I tell you Beirut, then what will you do?

You want to know what it was like when the war it comes? When our family it was broken?

I don't go back there. There is nothing there. What is important is right here.

MORKOOR crosses behind ARMEN into GARO.

Lights down on MORKOOR. Lights up on ARMEN. Lights soft-wash on GARO. Lights up on MUSICIAN. Cue MUSICIAN.

ARMEN is talking to the audience.

ARMEN: In the terror that still held the city we could not even decently mourn our dead. My father was buried hurriedly; his body, guarded by an escort of police, was carried through the streets accompanied by a few brave men who made their way past scattered corpses, beneath the black smoke from the burning wells. My little mother, homeless and a widow, gathered us around her to consider what should be done. Some decision as to our fate must be made at once.

GARO walks over to ARMEN, becoming the mother that she is talking about.

GARO: *(as mother)* As for you, my little daughter—

ARMEN: She said, embracing me tenderly.

GARO: *(as mother)* —you are to be married tomorrow.

GARO walks back to the desk.

ARMEN: This information surprised me very much. But as I learned that, even in the wreckage of our fortunes, a respected maker of marriages had found for me a husband in a young Persian.

Lights down on MUSICIAN.

Lights up on GARO.

ARMEN stays seated and starts writing on pages.

GARO picks up a few pieces of paper and refers to them throughout this segment.

GARO: Sophia was hurriedly married to a Persian-Armenian doctor, Haik Ter-Ohanian. Leaving her mother and the rest of her family behind, Sophia Ter-Ohanian moved to Tehran with her husband, but the marriage ended within a year.

Flips through pages.

It's interesting. In her memoir, she writes of some long, outlandish tale of her husband having an epiphany and leaving her to pursue god and help "the people."

But I met with a biographer of Armen's in Yerevan, and he said *she was the one* who left her husband. I didn't get a lot of clarity about how or why the marriage ended, but it is clear that she left him.

Apparently, also, Armen had a child during that marriage . . . *a child* that is not mentioned in *any* of Armen's writings that I have read so far.

ARMEN crosses out sections on pages, crumples, and tosses them. She walks back to desk. Lights soft-wash on ARMEN.

GARO crosses over and picks up the crumpled papers.

It's so interesting, these choices of hers . . . what to include. What not to include.

Pause. GARO makes some notes.

It *is* clear that after her marriage, Sophia fully pursued acting and, in particular, dancing.

ARMEN is packing.

While still in Iran, she perfected her "Oriental dances," which she toured through Egypt and then the Ottoman Empire. It was during her Ottoman tour that she was hired to perform in London, and then throughout Europe.

The first time she appeared on stage she was still calling herself Sophia Ohanian.

ARMEN is putting her hair up.

Makes a note.

. . . In the following couple years her name changed several times. From Sophia Ohanian to Armenuhi Ohanian to Armen Ohanian.

Pause.

GARO speaks while looking at ARMEN.

Armen. A clearly male-gendered Armenian name.

Pause.

Okay, so I'm trying to make links here, right?

And this is the part, in particular, that Schneider said was weak.

Lights up on ARMEN and GARO.

ARMEN moves downstage, reading her memoir. GARO moves downstage, reading their thesis.

But I'm going to read it for you anyways, okay?

So, in *Dancer of Shamakha* we see early examples of a budding queer identity. Throughout this memoir it is the relationship between women that is consistently foregrounded. The bulk of her memoir follows Armen's relationship with a Queen. The queen is apparently a fictional character—

ARMEN: Who swooped into my life to save me after I was left devastated and destitute by my husband.

GARO: —even though she really left him.

ARMEN: The Queen had renounced all men after her heart was broken by one, and instead we spent our time with other women in the bathhouses.

GARO: Okay, later in the memoir Armen is separated from the Queen, because she's dancing and touring. It's the Ottoman tour . . .

ARMEN: One night during my tour, I noticed this Turkish woman in the audience . . .

GARO: Who saw Armen perform and was totally enamored with her.

ARMEN: After my dance, she invited me back to her house, where she had a bath drawn for the both of us. As we were bathing each other—

GARO: Super platonically.

ARMEN: —she reached over and brushed her hand against my face, and said, "I wish that I were a man that I may more freely touch you."

GARO: Okay.

ARMEN has a moment with the memory, then goes back to her desk. She writes a love letter and puts it in an envelope.

GARO walk back to their desk.

Lights change, following ARMEN and GARO.

ARMEN keeps writing her memoirs, drinks, combs her hair. GARO talks to the audience.

Parallel to the time that Armen was writing this memoir, in her "real life" it is said that while in France, she had an affair with Natalie Barney, a very out and non-monogamous lesbian poet living in Paris in the early 1900s. There are newspaper clippings of Armen and Natalie arriving to a party riding on horseback. Armen clutching onto Natalie as they . . . I mean, yeah.

Incidentally, however, her biographer says it's unlikely that Armen was in fact queer. Because it's not well documented. Because, apparently, if something isn't well documented then it's not fact.

And then of course, there's the whole, *she wanted to be more gay than she really was.*

Okay, let's stick to the facts.

What we do know about her . . . Armen was a dancer, a writer, a poet, a choreographer, a translator. She travelled the world. Later in life, she started her own school. She was overtly political, involved as an artist and activist in communist and socialist movements.

Here's the thesis: throughout her life, Armen defied the gender roles ascribed to her, and importantly, she queered the traditional Armenian woman's narrative, and she did it over a century ago.

Lights down on GARO.

GARO walks downstage into GARINEH.

ARMEN: The dancer is more than a woman, she is a dream, and that to preserve it she should show the world only her unreal self.

Lights down on ARMEN. Lights up on GARINEH.

GARINEH: It's all the hidden things.

Like the places that hair grows when it shouldn't.

She takes off her shirt and exposes her armpit hair.

The shame. It lives in the hair.

All the girls at school shave. I did too. You know the routine. Razors, but my hair is so coarse and it gave me ingrowns; so then I tried creams, but this one time I left it on too long and it burned through my skin leaving brown patches for ages, which is grosser than the hair; so then, wax, but it's expensive.

Morkoor's friend, Aunty Maral, she got her hair laser removed. I wanted that soooo badly, and then one day I saw Mark's armpits during gym class. His big bushy armpits, and . . . well . . . I dunno, I got jealous.

How come he's *allowed* to have armpit hair? Like nobody even questions why it should or shouldn't be there.

And just like that.

Snaps fingers.

It was like my feminist awakening.

Laughs at her own joke. Serious again.

I mean, don't get me wrong. It's not that I have anything against removing the hair. Go for it, you know? But why do I *have to* shave? Like, it isn't really a *choice*.

She speaks directly to a person in the audience.

I know you know what I mean.

Pause.

Besides, I like the hair. It's soooo soft.

She strokes her underarms.

You should see how people react to it though. These little patches of hair. And the *physical* reaction people have. The *things* they say . . . That look of *disgust*. I mean, I don't really care what *people out there* think, or say. Not really.

Goes back to the stage.

But, in the house, I wear shirts with sleeves on.

Puts the shirt back on.

You know, I wouldn't want to ruin their appetites at the dinner table by accidentally lifting my arms and exposing myself.

Exposing my shame.

Goes back to bleaching the sheets. Lights up on MORKOOR.

MORKOOR *enters* GARINEH'S *space and starts cleaning up the room.*

(singing) We take the loofah and scrub until the skin comes off. We scrub so hard and scrape off the skin. And we make sure to remove all the hair.

We have to disinfect. We have to disinfect. Do you know why?

You know you know why!

MORKOOR: What is this business?

GARINEH is startled by MORKOOR's presence, and gets a bit embarrassed and walks away from MORKOOR.

Throughout this scene, MORKOOR and GARINEH are pushed and pulled toward and away from each other as their fight progresses.

Is this another of those poetry things you are writing? This artist business. *Ewwf.* Why you don't do your homework, instead of speaking to the walls and mirrors all the time?

We didn't come all this way and work hard for you to be artist, with no work and no real job. You must be realistic in this world, hokis.

GARINEH: Who asked for your opinion on this?! And why are just coming into my room? This is *my* space.

MORKOOR: You. Talking talking. Like these other girls you go to school with. With that mouth that says whatever it likes. At least them, they keep themselves dressed nice and comb their hair.

You. What you went and did to that head of yours? Inch amot. Hetch mdig ches ener. Inch bidi enem?

Goes to touch GARINEH's hair, and GARINEH slaps her hand away.

MORKOOR walks over to the dress tossed in the corner. She picks it up and shows it off.

Your cousin Taleen go and get you that beautiful dress. Expensive fabrics. You can be so beautiful in that dress. Why you won't wear it?

GARINEH grabs the dress from MORKOOR's hand and throws it aside.

So ungrateful. So stupid the waste.

You are breaking my heart. This heart, of mine. You breaking it piece by piece into small little pieces. I'm thinking, it's because you want to hurt me.

Hmmm. Garineh, is this why you . . .

GARINEH gets up to leave.

I am speaking with you . . . where you are going?

GARINEH: I don't have to sit and listen to this. It's not like you understand anyways.

MORKOOR: *(offended)* What I don't understand? What it is about you I don't understand? Eh? What, we don't do for you?

Explain to me, Garineh.

GARINEH: Well, we could talk about the fact that you're still calling me Garineh. My name is Garo. I've asked you repeatedly to respect the fact that I want my name to be . . .

MORKOOR: Garineh!

GARINEH: See what I mean. I just finished saying my name is Garo . . .

MORKOOR: This again? No. I will not call you Garo. You know that is a man's name. You are my most beautiful girl. I will not shame you and call you the names of a boy.

GARINEH: This is exactly what you did to Ara. Do you see history repeating itself?! Remember how long Ara fought with you about this?

MORKOOR: Why you are speaking of that now? Why you are mixing all this business? No. I tell you already, I don't talk about Ani or Ara or whatever it name is. You know I don't talk about that one. That is not our family. That is disgrace and shame to God.

GARINEH: Well, it seems like Ara and I have a lot in common then. Like maybe it's in the family genes.

MORKOOR: What you are saying?

GARINEH: Morkoor, come on. Don't pretend. We *have* talked about this. Remember, you, me, Uncle Raffi? We sat down for dinner. It wasn't that long ago. I said, look, I have something to tell you. Remember when I said, I'm like Ara. I'm a big queerdo, and I'm also . . .

MORKOOR: You?

She's shocked, as though hearing this for the first time, and very hurt, shaking her head.

Voch. No.

I will not believe it. You are my Garineh.

Changes tactics, while GARINEH *rolls her eyes.*

I do everything for you. We come all this way and do all this things for you. And this, this is how you repay this family?

Again shifting approaches.

Ummaa. You are crazy. That is what happen. My poor Garineh, she is crazy.

And what I'm supposed to tell the family? What I'm supposed to tell your cousins and your uncle Raffi?

GARINEH: Tell him whatever you want! I have already told him. You're the only one who's still in denial.

MORKOOR: *(upset now)* You.

You are just like your mother.

You do whatever you like. You have no appreciations for the family.

How you can know? You are so young. It's that Ani that put these ideas into your head.

GARINEH is fed up. She picks up her notebook and starts walking out.

Again, you are walking away. No respect. Where you are going?

GARINEH: Where I'm going?

Anywhere but here.

MORKOOR starts violently folding strewn clothes.

Let's not do this again, okay? I told you I didn't want to talk about this. *(frustrated)* I mean really . . . Ani? You still can't bring yourself to say their name? You can't stand to talk about Ara?

GARINEH gets into MORKOOR's face.

Yes! Ara! A-r-a. Remember them? Your child.

MORKOOR's mood dramatically shifts. She is sad and thoughtful. She moves away from GARINEH.

Your child who used to live with us? The one who was your favourite-could-never-do-anything-wrong-in-the-world, until one day your precious baby disappointed you, right?

MORKOOR goes to GARO's desk and starts tidying.

Oh, now you don't want to talk?

You just want to forget about the whole thing, hey?

GARINEH speaks to the audience. Her mood is nostalgic.

I remember. Ara. My cousin. Who asked me questions that didn't involve my plans for marriage, or Armenian men, or the length of my hair, or some stupid dress.

Ara. My cousin.

(to MORKOOR*)* Your kid.

The person in this family who actually talked about . . . hopes, concerns. Politics, history. Art.

You know, *real things!*

Ara, the person who was actually supportive. Who when they saw me writing or making art would say really nice things, instead of *what is this artist business?!*

Like that time they said, "Hey, Gar, have you thought about writing? You're a great writer." Or, "Yeah, totally, we need to know the story of who we are, to know about the story we want to become."

Pause.

She speaks directly to MORKOOR*, and gets more in her face.*

And what happened to Ara, Morkoor?

Right. Ara left.

Back to the audience.

Does anyone else care or see that the people who are *different* in this family leave?

(to MORKOOR*)* Why is that *okay with you?*

And why did Ara leave, Morkoor? Oh that's right. Because of you. They left because *you* wouldn't listen to what they had to say. Because you didn't like them. You didn't care about their feelings or what they thought . . .

MORKOOR *stops and is agitated.*

MORKOOR: What is this they?

GARINEH: They! It's a pronoun, Morkoor. You know, like she or he, only they. Gender neutral. We've talked about this a million times. We don't even have a she or he pronoun in Armenian. It's not complicated. *(patronizing tone)* Gender as a spectrum. Not only Boys or Girls. Not only Men or Women. There are a lot of different people. A whole rainbow.

I know that's hard for you to understand. It's hard to understand that some of us don't want to be put into boxes. But just try. Ara uses they pronouns. And for that matter, *so do I.*

Repeat after me: They

MORKOOR: She

GARINEH: Them

MORKOOR: Him.

GARINEH: Theirs!

MORKOOR: *(with a look of disgust)* It.

GARINEH: Not *it*! Them.

MORKOOR walks across the stage, holds it a moment, then turns into ARMEN. Lights down on MORKOOR.

MORKOOR soft-wash to ARMEN.

(defeated) Ahhh. Great. Forget it. I said I didn't want to talk about this. Is this what you wanted? To get here? I can't stand this.

(after MORKOOR) Why does it have to be like this?!

GARINEH falls to the ground. Lying on her back she stares up. Lights soft-wash to GARINEH.

Lights up on MUSICIAN. Cue for MUSICIAN. Lights up on ARMEN.

ARMEN: Oh my queen, the vaults of these rooms begin to oppress me as much as the heavy beams of our patriarchal houses. Let us go away! Let us go far from this place, to the place where all the women are free, free to live fully every hour of their lives!

But Freedom. What was it? I did not know.

ARMEN moves downstage and into the audience. She speaks directly to the first AUDIENCE/LOCAL ARTIST.

I knew only that something hidden in me that had been growing unnoticed had suddenly thrust leaves and blossom into the daylight. And its blossom was a desire to escape from all walls, to be free. Freedom? What was it? I did not know, but I desired it.

Lights down on MUSICIAN. GARINEH sits up.

ARMEN sits next to AUDIENCE/LOCAL ARTIST. Lights down on ARMEN.

Lights up on soft-house/audience light.

SCENE 4

A voice from the audience begins sharing a piece—spoken-word poetry, reflection. Content will likely be about intersectionality, gender, sexuality, gender justice, and equality. Will be a local artist/poet/activist.

When audience pieces are finished, ARMEN *thanks them with a smile and a nod of the head, and returns to her desk, working.*

House lights down.

Lights soft-wash on ARMEN. *Lights up on* GARO.

SCENE 5

GARINEH stands up and turns into GARO, *and walks to their desk.* ARMEN *opens an envelope and reads a letter.*

GARO: It's an unravelling. Like peeling back the layers of an onion.

Gynt had it wrong, though. At the centre is not nothing. Quite the contrary. If we wait long enough, at the centre of the onion is . . . another onion. Mise en abyme. A feedback loop. The cycle of life.

Beneath all the layers, are . . . more layers.

Tosses the pages so that they scatter. Pause.

In her biographical details, I found out that Armen studied theatre and visual arts in Baku. But in her book/memoir, she just miraculously begins dancing—as though she never had to rehearse a day in her life.

Pause.

Apparently, she co-founded the Union of Iranian Theater-lovers just before the Revolution, and in 1910 she was part of organizing a musical and literary gala, which was supposedly one of the first times women appeared on stage in Tehran.

But again, in her memoir, none of this appears.

In fact, for someone who was involved in so many overtly politicized actions, the absolute lack of analysis in her book . . .

God, when I first read her "memoir" I was really disappointed. She sounds like some bougie, spoiled, overly sentimental . . .

I mean, I almost dropped this project. Like thanks, Naiyiri, yeah, Armen Ohanian. Great.

But of course, context makes all the difference.

Puts down pages. Picks up a book and holds it up . . .

Context.

The Dancer of Shamakha. So, Armen wrote this "memoir" post-WWI, while she was living in France, and her dances were not making her enough money to live on. But writing about the "Orient" seemed to be selling a little.

Based on that, we can make inferences, right?

I mean, how do you talk about revolution to an audience that is largely exhausted of war and now wants tales and escapades? Where do you talk about "the movement" when your meal ticket is contingent on exotic Arabian nights and magical dances for queens?

This is entertainment for a price, right?

She was smart . . . couched inside is a narrative that unveils truths inside of fantasy.

Lights soft-wash on GARO. Lights up on MUSICIAN. Cue MUSICIAN.

Lights up on ARMEN.

ARMEN is ripping up the letter.

ARMEN: Needless to say, we took all precautions against being suspected of revolutionary sympathies. We suppressed so completely all use of the words "liberty," "revolt," or "the people" that not even among ourselves, hardly in our own minds, did we utter them. Those words, found by chance in the most innocent correspondence, or overheard in the most casual conversation, cost months in prison.

Lights soft-wash on ARMEN. Lights down on MUSICIAN. Lights up on MORKOOR.

GARO as MORKOOR has cloth in hand, and throughout the scene, as characters flip in and out of MORKOOR, they exchange the cloth.

GARO: *(as MORKOOR)* Freedom. Revolution.

This one, she is just like her mother.

She refuse to be realistic. Always reading some things. Always thinking the answers they are better out there. Always thinking the enemy is inside the house. That I am the enemy.

Like you know what is an enemy.

Pause.

You want me to speak of old times, and you, you don't even remember when we first get here. You was such small baby. What you can remember?

All of the cousins and the aunties and uncles. All of us in that one room. More of us coming from Beirut. In that small apartment with the bugs everywhere. You don't remember when we lock the kitchen because Hagop was more hungry than the foods that we have.

You grow up here. And you grow up when the things they get better.

We grow you here. Your uncle Raffi, working all the days and the nights. Me. In those hotels. Cleaning. Cleaning. Until my feet hurt. Until my back it hurt.

Working for those stupid peoples.

And Raffi, after what they did to him. After how they treat him. The names they calling him. Still, he getting up every day and he go out there and he do his works and . . .

Where your mother was then? With those books she is reading and the freedom she is fighting. What freedoms? Who got the freedom?

Pause.

ARMEN-*as-*MORKOOR *enters abruptly and grabs the cloth from* GARO-*as-*MORKOOR, *who then becomes* GARINEH.

ARMEN: *(as* MORKOOR*)* Ewwf. After all of this, and you. You are worst than your mother. You grow up in this place and these people you go to school with. Spoiled. You don't know what we know.

You make me tired with all these things you are saying always. All these things I need to understand. Like I am born yesterday.

We come here and work hard, this I understand. And you . . .

You get angry with *me* that I don't remember. What *I* don't remember? What I'm supposed to remember? I'm supposed to remember every things you tell me with that mouth?

These words. *You* go and disgrace god, and then you want *me* to listen.

Pause.

GARO: *(as* GARINEH, *reacting to* MORKOOR*)* And just like that, I go from caring about what you were saying, to . . .

Disgrace god? I don't . . . I am *not* a disgrace to god. Is it that hard? *Really?*

You're forcing me to choose, you know that, right?

ARMEN: *(as MORKOOR)* What forcing? How I'm forcing you?

GARO: *(as GARINEH)* At least out there, with the odars. At least with the odars, I don't care. It doesn't hurt the same way when they don't get it or they say hurtful things or bully me.

But here, this is just . . .

MORKOOR & GARINEH: This makes me want to scream

GARO and ARMEN switch; ARMEN becomes GARINEH, GARO becomes MORKOOR.

ARMEN: *(as GARINEH)* Fuck. I am not the good *Armenian girl you want me to be*!

GARO: *(as MORKOOR)* How you can say these words to me? How you can use this language?

ARMEN: *(as GARINEH)* Do you get it? That doesn't make me *bad*.

GARO: *(as MORKOOR)* You don't listen. You don't see how we sacrifice . . .

ARMEN: *(as GARINEH)* And, I won't hide. If that's what you're asking me to do, or hoping . . . *I won't hide.*

Because *you're ashamed* of what they will think?

GARO: *(as MORKOOR)* Shhhhhhhhhhhh. Garineh. You are speaking so loud. They might hear you.

ARMEN: *(as GARINEH)* You think this is loud? This isn't loud. I can talk really loud, if you want.

GARO: *(as MORKOOR)* Garineh!

ARMEN: *(as GARINEH)* No! *I will not lower my voice. Let them hear!!!*

Let them hear!!!

MORKOOR & GARINEH: What will they say?

GARO and ARMEN switch, and switch back and forth frequently.

GARO: *(as GARINEH)* Who cares if they hear me?! Who cares what they think!

Pause.

ARMEN: *(as MORKOOR)* You're always pushing.

ARMEN and GARO are circling as they switch back and forth between MORKOOR and GARINEH.

GARO: *(as GARINEH)* Pushing everyone away. Go on, push, Morkoor.

GARINEH & MORKOOR: Push.

GARO: *(as GARINEH)* One of these days, you're going to push so hard I'm gonna leave, and I won't come back.

> *Pause.*

ARMEN: *(as GARINEH)* You should take some of your own advice.

GARO: *(as MORKOOR)* Family is the most important thing, right?

ARMEN: *(as GARINEH)* What about when we have to face things we don't like about each other.

GARO: *(as GARINEH)* Then what?

ARMEN: *(as GARINEH)* How important is family really?

GARO: *(as GARINEH)* If you want to hide and be ashamed, do it.

> *They stop circling.* ARMEN *and* GARO *face each other.*

ARMEN: *(as GARINEH)* You hide under your masks. Don't expect me to.

> ARMEN *as* GARINEH *exits.*

> GARO *as* GARINEH *turns into* MORKOOR *and begins pacing around the stage, moving in and out of characters.*

MORKOOR: What is hiding? You thinking this is game, like hide and seek or some things? You have no respect.

GARINEH: What do you mean, I have no respect?!

MORKOOR: Do you thinking what it was like for us? You thinking because you go and cut your head, err, your hair, you knowing what it is when the things they are hard.

GARINEH: Is this where you compare me to my mother again?

MORKOOR: Your mother?! She leave us. Do you understand that?

She stay in that war. She stay there and we don't know what it is that happen. You thinking that is some big hero things she is doing? You thinking she going and fighting and leaving the rest of us is some big answer?

GARINEH: Yes, badaskhan chem pndrer gor. Yes, mamas ge pdrem gor.

MORKOOR: Toon shad medz peran oonis, yev inch e vor toon kides ays gyankin masin? Eh?

GARINEH: Wait! That is not what I'm saying. I'm saying that . . .

MORKOOR: What it is you knowing about what you saying? I am doing all of these things for you.

GARINEH: You don't like what I am doing. I don't care what you say.

MORKOOR: I tell you to take care of you. You don't want to do it like I say, what you want from me?

GARINEH: What do I want from you?

MORKOOR: I want you to stop making me into whatever it is *you* want me to be.

GARINEH: I want you to understand!

MORKOOR: Garineh. I was younger than you are now when my mother she died. I raise your mother, and our brothers, and I taking care of my father. And your uncle. And Ani. We moving us from Beirut to this Canada. We learning to speak this English.

What I am hiding from, eh?

GARINEH: What mask do you think I'm wearing?

Do you think I am lying about these things?

MORKOOR: That I am not knowing anything? That I don't . . .

GARINEH: . . . understand.

I don't tell you these things because . . .

MORKOOR: *I want these things they are different for you.*

GARINEH: I am not the enemy you think I am.

MORKOOR: I love you. I raise you.

Blackout.

Cue sound, THE VOICE OF ARMEN.

THE VOICE OF ARMEN: I must present myself under this mask. The most striking of all are my eyes. They are those of an enraged tigress.

SCENE 6

MASKED PERFORMER enters in darkness. Cue music.

Lights up on MASKED PERFORMER (stark/harsh light).

The dance is slow and creepy, with subtle creature-like movements. MASKED PERFORMER has a gold mask with a papier mâché mouth overtop of their nylon-covered head, wearing a black lace dress that covers them from neck to ankles. During the dance, MASKED PERFORMER undresses, revealing a black lace bra and pantyhose (no underwear).

They transform into a more rabid-like creature, dancing close to the ground. At the end of the dance, MASKED PERFORMER removes their mask, letting it drop to the ground, clutches their stomach as though sick, lifts the nylon halfway up their face, and vomits out saliva-covered rose petals. They breathe heavily. Pause.

Blackout.

MASKED PERFORMER exits in darkness.

SCENE 7

Lights up on GARO. Lights up on MUSICIAN. Cue MUSICIAN.

During this scene, GARO becomes ARMEN. They put makeup on their face and cover themselves with a piece of red fabric. They begin to conflate the different areas of the stage, moving all around. MUSICIAN accompanies these excerpts.

GARO: The whole kingdom talked of me. A thousand stories were invented about me, to thrill the bazaars and the baths. No one doubted that I had become a traitor to my religion. It was not true. I was, and I remain in spite of everything, a good Christian who believes in god and paradise . . . But my piety, different from that of others, was in my own soul. The Christian world called me a heretic and a courtesan, and these terrible epithets were crowned with the name "Daughter of Sodom and Gomorrah."

These indignities penetrated like a blade of steel into my Armenian soul. All innocent as I was, I felt myself lost. Shame troubled my soul. I feared even violence, and left the house of Envar-ed-Doule only disguised or under cover of night . . . I must leave . . . But to do that, I must go away from Persia. I valued too highly the respect of our patriarchal Armenian society to be able to endure returning as a sinner. Where could I go? Fearful, I hesitated. Imagine how much courage I needed to go, alone, into countries far beyond the borders of everything I knew.

"Your feet are set upon a downward path, my daughter," he sighed. "You will soon be changed from an honest woman to an artist. Your fall is inevitable. You are young, you are alone, you dance . . . One sees your face, your naked feet . . . Corruption awaits you. I see it."

Courage, the four walls of a garden are no longer around me, the patriarchs no longer watch over me. Then deeds, not lamentations! Guide me toward new horizons. I must submit. Farewell to my dreams, farewell to my sun! I am now become an artist.

From that moment I became independent, that is to say, thrown to the mercy of events. Independence! Proud word, created to reduce the proudest to slavery.

Asia! I leave you, perhaps forever. Will I be able to live without you? To what does this huge ship, this sea monster, carry me away? And the Europeans, enclosed with me upon this ship, how ugly they are! These blond people with unnatural, colourless skins, who smile at me—how I detest them! One of them wishes to speak to me, O Heaven! I fled into my cabin and began to weep, my face sunk into the cushions of my bed. As in the agony of the drowning, all the countries, all the houses that I had known, all the living and dead faces, all that was dear and terrible to me, rushed before my eyes from I know not where.

Laughing and weeping, I wiped them away with my burning hands, but they returned.

Among the others, a face with luminous rays rested upon me two sorrowful eyes. It leaned toward me, and I felt a kiss on my forehead. My mother, my adorable mother! At this very hour, without doubt, she was praying for me, far, far away among the mountains of my Caucasus.

Mother, where am I going? Oh come with me; I am afraid! Eternal Saviour, God of Kindness, God of Mercy, what horrors dost Thou reserve for me in the unknown lands of the Occident? I am alone. O Great God, watch over me, protect me!

SCENE 8

Enter MORKOOR *through audience.*

MORKOOR *is carrying flour and a rolling pin in a big bowl.*

MORKOOR: What is this girl talking about? Can't you see we have guests?

Lights down on MUSICIAN. *Lights soft-wash on* GARO. *Lights up soft-house.*

GARO *walks back to their desk.*

They are dying of hunger. Look at this one, she's so thin. Practically begging for a piece of bread. You don't want to help me cook? Fine, I'll do it all by myself as usual.

What is this darkness?

Addresses the technician.

How can you expect me to make dinner in these conditions? Please. Turn some lights on.

Lights up full-house.

And where is my table? You—

Addresses the MUSICIAN.

—bring me a table! Where do you like me to cut the onion, on top of my head?

MUSICIAN *brings a table for her.*

Good, now we have to start preparing the foods.

She turns toward the audience members as she covers the table with a tablecloth.

This one, she is just like someone I know. Never help me in the kitchen, always in her room like how she is now. And you?

Addresses a specific audience member.

What are you doing over there like a lump on a log? Come help me, the onions need to be clean and cut. Come make yourself useful.

She gets an audience member she perceives to be a woman to join her and help cut onions.

No not like that. No! Faster. They are starving, can't you see? Faster. Oh God. You're going to drive me crazy . . . did your mother not teach you how to cook properly? Ewff!

(to another female-perceived audience member) You, yes you, come here, you think I am joking? The garlic has to be clean and cut as well. Yalla. Come, come my daughter.

Like this. Yes. Exactly. Bravo. Very good my daughter . . . Unlike a certain someone . . .

She tilts her head at the first audience member, who is cleaning the onion.

You could learn a thing or two from this one!

She turns back to the second audience member.

You're so pretty, so pretty!

Rubs her head.

Are you married? How old are you? . . . What? Is everything normal? Don't worry, we'll find you a nice Armenian husband.

Faster, faster, we're going to be here all day with this onion! No, not you my darling, you continue doing what you're doing, you're doing a great job.

Now for the dough . . .

She pours flour into the bowl and cracks an egg into it, begins to mix it with her hands.

Agh, my back hurts.

Turns to a male-perceived audience member.

Come give me a hand, will you? I can't knead this dough anymore. Go ahead, don't be scared. Yes, go. No, no. Not like that. Like this . . .

She feels his arms . . .

Very nice . . . Are you Armenian?

If they answer yes, she squeezes him and the second "pretty" female-perceived audience member together, and pushes the first female-perceived audience member away.

Yes, just like this, perfect.

If they answer no:

Oh, I'm so sorry for you.

She turns to the second female-perceived audience member.

It's okay, we find you someone else.

She turns to first female-perceived audience member.

For you, not so much.

Walks away from the table and sits in an audience member's seat, or at the edge of the MUSICIAN's *area.*

This is how it's done . . . watch and learn! Such good helpers . . . thank you very much, yes. Such good helpers. You can sit now, you have been so good, thank you. Thank you, yes, yes. Sit now, sit.

Pause.

It is so nice to have the helpers in the kitchen. So different from the way it was before. When I have to take care of everything.

I am not complaining . . . I do these things and I do them good. I take the things they are given and I make a home with those things. I take the mess the people they leaving and I make it nice.

Her mother leave, and I take care of her. It was not all good, but I do a good job.

Look, she come back. After all these times we never talking, but now she is home again.

House lights dim. Lights up on GARO.

GARO *is at their desk, talking to* TY.

GARO: Babe, it's really strange being back here. So many things are the same. This room. This desk. The smells. Her kitchen. I haven't thought about this stuff in I can't even tell you how long.

TY: That must be super weird, hey?

GARO: Yeah, it's weird. This room is . . . haunted by the way things were. It's like the two of us are alive in here.

TY: At least your thesis presentation is sounding good. That's gotta feel like progress?

GARO: I mean, you're sweet. But it's a mess . . . and it's not easy to work on it while here. I just have so much to do, and no there isn't a ton of time.

Because it's Uncle Raffi's anniversary, we've been seeing family. We went to church with everyone. There's more people coming over for dinner again tonight. It's a big production. I mean, *I* went to church.

I don't know if I'm going to pull this presentation together, and who knows what Schneider is going to say when she realizes my academic paper is turning into a piece of creative non-fiction/fiction. But fuck it. *This is the whole point of this work.* I'm trying to get a *handle* on what broke.

Lights soft-wash on GARO. Lights up on MORKOOR.

MORKOOR goes to the table and starts kneading dough.

MORKOOR: Yes, yes. She is coming. She is working on the homework.

She is going to be doctor, you know? All that reading with her nose in a book, and now she is going to be doctor. It is not doctor in hospital or medicine, and I don't know of other peoples going back to the school when they turning thirty, but she's doing good works.

You know, she is writing about Armenian family. I always telling her, family is the most important thing, and now she writing about our family. And this Armen Ohanian.

You hearing about Armen Ohanian? *(tutts)* I never hearing about this one, too. But what we knowing? What Armen Ohanian they teaching us? We don't go to school. I stop going at twelve years old. And Raffi, he don't even go that long.

Gets distracted by thoughts of Raffi.

I wish that Raffi can be here. Asdvads hokin lusavore.

She crosses herself.

If only Raffi can see how big she get. He can see from the place is now.

She points to the heavens.

He can see how smart this one become, huh? Then he know we do okay. That this one will come home again. Before he getting sick, he saying that this house is too quiet. After he . . . it getting even more quiet.

Lights soft-wash on MORKOOR. Lights up on GARO.

GARO: It's super weird without my uncle Raffi here. I mean, it's not like he was ever home a lot. But it's different now that he's gone. It's like you can feel it in the house that he's not *going to come back.*

And it's so intense to see how much she has aged. Her hands. But she's still living in this house, by herself, and she's been doing all the cooking and cleaning for guests and family coming over.

TY: How has it been seeing all the family? Do you think you're going to want to visit again?

GARO: I don't know how any of this will go when you and I visit together. Or if I do decide to take hormones. But for now . . . it's okay.

Lights up on MORKOOR. GARO lights same.

MORKOOR: We all finding ways to live with the things they happen. The time it is going too fast.

Back with GARO.

GARO: Listen, Ty, I should go, we're going to eat soon and I should go help with something before she thinks nothing has changed.

I love you. Talk later?

TY: Okay, hon. Yeah. Let's talk later.

I love you, too.

GARO: Okay, bye.

GARO hangs up the phone/Skype. Lights down on GARO.

GARO walks behind MORKOOR.

MORKOOR is still talking to guests and doesn't hear GARO come down behind her. GARO overhears MORKOOR talking about them.

MORKOOR: I don't understand these young people.

But you know, my baba say the same things about us when we young. Ach, look at this time. Okay, we are all hungry?

(yells) Garooo, dinnnner.

GARO: I'm right here, you don't have to yell.

Startles MORKOOR. She turns to look at GARO and knocks over a thing of flour, and it falls everywhere. GARO quickly bends over to help clean up. Throughout this scene, MORKOOR and GARO banter back and forth about who should clean up.

MORKOOR: Ewwwwf, Raf, Tal, An, errr, Garo. Hima nor makretsi amen asi. Okay, go getting me that cloth.

Already walking back with the cloth, GARO exhales with irritation. MORKOOR bends down and starts collecting the flour with her hand.

GARO: I know, Morkoor. Come on, let me help.

MORKOOR: Give me that cloth. You don't know how I like it.

GARO joins MORKOOR on the floor as they both struggle to be the one to clean the mess.

GARO: *(smiling)* I know how to clean a floor.

MORKOOR: Yes, yes. You clean like you, but . . . okay go get the brush.

GARO: Great. Where is it?

MORKOOR: In the closet. You see?

GARO: Yup, I got it.

GARO helps MORKOOR *finish cleaning up the flour. Lights down softly as* GARO *is sweeping.*

Curtain call.

NO STRINGS (ATTACHED)

SUNNY DRAKE

ACKNOWLEDGEMENTS

I am deeply grateful to my wonderful creative team: it is strange to call this a "one-person show" considering how many talented people it took to bring the work to life. Thanks particularly to director Gein Wong, who brought out new depths in the work, to collaborators Catherine Hernandez and Hisayo Horie who were instrumental in its early creation, and to artists who gave feedback and/or hosted work-in-progress showings including Awilda Rodríguez Lora, Michelle Nonó, Lydela Leonor, Patio Taller, Chanelle Gallant, Roxanna Vahed, nisha ahuja, Annah Anti-Palindrome, Rachel Mishenene, Ma-Nee Chacaby, Aiyyana Maracle, Trish Salah, Writing Trans Genres, the University of Winnipeg, Sze-Yang Ade-Lam, Ravyn Wings, kumara giles, ILL NANA/DiverseCity Dance Company, Donna-Michelle St. Bernard, Jiv Parasram, New Harlem Productions, Eventual Ashes, Tania Anderson, Hannah Pepper-Cunningham, Nick Slie, Celiany Rivera-Velázquez, Reena Reddy, WPIRG, Rosina Kazi, Nicholas Murray, Unit 2, Morgan M Page, the 519, and many generous audience members.

A big thank you to all of the fabulous presenters who brought the show to many cities and towns across the world, to Bee Sack, my wonderful audience development and touring administrator; my stage managers Katherine Belyea, Abbie Trott, Beth Wong, Chase Tam, and Chanelle Gallant, who shared many adventures in Toronto and on the road; and to Brendan Healy, Evalyn Parry, and all the Buddies in Bad Times Theatre staff.

Finally, I'd like to acknowledge development and touring financial support from the Ontario Arts Council, an agency of the Government of Ontario; the City of Toronto through the Toronto Arts Council; the Canada Council for the Arts; Arts Queensland; Volcano Theatre; the SummerWorks Performance Festival; and the many individuals and groups who donated money to accessibility costs such as ASL/AUSLAN interpretation and tickets for people on low incomes.

CONVERGENCES

BOBBY NOBLE

If I had to describe the content of *No Strings (Attached)* in one word, I would choose *convergences*. Of course, there are others: *intersectionalities*, *non-binary*, *deconstruction*, and by necessity, *trans-ed*.[1] But for me, convergences sets the tone that I want to detail.

As evidenced by this list, *No Strings (Attached)* is very much interested in asking you, reader and collaborator, to *co-produce it* in ways neither easily accessed, available, encouraged nor rewarded. *No Strings (Attached)* is, by definition then (that is to say, both performatively and in terms of performance) labour-intensive—a labour of love. As it should be.

Sunny Drake is a Toronto-based playwright, producer, and actor/performer who wrote, staged, and performed this gem of a play about the follies and impossibilities of romance in modern times. The main character, Jimmy, navigates his way through non-monogamy, online dating, trans-ed polyamory, and all of their affective dis-orientations, coming to no startling conclusions in the end. But conclusions aren't really the point of this fast-paced, multimedia, one-person show. It bears repeating here that as with much really good drama in the twentieth and twenty-first centuries, indeed the medium is the message. And that medium? Not just a long tradition of the one-person show but also the very convergence of the processes of romance turned inside out and crafted for all to see.

But lest one fear that "one-person show" is the same as "monologue," Drake reminds us in *No Strings (Attached)* that the best one-man shows are deconstructive and dialogic, not just chipping away at that fourth wall separating stage

---

1   Susan Stryker, "The Transgender Issue. An Introduction," *GLQ: A Journal of Gay and Lesbian Studies* 4, no. 2 (1998): 145–58, https://read.dukeupress.edu/glq /article/4/2/145/69263/The-Transgender-Issue-An-Introduction.

from audience but actively recruiting audience members into the multilingual text itself—to insist that fourth wall safeties and their attendant distances not be possible. "Unfinalizable" becomes the intended outcome of both medium and message, surpassing the neat beginning-middle-end conventions of storytelling that can all but erase meta-content in favour of the neatness of "content." In other words, time is all time; gender is all genders; staging becomes scene; process becomes the end; and Jimmy, our intrepid one-person of the "one-person show," is both one and not one in his desire for desire.

Converging in the stage scenes of *No Strings (Attached)* are not just Jimmy's love objects but love itself as an object circumscribed by gender and imperatives of monogamy, possession, and unmediated in-person narratives. In this reiteration, though, the idealizations of polyamory-as-resistance are somewhat tentatively explored—bracketed, if you will—as labour-intensive. The literal parentheses around "attached" in the title suggest for us that courses of counter-resisting love practices don't run smoothly, even as run they must. If monogamy is about possessive attachment, unexamined and assumed, then in polyamory "attached" needs to stand alone; however, what it is attached to remains a significant question, one which Drake explores with full intent. As he posits in the play, attachments happen; how, why, in what capacity, and via what converging modalities are the things to be ferreted out—not their absolutes, rightness, or wrongness.

The context of those examinations is particularly clever. The play opens with Jimmy attending a Romance-aholics meeting where the audience functions as part of the group scene. While it is too easy to be dismissive of such socials as clichés of the modern self-help movement, that the structure (Alcoholics Anonymous) is juxtaposed with romance as the content creates a picture of romance as equal parts enticing and potentially as dangerous as excessive alcohol consumption. The anonymity and repetitions of this structure and social, though, are both framed as one of the ways to grapple with imperatives produced by such social structures, and then consolidated individually. The solution to their toxicities is similar: group process, individual responsibility, and contextually specific support. The "fill-in-the-blank-aholics" social-as-context is one step away from a social movement, and it is here where Drake weaves, with a great deal of skill and ingenuity, the needs of the individual to recover from such structures into and through the potentialities of larger socials with shared values, wishes, and desires. It is a dangerous mistake to presume individuals harmed by social worlds do not need time and space to process trauma; it is equally dangerous to presume such recoveries constitute politics in and of themselves. Both the personal and the political are necessary for the other to function.

To frame this differently, instead of the monolingualities of the examined self as the mode of attachment under interrogation, the text—and Jimmy—is driven by intersectional modalities or grammars of being that defy mandated singularities. In fact, they deconstruct singularities and binaries alike. Jimmy discovers, as the consequence of living such an examined life, that who he is and how he desires to attach are constituted by selves long forgotten but still awake, still overdetermining, albeit unconsciously, the "choices" he makes in his complex navigations through everyday worlds. Only a structure, process, and indeed culture of self-reflection can undo the work and harm created by binary logics that mandate such things as unnecessary. We learn from Jimmy that the truth is just the opposite.

It is in these non-binary cultures and practices where we see Jimmy undo who he is supposed to be, post-gender transition. As an FTM trans man, Jimmy is supposed to be non-queer and masculine; his attractions to other men undo the often mandated heteronormativities of gender transition. His inclination as a romantic is supposed to produce monogamy as its outcome; Jimmy instead cultivates not just non-monogamy but also flamboyant polyamory. His identifications as queer and polyamorous do not preclude his attraction to romance. Nothing *is* what it is *supposed* to be. In that non-binary logic of *otherwise-as-scene*, not only is Jimmy trans-ed but so too is the play itself. *Unfinalizable*, it is text as both context and subtext where form is equally *otherwise*. The play is Facebook; reality TV; a game show; fantasy and everyday; text message and script where content is the scene of staging. To step into Jimmy's world is to step into and out of the worlds within the world, *otherwise* and all at the same time.

To read the way these all converge on the page—or on the stage—is to *be otherwise*, with Jimmy and Sunny both. These are love's labours, labours of love robust, intentional, deeply political—and most certainly not for the faint of heart.

The play has toured to thirty-seven cities across Canada, the US, Europe, and Australia. Premiering in 2013, the initial version of the play was entitled *Transgender Seeking . . .* This script is based on the later version at Buddies in Bad Times Theatre in Toronto, 2016.

Director: Gein Wong
Writer and Performer: Sunny Drake
Dramaturg: Catherine Hernandez
Video: Gein Wong, Laura Warren, Alex Williams, and Hisayo Horie
Set and Costume Designer: Joe Pagnan
Lighting Designer: Michelle Ramsay
Immersive Space Designer: Jade Lee Hoy
Composer: Njo Kong Kie
Other sound: Miquelon Rodriguez
Puppet: Ann Powell
Stage Manager: Beth Wong
Touring Stage Manager: Katherine Belyea (Canada) and Abbie Trott (Australia)
Audience Development and Touring Administrator: Bee Sack
Technician: Jazz Kamal
ASL Interpreters: Sage Willow and Tala Jalili
Romance-aholic Anonymous Greeters: Jackie Cooper and Jarrod Clegg
Ballroom Dance Consultant: Mario Piñon
Assistance with Props and Costumes: Shawn Henry, Joce Tremblay, Erica Meyers, Jenny So, and Michelle Tracey

CHARACTERS

Jimmy
Gameshow Host
Anti-Monogamy Police
Expert Guest
Date
Brian
Dad

NOTES

This was written as a one-person play. In multi-character scenes either the actor played all roles live, or as indicated for select scenes, one role was filmed and then video projected and the other played live. This use of video was a dramaturgical decision rather than an acting solution.

If you would like to stage the play yourself, you could stage it with or without video, and as a solo or multi-actor work. You can change the following references to suit your local context: Craigslist, OK Cupid, the Toronto International Film Festival, and Buddies in Bad Times Theatre.

The set was a wedding dress with a wedding cake attached as though it was a head for the dress. The wedding dress had a train of three satin panels with lacey borders trailing from the base of the dress up to the ceiling. There was a multi-coloured paint stain on one of the panels.

"/" within a line of dialogue indicates overlapping lines and where the next character's line starts.

The audience entry and seating area resembles the meeting of a fictional group: Romance-aholics Anonymous. Posters and slogans instruct "no flirting," "exchange phone numbers only for recovery purposes," "one ~~date~~ day at a time," etc. The space looks like Romance-aholics have attempted to make it unromantic, yet have failed: it is "accidentally" romantic.

As audience members pick up their tickets, they are given a flower. When they enter the space, a greeter welcomes them to the Romance-aholics Anonymous meeting and has a short interaction with them: confiscating the flower, threatening to confiscate any other romantic items posted on a contraband list, and handing them a romance sobriety chip—1 minute sober, 1 month, 5 months, etc.

A full moon rises slowly in the audience area.

A chair on the stage.

JIMMY bursts through the audience entrance door, clutching flowers and a small well-worn suitcase. He screeches to a halt underneath the full moon.

JIMMY: Sorry I'm late everyone! Has the meeting started?

Senses something behind him.

Huh?

He spins around just as the full moon evaporates into a new moon and then disappears before he sees it.

This is the Romance-aholics Anonymous meeting right?

He sits down in the audience, preferably in a seat a few audience members in, so he is surrounded.

Do any of you want to share first or have you already gone?

Has everyone finished sharing? Wow, I'm later than I thought. I guess I should share then? . . . Sorry I'm a bit nervous.

He shuffles onto the stage.

I have been to a few of these meetings, but this is my first time actually getting up here. I just got myself a sponsor—Sunny Drake. Oh, sorry, my name's Jimmy and I'm a—well at least I think I'm probably a romance-aholic? I am constantly doing romantic things for people. I create elaborate multi-stage dates each with their own soundtrack. I keep a spreadsheet with every detail about what my dates do and don't like. Well I am practically a nun next to my ultra-slutty ex, Brian. The problem is—well I always thought I'd be able to stop if I wanted to, but I can't seem to stop! I'm serious this time: I'm quitting, cold turkey. That's why I've come to this group. Well I may technically have heard about the group on the Transgender Seeking section of Craigslist—but I was on there looking for help, not for dates.

Last weekend, I guess I hit my rock bottom. I had a stupid crush on this guy, so when he asked if I was into *medieval live action role play*, instead of just saying, "what the hell is that," I found myself saying, "I *love it!*" I thought he at least meant something kinky. We went on a two-day trip to Medieval Land. I had to dress up as a gnome because that was the only role for a short trans man. I mean couldn't I have at least gotten to be the water sprite? You'll never believe who randomly happened to be there on a date with *my* housemate? My ex-partner, Brian! If that wasn't bad enough, then some dude dressed as a dragon tamer locked me in the basement where I spent a whole day and night all on my own. Do you know who I found out later was in on it? Mhm, Brian!

I looked after him better than anyone ever had—he said so himself. He was a complete mess when I first met him. I don't get it—I go to these elaborate lengths to find out exactly what my dates need and I give it to them. So why do they leave me? Brian will never cope without me. Selfish asshole. And where does all my awesome caretaking get me? Alone again . . .

JIMMY discards the flowers on the floor and eyes his suitcase. Delighted, he dips into the suitcase and old-fashioned music starts to flow out. He notices the audience and slams the suitcase shut, music halting.

It's just real world romance that I'm supposed to give up—my fantasy world's fine, right?

Panicky, JIMMY reaches into his suitcase, relaxing as the music resumes. He slides a long, lacey tablecloth from its depths up along his body. There is a paint stain on the tablecloth. He drapes it in the shape of a dance partner and swoops into a waltz with his fantasy partner, building into flamboyant twists and decadent turns. He sensually drapes the tablecloth around himself. As he continues talking, a sequence is projected onto the tablecloth, of silent images from a black-and-white romance film, A Farewell to Arms *(1932).*

I love every moment throughout the day when I get to wrap myself in a romantic fantasy about a—

Startles as he notices the audience—projections and music stop.

I was just thinking about a-a radical futuristic sci-fi non-monogamous love story, the visionary politics . . .

Drifts off again, music and projections fade back in.

The dramatic music. The forbidden lusting glances. The comfort of knowing exactly what's gonna happen.

A scene from A Farewell to Arms *is projected onto the tablecloth draped around JIMMY. JIMMY mutters both parts along with the characters—he's done this hundreds of times. He cradles the tablecloth as though holding a lover.*

HENRY: You're all right?

CATH: I'm fine. Poor darling. Let me look at you. Mmm. You're wet and tired. Tell me you haven't stopped loving me.

HENRY: You know I couldn't stop.

CATH: I like to hear you say it though.

HENRY: I'll never stop loving you.

CATH: Never? Not even . . . if I died?

HENRY: Never.

CATH: Oh, darling, I'm going to die. Don't let me die.

HENRY: Cath.

CATH: Take me in your arms. Hold me tight.

HENRY: You can't die; you're too brave to die . . .

CATHERINE dies and HENRY lifts her from the bed, long white dress trailing behind. JIMMY cradles his imaginary lover, tablecloth trailing to the floor in the same pose as HENRY.

JIMMY: Do something! Why can't you save her? Save her! Mom, Mom, *Mom!*

Black-and-white TV static cuts the film out and JIMMY *startles, realizing he's drifted off into his fantasy world. He sheepishly addresses the meeting.*

I know everybody fantasizes . . . Well I see it as a form of harm minimization: surely it's better to just fantasize instead of humiliating myself in real life begging for a new boyfriend. My friends say that I shouldn't beg, that I'm a real catch. I don't know about that, but I certainly wish I could find someone as caring as me. At one point I decided to try online dating. I'd used those online sites for anonymous hookups before, but I mean the type of dating where you like, talk and stuff. It took me forever to get my OK Cupid profile up—talk about complicated tick boxes. Male, female. Straight, gay, bisexual. I just needed a simple box to tick: Effeminate-Queer-Pansy-NonMonogamous-SparklyPrincess-SomewhatSlutty-Kinky-Trans-Man! Is that too much to ask for? I guess it's a good thing I'm quitting romance.

Besides, I'm really enjoying getting to know all of you. And I think I'm doing pretty well considering there're so many good looking people at this meeting and it's not like I'm gonna ask any of you on a date.

JIMMY flirtatiously sizes up an audience member.

Hey, how's it going? . . . Shit, my sponsor Sunny says it's a big no-no to flirt with other meeting members—sorry.

JIMMY startles as he notices a guy in the audience. Is that the guy who he? . . . Crap, yes it's him. Horrified, JIMMY *slips his phone from his pocket. He types a text message—his text conversation with his sponsor* SUNNY *is projected (we don't see the character* SUNNY*—just his text responses):*

JIMMY: omg I propositioned that guy online!

SUNNY: lol which 1?

JIMMY: to yr left

he never responded

SUNNY: awkward

JIMMY: humiliating! :(

what should I do???

SUNNY: just act casual!

lol that's not casual!

nope still not casual

JIMMY: omg don't know what version of my profile he saw!

A projection of JIMMY appears on the wedding dress and wedding cake (which is the central set piece). The live JIMMY snaps selfies with a large tablet and obsesses over each photo. Throughout the following, they flip between recording their own conflicting versions of an online dating profile to the audience, and arguing directly with each other.

PROJECTED JIMMY: Is-is this recording? Oh. Hey! Thanks for checking out my profile. I'm Jimmy. I'm thirty-two and very happily non-monogamous—so I'm into consensually open relationships. I think monogamy works for some people, but personally I love having a whole range of connections with different people. I'm mostly interested in men but not exclusively. I'm looking for something ongoing. Oh, but casual is fine—it's not like I wanna get married or anything. Not that there's anything wrong with marriage.

JIMMY: *(for the dating profile—i.e., to the audience)* Except that marriage gives benefits only to a particular style of monogamous relationship. We shouldn't have to get married to access resources like health care or immigration. And what about people with multiple lovers or partners? Or single parents, non-sexual best friends—there're plenty of different types of valid—

PROJECTED JIMMY: Yes I do know the anti-marriage arguments, but I still support people who get married for religious or economic reasons, or just because they feel like it.

(to audience) There's nothing wrong with a princess wanting a wedding dress.

JIMMY: That's funny, I thought you said you didn't want to get married.

PROJECTED JIMMY: Ah, sometimes you're so impossible.

JIMMY: You're so impossible!

PROJECTED JIMMY: *(to audience)* So I'm an activist and a filmmaker—

JIMMY: Okay okay! *(to audience)* Yes to marriage. But we need more than marriage. The danger is: gay marriage, tick, now we're equal. What about addressing violence against trans women of colour, decriminalization of sex work, ending the incarceration of thousands and thousands of—

PROJECTED JIMMY: Yes, but can we please save the politics for the second date?

JIMMY: I don't want to end up dating someone with terrible politics. Boner killer!

PROJECTED JIMMY: Well there's no point in having the boner in the first place if they flee straight out the door because you've scared them away *again* with your lengthy rants!

JIMMY: Ahh!

PROJECTED JIMMY: So I'm an activist and a filmmaker. I love watching edgy futuristic sci-fi films. I'm transgender. Trans. Transsexual. Whether or not you're trans, I'd love to know what words feel good to you to describe your body. For me, this is my chest. Or sometimes, affectionately, my boy tits.

JIMMY: Here's a tip for free: most trans men probably won't find it all that hot if you start heavy breathing in their ear about boy tits.

PROJECTED JIMMY: (clears throat) Down here is what some people mistakenly call my clitoris, but I experience it as my penis or dick. Beneath that is my boy hole, or inny bit, or front hole, then there's my asshole behind that. But don't stress out if you get any of that wrong.

JIMMY: You'll probably just cause lasting psychological damage.

PROJECTED JIMMY: Shhh! You're making me sound vulnerable!

JIMMY: Sorry.

PROJECTED JIMMY: If I'm your first trans man I'll totally understand if it takes you a while to adjust, particularly the first time you see me naked.

JIMMY: I call it "the Craigslist meltdown." Where we're on a date together and we take my clothes off and you're like, "Wow! This really fascinating! Wait, you're a trans *man*, so does that mean you were born with a penis or a vagina? Which of this is even real? This is so confusing!"

JIMMY imitates the date have a sobbing meltdown.

PROJECTED JIMMY: Get away from me! Sooooo, I get into either old-fashioned vanilla sex or I'm into some kinky stuff, too, so I'm happy—

JIMMY: But if pumping your penis in and out of me for two and a half minutes in the missionary position is the kinkiest thing you've ever done, you need to get out more.

PROJECTED JIMMY: Stop it! Maybe we can negotiate a scene, just let me know what sort of kink you're into and—

JIMMY: It really upsets me when people think it's kinky just that I have a boy hole. There is nothing abnormal about my body.

PROJECTED JIMMY: I'm just looking for a no-strings-attached good time!

JIMMY: And remember, I'm a filmmaker, so if you screw me over, I'll name a horrible character after you in my next film at the Toronto International Film Festival.

PROJECTED JIMMY: Okay seriously, would you stop that?

JIMMY: If you'll stop being such a pushover.

PROJECTED JIMMY: You're scaring them away!

JIMMY: Only the wrong ones.

PROJECTED JIMMY: *(to audience)* I'm actually really—chilled out and lighthearted.

JIMMY: *(to audience)* Don't fuck me over!

Both JIMMY and PROJECTED JIMMY attempt to record over each other's profiles:

PROJECTED JIMMY: I'm also excellent at making you feel uncomfortable— I mean comfortable! Comfortable! And safe. I'm really happy to roll with whatever you want to do—the most important thing to me is that you feel well cared for. Look, let's just get together and have a great time.

PROJECTED JIMMY: So just call me!

JIMMY: I'm serious. I am not going to try and save you anymore. I am sick of dates who take me for granted and only notice when I take my care away. Let's see how you cope without me. In fact, let's just not get started in the first place.

JIMMY: Don't even call me!

JIMMY and PROJECTED JIMMY slowly turn to glare at each other.

PROJECTED JIMMY: Why do you always have to do that? I'm just trying to put the most positive view forward and attract something good in my life.

PROJECTED JIMMY: Look, if I'm just caring and loving enough, eventually I'll find a husband, and then I'll finally be happy.

PROJECTED JIMMY: Ahhh! You're so irritating!

JIMMY: Why do you always have to do that? I'm just trying to put the most *honest* view forward and attract something good in my life.

JIMMY: You're so incredibly needy and then you wonder why your dates push you away.

JIMMY: Ahhh! You're so irritating!

Projection fades out. JIMMY resumes the same awkward pose at the chair as previous, staring at the meeting member he recognized. He starts texting with SUNNY again.

JIMMY: he probs thinks I'm desperate

he's so cute!

should I facebook friend him?

SUNNY: Bad idea!

JIMMY: just 2 see what events he goes 2, then I could run into him . . .

SUNNY: facebook stalking BAD IDEA!

Speaking instead of texting.

JIMMY: Like maybe I could run into him at a party . . .

Old-fashioned music fades in as JIMMY *drifts off into a fantasy. He dances with the chair as though it is a person, while speaking his fantasy aloud. The music becomes a mashup of a more contemporary dance club beat with the old-fashioned music.*

With dancing. And all my friends there. And I see him across the other side of the dance floor: leopard print shorts stretching across his astounding ass. The crowd circles up, and I throw my head back and sultrily strut over to thrap my thighs into his. We unite in hypnotic hips and fancy footwork. Everybody is watching us mould the music, thigh throbbing thigh—

While trying to lap dance the chair, JIMMY *accidentally crashes the chair to the ground and the music cuts out.*

Shit, I'm terrible at dancing with other people. Shut up! This is a fantasy!

Music resumes.

Thigh throbbing thigh, chest chaperoning chest. I ride him across the dance floor and then spin him away until he whirls to a stop, our eyes fixed in fixation. He runs toward me leaving a slow-motion trail of silver glitter then leaps. I catch his hips and thrust him into the air as I silently mouth *nobody puts baby in the corner*!

My friends have all seen it. They've all seen how this babe-ilicous man desires me.

JIMMY *makes out with the chair. The music fades out while he passionately continues until suddenly noticing the meeting members and realizing he has drifted off again.*

I am very political. I'm an activist. I've done a lot of important projects. I was even on TV once . . . Well that wasn't so much for my political activities per se . . . It may have been a gay reality TV show. It wasn't my idea though: Brian insisted we go on it together after we first broke up.

JIMMY's character morphs into the GAMESHOW HOST. The actor flips between playing the HOST and JIMMY. The transitions are very rapid, mirroring the pace of a gameshow quiz.

HOST: Welcome to another episode of *The Games We Play*! Where we pit recent ex's in a battle against each other, to see who's gotten over the break up faster and who's really "Great! Fine! Never-been-better!" You, our seasoned and triumphant game players, are tonight's expert judges. We have a fabulous pool of prizes including the new Queer-Web app that utilizes quantum mechanics technology to keep track of who's dated who—who's-dated-who—who's-dated-who—who's-dated-who. The dude-buster-genital-implant, which delivers a little zap to the private parts of your dates for sexist, ableist, racist, or classist behaviour. Ouch! And our grand prize, our special hetero-normative package! Complete with 2.2 bratty kids, a seventy-three-year mortgage, and a lifelong stifling gay marriage with someone you never particularly liked anyway. Yes that's right—give up that bathhouse membership, put away the leather chaps, sanitize those golden showers, we're showing the straight people we can be as every bit as soul crushingly repressed and boring as them. Not to mention, petty, manipulative, and vengeful. And that's what it's all about on *The Games We Play*, so let's get started. Tonight's recent ex's are Jimmy and Brian. Experts, let's give a warm welcome to the first half: Jimmy!

HOST whips the audience up into louder applause if necessary.

Jimmy, it's great to have you on the show. First up, it's time for our thirty-second rapid-fire he-says-you-say quiz! Jimmy, your time starts . . . Now! He says, "How are you feeling about us breaking up?" You say?

JIMMY: Great, fine, never been better.

HOST: Correct! He says, "Can I have my toothbrush back?" You say?

JIMMY: But that's the last thing I have of yours.

HOST: Incorrect.

JIMMY: Ah, I probably already threw it out?

HOST: Correct. He says, "I need some space." You say?

JIMMY: For how long?

HOST: Absolutely not!

JIMMY: I-I'll just hang out in the tree house in case you need me.

HOST: The correct answer is, "Whatever! I'm really busy anyway!" He says, "Do you mind if I bring my new boyfriend to your party?" You say?

JIMMY: Wait, this is hypothetical right? Brian hasn't actually got a new boyfriend has he?

Beat.

HOST: And that's all we have time for! . . . Or is it? Let's go directly to the source of all knowledge—Facebook—to answer that question. Ah, judging from Brian's new profile pic it looks like he's having an awfully good time backstage with the makeup artist. And he gets a bonus ten points for wearing Jimmy's favourite hat, which he never returned. Jimmy, how does this photo make you feel?

JIMMY: I-I feel—great. I feel fine. I've never been better.

A helicopter and a siren are heard as the ANTI-MONOGAMY POLICE *appear—a grid of large eyes and mouths projected onto the wedding dress and long satin wedding trains. A flashlight sweeps the space searching for* JIMMY, *who tries to escape. A twin set of giant mouths projected onto the wedding dress begin talking.*

ANTI-MONOGAMY POLICE: This is the Anti-Monogamy Police. Put your hands in the air. If you cooperate we will be lenient.

JIMMY: What's the charge?

ANTI-MONOGAMY POLICE: Do you admit to experiencing jealousy?

JIMMY: No! . . . Well, I guess so.

ANTI-MONOGAMY POLICE: Under what circumstances?

JIMMY: Just like every now and then really occasionally like it's not that big a deal I'm not actually—

ANTI-MONOGAMY POLICE: More specific information is required.

JIMMY: Okay . . . I can get jealous when an ex gets a new significant partner before I do. I get this horrible feeling in my guts, like I've been replaced. Not to mention, what if they're better than me in bed? I can just imagine them lying around post-fuck talking about how it was the best sex ever! How humiliating.

ANTI-MONOGAMY POLICE: Hands in the air!

JIMMY: One of the final straws with me and Brian was when he started dating this new guy, Joel. But he already had two other boyfriends! He reckons instead of admitting I was jealous, I may have passive aggressively punished him by pushing him away, which at least made for a nice change from his usual complaint that I was too needy. It worked great when it was just me and Brian and his other two boyfriends. But Joel was such an asshole, and then Brian went completely AWOL and well . . .

Looking at a photo on his phone.

I missed him.

ANTI-MONOGAMY POLICE: Cease Facebook stalking immediately or I will handcuff you!

JIMMY: All right. It's just that I thought, well, if Brian has three other dates I should find three other dates, but of course Brian's a total weirdo who rarely got jealous about anything, which sometimes made me wonder if he even cared about me at all, and then the more *insecure* I got the more *secure* he got because if I'm worried about him leaving me then that shows him that I really wanna be with him I mean how was I supposed to know that he wanted to be with me?

ANTI-MONOGAMY POLICE: This is not a counselling session. According to section 432 of the Queer Radical Relationships Act, radical people do not experience jealousy.

JIMMY: That's not what it says in *The Ethical Slut*—I read that book cover to cover.

As the ANTI-MONOGAMY POLICE quote the following, JIMMY begins to pray—he's done this before. He recites along with them, tentatively at first, and then builds into a fervent oration, a giant mouth taking him over.

ANTI-MONOGAMY POLICE: I will quote from the New Questament, chapter 17 verse 44: "Then the great Many said, when you feel jealous, look to where it arises from. Do not be tempted by the eternal fire of capitalism. The Capitil would tell you that love and sex are scarce commodities that can be owned. He will tell you that to love someone you must possess them. That your lover loving somebody else means they love you less. My children, beware the nuclear family unit! For it forms one of the axes of evil, forged by the hands of the Capitil himself to encourage individualistic preoccupation thereby eroding the development of genuine extended community, *which may result in collective liberation*!

An exuberant JIMMY thrusts his arms toward the Radical Heavens. He searches the Radical Heavens and finds . . . wait, it's slipping out of his grasp. He comes crashing back to Earth.

JIMMY: But I still get jealous. I can't help it.

ANTI-MONOGAMY POLICE: I am issuing you an on-the-spot fine involving a public shaming. / You will be monitored in all future situations for further breaches.

JIMMY: A shaming? No no no no.

Pleading directly with audience members.

I'm not really that jealous! I'm good at open relationships. Sometimes I help my dates compose text messages to their other dates. I'm not that jealous! Look, as long as everybody likes me the best, I'm fine!

ANTI-MONOGAMY POLICE: Calling for reinforcement, the offender is getting agitated. Repeat, calling for reinforcement.

JIMMY: I was just joking! It was a joke! Joking! I'm great! Fine! I've never been better!

JIMMY's face freezes into a fake smile. Most of the ANTI-MONOGAMY POLICE fade, leaving one creepy eye following JIMMY's movement across the stage as he forces laughter. Sobs threaten to overtake his laughter.

JIMMY's character morphs back into the GAMESHOW HOST.

HOST: And that's how we roll on *The Games We Play*, great, fine, never-been-better! Next up, it's time to get one of you, our expert judges, up on stage to try out your best game-playing strategy with contestant Jimmy. In a moment I'm going to call for a volunteer, and if that lucky person is you, your job will be to read out your highlighted section of this script. There will be absolutely no physical contact, unless you want to consensually take it backstage later of course. Who wants this once-in-a-lifetime opportunity to be our Expert Guest, put your hand up!

If needed, the HOST coaxes the audience for a volunteer. The volunteer comes on stage and the HOST introduces them to the audience. The HOST asks them to put on a hat and gives them a written script from which to read.

(to audience) Now let's welcome back to the stage, Jimmy!

The actor transitions from the HOST to playing JIMMY. JIMMY picks up the suitcase and flowers, and excitedly skips over to the volunteer.

JIMMY: Hey, nice to meet you!

EXPERT GUEST: You too!

JIMMY: You've got the exact same hat as my ex. Shit, sorry, you probably don't want to hear about my ex . . . Can I take your baggage for you?

EXPERT GUEST: That's not mine, it's yours.

JIMMY: Oh. Right. Sorry, of course it is . . . I can't quite believe I just said that.

EXPERT GUEST: How am I supposed to push you away if you're all the way over there?

JIMMY: I can come back over there if you need me?

EXPERT GUEST: No, my dear, it's you who needs to be needed. What I need is some space.

JIMMY: For how long? Wait, I'm confused. Do you want me to come back over there or not? I could tell you how much I love you.

EXPERT GUEST: Um, if you need to.

JIMMY: I know you like to hear me say it.

EXPERT GUEST: I guess so.

JIMMY: I'll never stop loving you.

EXPERT GUEST: That's ridiculous. What if I died?

JIMMY: Never.

EXPERT GUEST: Cool . . . I guess.

JIMMY: Ah, would it trouble you too much to put away your newspaper while we're trying to have this tender moment?

EXPERT GUEST: But if I look away from the script, how will I know what to say?

JIMMY: What script? Why are you reading a script?

EXPERT GUEST: Well it's your script about how you try to save people and instead get pushed away over and over. At least you get to be right and control everything.

JIMMY: I don't try to control stuff. Why do you always have to think there's something wrong with me?

EXPERT GUEST: Here we go. Now all you can hear is that there's something wrong with you.

JIMMY: Wow, it's almost like I don't even know who you are anymore.

EXPERT GUEST: Um, we just met a few minutes ago.

JIMMY: Right. Yes, right.

EXPERT GUEST: There's something wrong with you.

JIMMY: Ha! See? You do think there's something wrong with me!

EXPERT GUEST: There is definitely something wrong with you.

JIMMY: Wow.

EXPERT GUEST: Something *wrong* with you. Something wrong with *you.*

JIMMY: I knew it.

EXPERT GUEST: Hello? Can you hear me?

JIMMY: I hear you loud and clear.

EXPERT GUEST: Well what are we going to do about the mess on the tablecloth?

JIMMY: The tablecloth?

EXPERT GUEST: I just spent five minutes telling you . . . Never mind.

JIMMY: Look, maybe this isn't going to work out.

EXPERT GUEST: Are you about to change scripts?

JIMMY: Huh? Give me that.

JIMMY grabs the script and reads from it.

Jimmy grabs the script and reads from it. Expert Guest contestant takes the hat off, drops it on the stage, and goes back to their seat. No matter what Jimmy says, Expert Guest leaves the stage?

What is this?

JIMMY follows the volunteer back to their seat in the audience.

Why are you leaving me? If this is about me, I can change. Just tell me what it is and I'll change. Wait, don't say a word—this is about space, isn't it? I can give you space! I'm actually really busy anyway. I'll just hang out in the tree house in case you need me.

JIMMY hurries back on stage and stares at the audience volunteer. His suitcase lurches away from his hand. What the? . . . JIMMY examines the suitcase and it lurches again. The suitcase leaps away a third time, dragging JIMMY across the stage.

He opens the suitcase a crack: playground sounds and children's laughter spill out. A child's voice echoes: "Even your own mother left you." JIMMY slams the suitcase shut. Was that really? . . . No, his mind must be playing tricks on him. He opens the suitcase again: more laughter and another child repeating, "Even your own mother left you." He slams the suitcase. This is horrible.

He makes a decision to face whatever is inside the suitcase and opens it all the way. Inside the suitcase, an old fashioned video plays on a lacey tablecloth with a paint stain and a bundle of lace. The video footage is from a 1960s documentary on homosexuality.

PSYCHIATRIST: Homosexuality is in fact a mental illness, which has reached epidemic proportions.

STUDENT: I was wondering if you think there are any, quote, happy homosexuals?

PSYCHIATRIST: The fact that someone is a homosexual, a true obligatory homosexual, automatically rules out the possibility that he will remain happy for long.

CLERGYMAN: I have this problem in my own emotions, whenever a homosexual comes to me. I have the reaction of tending to pull away and to not wanting to come into physical contact. There's something that is just wrong and perhaps even a little dirty.

PSYCHIATRIST: Bitterly aware of his rejection, the homosexual responds by going underground.

JIMMY slams the suitcase shut.

He proudly holds up a sobriety chip as he skips back to the chair.

JIMMY: I'm Jimmy! Romance-aholic. I just got my five-month sobriety chip today! I didn't think I'd need to come to meetings for more than a few months, but it's taken me this long to realize that me and my ex were never actually that compatible. I think I got carried away with how totally comfortable he was with himself, and being with other dudes. Even dudes like me . . . He was the first date I ever had who saw my body in this way that just felt—right. Like, he actually believed that I'm a man. I don't mean close your eyes and imagine my body is different, but that *this* body *is* a man's body, my boy tits, my junk and everything. It was really jarring to go from that sort of validation back to dating people who see me as a woman. Don't get me wrong: women are totally awesome, it's just that—well I'm not a woman. The first date I went on after me and Brian broke up was with this non-trans guy who I met online.

JIMMY throws the sobriety chip across the stage and leaps to catch it, transforming into the DATE character. The actor flips between playing the role of the DATE and JIMMY.

DATE unbuttoning his shirt.

DATE: I meant it as a compliment. I think you're really hot!

JIMMY: Thanks . . .

Also unbuttoning his shirt, halts.

You mean I'm a hot *man*, right?

DATE: Oh I'm not gay: I date women. Although I've had this fantasy about doing a trans man.

JIMMY: I'm trans, yes and I'm proud of that. But I'm also just a man. Are you saying—

DATE: What I'm saying is that I just can't get into cock, okay?

JIMMY: Ah, did you actually read my online post?

DATE: Of course I did . . . Oh, sorry—you call your clitoris a cock. But you know what I mean. To be totally honest, when you first knocked on my door, I was a little bit confused. I know you described your—*anatomy* in the email, but to look at you, I just can't believe you actually grew up a girl.

He has unbuttoned his shirt all the way and pulls it off his shoulders.

JIMMY pulls his shirt back over his shoulders.

JIMMY: I wasn't exactly—never mind.

DATE: But wait, this is really interesting.

JIMMY: Um, I—

DATE: Are you saying you insisted that you were a boy when you were a kid?

JIMMY: Look, I don't really—

DATE: Did everyone treat you like a boy?

JIMMY: Could we just—

DATE: Like let you use the boy's toilets and stuff?

JIMMY: *(laughing)* Could you please stop talking! Seriously, could we just? . . .

JIMMY starts cuddling his DATE. DATE returns the stroking.

DATE: *(sexy voice)* Mmmm . . . You're soft and hard. So sexy . . .

(normal voice) But wait, I just still don't get it. If other people didn't treat you like a boy, doesn't that mean you were socialized female?

JIMMY: Fine: I socialized myself male. I watched how the boys were supposed to behave, and even if I wasn't always allowed to act it out, those are the messages I internalized.

DATE: Calm down! I think considering you're so—*unusual*, I am entitled to ask a few questions.

JIMMY: You're entitled to . . . ? Look if we're going to talk rather than fuck, let's talk about how as white dudes we seem to feel entitled to everything.

DATE: Ah! All I want to know is are we going to get it on?

JIMMY: But you're the one who . . . I think I'm just gonna go home.

DATE: What the hell is wrong with you? Your loss.

JIMMY slumps back in the chair, and addresses the meeting again.

JIMMY: And if the date itself wasn't crappy enough, it was a shock to arrive back to an empty home. No Brian. We always used to gossip about our other dates—like debrief about the shitty stuff. Although my favourite was when we'd share the sexy details. Um hello: my boyfriend getting it on with other men, big time boner! Getting to enjoy each other's other relationships was really cool—I'd never had a partner before who could just be happy for me to connect with others. We always used to say to each other "happy wife, happy life!" We tried "happy husband, happy life" for a while, but it just didn't have the same ring to it . . . Brian had this sweet side that not a lot of people got to see because he can be a little blunt. I loved that combination: sweet and blunt.

The actor flips backwards and forwards between playing the roles of BRIAN and JIMMY. BRIAN is very masculine.

BRIAN: Aw, Jimmy, it's really really hard being a white guy, isn't it?

JIMMY: Shut up, Brian!

BRIAN: It's so exhausting being so popular and having people throw themselves at you.

JIMMY: Insert Brian rant number 642.

BRIAN: Come on, Jimmy, so what if people don't see your gender and your body exactly how you want them to? At least you could go on a date and get laid every other day if you wanted.

JIMMY: Not with gay men.

BRIAN: Um excuse me? I seem to recall getting you off pretty regularly, bubs.

JIMMY: I'm talking about non-trans gay men.

BRIAN: Ouch.

JIMMY: You know that's not what I meant.

BRIAN: Whatever, Jimmy. You spend so much time feeling sorry for yourself—yes you do have to deal with transphobia but it also doesn't help your dude score list that you're a such a flaming pansy.

JIMMY: I'll show you a pansy.

Prances around and sings.

I'm a pansy! I'm a pansy!

BRIAN: Don't get started—

JIMMY: Oh I am started and I am not going to stop until you say you love it. C'mon say it, say it!

JIMMY chases and tickles BRIAN.

BRIAN: Okay—okay—you're beautiful! Stop tickling! I love that you're a pansy! I love it! . . . Seriously though, Jimmy, you said yourself that the stereotype about gay men being effeminate doesn't change the reality that there's a hierarchy in the gay world too, and masculinity is definitely at the top. You'd know way better than me, babe—straight people, gay people, queers—this world shits all over femininity. So do you wanna be your fabulous effeminate self or do you wanna get laid?

JIMMY: I shouldn't have to choose.

BRIAN: No, babe, you shouldn't, but at least you can choose: Mr. able-bodied white dude. Not everyone can just chuck on some masculine clothes and suddenly be considered hot. Or at least how this world has trained us to define hotness.

JIMMY: Brian, is there nothing beyond fucking politics?

BRIAN: Well fucking is certainly not beyond politics. Come here, my little pansy.

BRIAN and JIMMY dance until JIMMY whirls back in the chair. He plays "he-loves-me, he-loves-me-not" with the flowers, plucking them off one petal at a time.

JIMMY: Me and Brian have started hanging out a bit again. Oh just as friends— it's not like I want to get back together or anything. Although after months of hating everything about him, I'm finally remembering some of the stuff I liked about him. Like I just kind of miss . . . well it's silly really. I mean you'd think I'd miss the sex or conversation or something. But mostly I just miss holding him . . . Like really holding him.

Music starts as JIMMY melts down into the chair, sensually stroking and holding it. He cradles the chair in his arms and begins to dance with it until he notices Brian's hat on the stage, where the audience volunteer left it. Ah, Brian! He retrieves the hat and begins to dance with his imaginary Brian. The movement is cinematic, moving in and out of slow motion. He spins behind the wedding dress and his imagination conjures a couple dancing from a 1950s film. We see JIMMY appear high up behind a transparent section of the set, spinning with the hat. He re-emerges and flings the hat on the wedding cake. Music fades out.

The wedding dress and cake become BRIAN. Throughout the following, JIMMY tucks BRIAN in to one end of a lacey tablecloth/sheet and himself into the other, creating a vertical bed scene.

Brian, are you propositioning me? Nah, I'm just kidding, I know this is a friend sleepover. I mean it makes sense: it's way too late for me to go home. Besides, we've slept in the same bed literally hundreds of times. It'd only be weird if we went back to our old sides of the bed: you sleep on that side . . . I have missed you. Although I'm totally fine. Great in fact. I've actually never been better. It's just that I've been thinking—well, maybe we could be sort of more like friends with—you know friends who-who—well now that we're in the same bed together, would you want to . . . are you awake, Brian?

> *Seeing that* BRIAN *is asleep,* JIMMY *sighs. He indulges himself for a moment, playing both roles in his fantasy.*

Tell me you haven't stopped loving me.
(whispers) You know I couldn't stop.
I like to hear you say it though.
(whispers) I'll never stop loving you.
Never? Not even . . . if I died?
(whispers) Never.

> *He tucks the sheet up around* BRIAN.

Goodnight, my love.

> *He drifts into sleep and is overcome by a strange dream. Old black-and-white footage is projected onto the bedsheet/tablecloth: a long line of newly married couples march in a zombie-like procession. Asleep,* JIMMY *slowly rolls toward* BRIAN *until he is snuggled into his side. He wakes.*

Oh hey . . .

> *Looks toward clock.*

Three a.m. We're cuddling. That's cute . . . Well that's because you're on my side of the bed! This is nice. Remind me why we broke up? . . . No, I loved it when it was just you and me and Amir. He may have *technically* been your boyfriend, but he felt like family. When you added Brad into the picture it was a bit of a stretch time-wise at first, but I loved seeing you so happy. Happy wife, happy life! It ended up surprisingly liberating when it freed me up a bunch of time to focus on my work: you finally stopped complaining about me being a workaholic. Then came boyfriend number four: I hated Joel, he was such an . . . Don't tell me to calm down! You never hear my side of the story . . . Bullshit, your side is on loudspeaker blasting the bedroom door open! . . . Nobody's gonna make a show out of my side of the story and perform it at Buddies in Bad Times Theatre . . . Yes, I may be the one who expresses actual human emotion, but in reality it's all about you because you just go out and do whatever you want without even considering me, and then I'm the one who ends up doing all the emotional work. You know what, this was a massive mistake. I'll be gone before you wake up.

> JIMMY *momentarily tucks himself back in, then wakes and flings away the bedsheet/tablecloth. Throughout the following, he pulls scissors from his suitcase and deadheads about half of the flowers.*

Jimmy, romance-aholic, but who should really be coming to these meetings is my ex. He was constantly chasing a million people, including my housemate who he reckons he only hit on *after* we broke up, but frankly he is full of shit. And now he's got the nerve to ask *me* for space! Whatever. I'm really busy anyway. I bet he only wants space because I called *him* out for the ways *he* hurt *me*. I wasn't even asking for much. It's not like I want him to suffer like I did. No, I wasn't trying to punish him. Punishment doesn't fit with my politics—I'm a prison abolitionist. Prisons and police are a tool by people in power to keep anyone who might threaten that power out of the way—aka people of colour, Indigenous people, trans women, sex workers. Prisons are a business: it's in their interests to keep people locked up and isolated . . .

> *Notices he has been deadheading the flowers.*

Well it's not like I want Brian to go to solitary confinement. Just for everyone to stop talking with him. Stop inviting him to things. At least until he apologizes. I don't know what his problem is—it's not like there's some sort of permanent queer bad person list. That would be counter-radical because then everyone would probably just deny the shit they do, so they don't get on the list, and what good would that be?

When I see people genuinely own up to it when they've hurt someone, it can create this powerful opening to transform themselves and their relationships. It's actually really amazing! . . .

Look, even though Brian was a complete asshole, I guess I did have a role in stuff that went down, too. Like how I . . .

> JIMMY *looks down, surprised that he's been pulling a line of lace out of the suitcase. He tries to hide the lace. He slips his phone out and starts typing a text. The text conversation is projected:*

is this a bad idea?

the bad person list . . .

Audio of applause as the actor spins into the role of GAMESHOW HOST. The HOST steps down into the audience and saunters around talking directly to individual audience members.

HOST: Let the games continue! It's time to play Dodge the Bullet. Jimmy, you may have noticed we've brought into the studio every single person you've ever dated. Now our studio of ex's, you're going to fire off your endless complaints about the crappy things Jimmy did while you were dating, and Jimmy's job is to come out unscathed and unphased. Some time-tested strategies for Jimmy include denial, blaming the other person before they can blame you, faking serious injury or possibly even death, or my personal favourite: faux-responsibility. When someone complains about you, you simply nod politely, deliver the carefully rehearsed speech you plagiarized from *The Revolution Starts at Home*, and then continue with the exact same shitty behaviour. Genius! Jimmy, your time starts now!

The actor spins back onto the chair and becomes JIMMY again. JIMMY struggles with what to confess. He glances at the lace busting out of the suitcase, then hides the lace under his shirt.

JIMMY: Like this one time with Brian I pretended I was listening when I really wasn't listening at all?

Children's laughter creeps in as JIMMY's gaze is drawn to the bundle of lace under his shirt. His shaky hands pull on the lace—a long lacey stream sliding out from his bellybutton, attached also to the suitcase. White lace gives way to paint-stained lumps of lace ending in a tangled paint-soaked clump.

Sobs rack JIMMY's body and he becomes a man-baby version of himself. Tangled in the lace and clutching the suitcase, he rocks himself over to the wedding dress. He clings to it. A dishevelled PROJECTED JIMMY tries to shoo JIMMY away.

(baby-whining voice) It's not fair! I'm the only one who got made to say anything and now I look really bad, but I bet they did way worse things. And now nobody's gonna invite me to their parties and I'll probably die all alone and I'll never have another—

PROJECTED JIMMY: Okay, stay, just be quiet though.

Recording another online dating post, PROJECTED JIMMY tries to ignore JIMMY as best he can.

Hey! Some of you may have noticed I took my profile down for a while—I'm back. I'm Jimmy. Thirty-two years old. I'm very politically onto it and / emotionally mature.

JIMMY: Emotionally mature.

PROJECTED JIMMY: I'm committed to doing emotional labour in relationships, like checking in about how things are going, being responsible for my own emotions. Although sometimes / it's not—

JIMMY: It's not my fault! Why should I have to be responsible if it's not even my fault!

PROJECTED JIMMY: *(drowns out JIMMY)* I also give a lot of support in relationships and consider how my actions impact my dates. Look, as long we live in this messed-up world, I don't believe that it's possible to *arrive* at being a feminist, anti-racist man. I know it's gonna be a lifelong process and I'm totally committed to that. / Well and the thing is—

JIMMY: Well and the thing is I just put feminist and anti-racist all in the one sentence, so where's my gold medal?

PROJECTED JIMMY: But being careful to not hijack the attention vying for praise or obsessing about myself.

JIMMY: But it's really hard!

PROJECTED JIMMY: It's not even that hard.

JIMMY: Why can't I have some attention?

PROJECTED JIMMY: *(whispers)* Look, it can't be all about you, all the time.

JIMMY: I never said it was all about me!

PROJECTED JIMMY: *(to audience)* Yep, no man-babies around here.

(to JIMMY who is sobbing again) What is it?

JIMMY: You called me a man-baby. That hurt my feelings!

PROJECTED JIMMY: Would you stop that? It's making me look really bad.

JIMMY: But couldn't you just—

PROJECTED JIMMY: Shh!

JIMMY: Couldn't I just have some—

PROJECTED JIMMY: No!

JIMMY: Ah! Next time you're going to say something hard, you could at least give me some chocolate first.

PROJECTED JIMMY: You're not my responsibility.

JIMMY: But I am you! We're the same person!

Beat.

PROJECTED JIMMY: Oh yeah.

JIMMY: I'm sick of you pretending I don't exist, just so you can look good.

PROJECTED JIMMY: You're right. I was just . . . I'm sorry.

JIMMY: Well, it hurt because—

PROJECTED JIMMY: I can't believe I did that. I feel so terrible.

JIMMY: I just felt like—

PROJECTED JIMMY: Not only was I irresponsible, but then I completely denied being irresponsible so I further hurt you. I'm so sorry.

JIMMY: Well I just wanted to say that—

PROJECTED JIMMY: Wow, I totally suck.

JIMMY: Hello! Do you wanna know how I feel?

PROJECTED JIMMY: Ahhhhh crap! Now I did that thing where I made the apology all about me! Okay, I'm really listening this time.

JIMMY: I was just going to say that when you said that thing about me being a man-baby—

PROJECTED JIMMY: *(mutters to self)* Man, I'm really gonna have to work on that. I'm usually so much better at giving support. Okay, I'll do a bunch more reading, I'll make a checklist . . .

JIMMY: You're not listening! I want some attention attention attention!

PROJECTED JIMMY fades out.

JIMMY collapses on the Romance-aholics Anonymous chair. Soaked in shame, he is barely able to look audience members in the eye.

Jimmy. Romance-aholic . . . It's been a few weeks since my last meeting, so some of you probably guessed: I relapsed. My sponsor Sunny says that the program will never work unless I share *everything* at meetings. There was this time. I was a kid. Seven. I was at my dad's house painting a birthday card for my mom. I didn't know the lacey tablecloth I was painting on top of had been a wedding present for my parents. I didn't even know they'd been married. All I remember my mom saying about my dad is there's no such thing as forever—you're with someone for as long as you're meant to be and then you move on. Anyway, the birthday card. I guess I must have got paint all over the tablecloth, because when I turned around, my dad said:

The actor flips between playing DAD *and a seven-year-old* JIMMY. *The* DAD's *presence is larger than life. The characters are connected to the suitcase by the line of lace, which stretches out as they move across the stage. The clump of paint stained lace hovers in the line of lace.*

DAD: Ah, I can't believe it.

JIMMY: What?

DAD: That was the last thing I have of your mother's.

JIMMY: I'll fix it.

DAD: Look, I need some space. I'm taking you back to your mother's.

JIMMY: For how long? Wait, can't I just stay in the tree house? I'll be really quiet.

DAD: Sweetie, it can't be all about you, all the time. Just pack your bags please.

JIMMY: But Mom said I had to stay here.

DAD: *That's because she's sick of you too!*

Beat.

JIMMY: Mom's not sick? . . . Is she?

DAD: There is something very wrong with you. Your mother's depressed and she nearly killed herself, and you're so bloody selfish you didn't even notice, did you?

Drags suitcase in by the lace.

JIMMY: But it's not my fault! . . . I never painted on her tablecloth.

Beat.

DAD: Look, I'll buy you some chocolate. Just . . . get in the car.

JIMMY *slumps back on the chair.*

JIMMY: I never saw my mom again. If only I could have just been . . . Wait, I was a kid. There's *nothing* I could have done to save her . . . I've spent my entire life obsessively caretaking other people to try and prove that I'm not selfish, when I actually wasn't even selfish. Even my mom used to say: I was a really sweet kid. That-that last birthday card I made for her, I found it the other day, it's really cute: there's these two little stick figures of me and my mom and then a yellow full moon. There was this time—well my mom used to work the day shift then she'd come home to sleep then go back for the night shift—it was actually poverty that killed my mom. But there was this one time she called in sick and she let me stay up really late and we climbed up onto the roof, and there was this huge full moon and my mom said, "Make a wish. Anything you want. Anything in the whole world . . . "

JIMMY presses his eyes closed, full of hope, and thinks of a wish. He leaps into his wish. He lands with a thud.

I wished for a bike. A stupid fucking bike. Was I? . . . No, kids want bikes. But as an adult, denying that all this shit has been going on in the background has probably meant that I *have* done some selfish stuff. Brian said this thing when we were breaking up about the way I care for people being secretly controlling. He said I give care and attention so that people are in debt to me and then they won't leave me. I've always thought that was just Brian being an asshole, but . . . I hate him . . . and I love him. I don't know if I love him: maybe I'm just lonely. I guess I've been trying to shove intimacy and relationships into the void that Brian left, that my mom left, rather than spending time creating my own amazing life with my friends and family, and waiting for the right man to . . . I know I'm supposed to be quitting romance, but maybe one day in the distant future when I'm fully recovered: I might like a partner again. Or a husband. Or even more than one husband. I don't think it'd look like forever though.

A knock at the door.

That's my date! Oh, I mean, my friend date, like a-a datish-sort of friend. Friend-friendish date? I am quitting romance. Quit! I've quit! I'll see you at the next meeting.

(to door) Hang on, I'll be there in two ticks!

JIMMY gets dressed with nervous anticipation—he flings on a vest and a pink cravat with white lace, brushes his eyebrows, checks his breath, etc. He grabs his suitcase and the half-butchered flowers and bounds over to an imaginary door. He takes a moment to snap out of his puppy dog excitement, manufacturing cool, casual body language, then opens the door.

It's so good to see y— Hello? . . . Hello?

JIMMY searches the front stoop—nobody is there. His face crumbles. Stood up, again. In his devastation, he absentmindedly stuffs flowers into his mouth, binge eating them until he is numb.

A rustling comes from the suitcase. JIMMY is drawn to his knees, his mouth still jammed with flowers. Uncertain, he hovers with hands outstretched toward the suitcase. With a deep breath, he pries the suitcase open. Light streams out—the sight inside washes him in awe. He cinematically spins the suitcase in a few sweeping spirals, revealing glimpses of the lace and light installation inside.

A miniature version of JIMMY *emerges from the suitcase: a man-baby puppet dressed in the same outfit as* JIMMY. *The puppet cinematically spirals around to confront* JIMMY. *Surprised to see flowers spilling out the sides of* JIMMY's *mouth, the puppet thumps him on the back of the head until* JIMMY *spits out the half-chewed flowers.*

The puppet tries to lead JIMMY *outside, but* JIMMY *wallows back in his hard luck. The puppet dries the tears from* JIMMY's *eyes with a lacey handkerchief then coaxes him outside, whispering in his ear.*

The puppet eyes a full moon rising and turns JIMMY's *head toward it.* JIMMY *takes in a sharp breath. The full moon transforms into a new moon.*

JIMMY *closes his eyes, makes a wish, and, together with the puppet, leaps.*

The end.

At the end of the curtain call, "(I've Had) The Time of My Life" plays (Dirty Dancing *soundtrack) and* JIMMY *and the puppet dance off stage together,* JIMMY *thrusting the puppet into the air in the iconic* Dirty Dancing *pose from his fantasy.*

ANDROGYNE

D'BI.YOUNG ANITAFRIKA

PERFORMING QUEER MARRONAGE: THE WORK OF D'BI.YOUNG ANITAFRIKA

HONOR FORD-SMITH

In d'bi.young anitafrika's *word! sound! power!* a young poet is arrested and tortured by the police on the eve of a Jamaican election. As her interrogators work to extract information from her about a plot to incite revolution, she fights to find the resources to withstand the torture. In her dissociative response to the physical abuse, she makes a journey to the heartland of maroon[1] communities, which symbolize the interior of ancestral Black decolonial struggles from which multiple forms of resistance, including guerrilla wars, were waged against enslavement in the African diaspora.

As in this example, d'bi.young anitafrika's performances and writings remember, celebrate, and interrogate enduring and plural Black and Caribbean radical traditions while also dramatizing a quest for courage and the strength to survive, love, struggle, and hold space in the midst of extraordinary violence. Her work seeks out what is incomplete in past emancipation projects and rehearses ways of extending these—telling stories, amending experiences, and inserting questions into the gaps and fissures of past struggles. She frequently draws on maroon narratives of resistance, underlying ideas of Caribbean decolonization and she reworks these so as to queer insurgent Black identity and women's struggles, and to inspire work for emancipation in the present. The result is

---

1   Maroon communities were and are autonomous communities of free Africans that established themselves throughout the Caribbean and the Americas. They came into being alongside plantations and in many cases were linked to earlier forms of Indigenous resistance in the Americas. During the long period of enslavement, maroons carried out sustained and often armed resistance to slavery and colonial domination. Jamaican maroons won land grants from the British, but like the Garifuna of St. Vincent they too suffered deportation. Such deportation saw them transported to Canada, and from there to Sierra Leone in 1800.

work that contributes to what Ronald Cummings has called "queer marron-age," a term he uses to theorize a layered and often transnational process of resistance and liberation that requires engagement with "multiple flows, infinite crossings, unstable crosscurrents and its transgression and renegotiation of multiple frontiers of belonging."[2] d'bi.young anitafrika combines choreopoem, drumscore, mime, dance, monodrama with trickster tales, ritual, and role shift to extend marronage beyond conventional borders of geography, and to insist on social formations that transcend and subtend the borders between nations and identities. In this way her work begins to enunciate imagined transnational communities of liberation.

Born in Jamaica in 1977, anitafrika moved to Canada when she was fifteen. Her account of her artistic development begins with the influence of beloved Jamaican performance poet and nationalist figure Louise Bennett, whose poem "Pass Fe White" appears as part of the play *androgyne*. Over her long and sin-gular career, Bennett consistently gave voice to the vernacular thought of Black working class women. She combined popular and often satirical performance poetry with a critique of social pretension while advocating for the Jamaican language, social progress, and national unity. "Miss Lou was who I wanted to be!" anitafrika explains. She also traces her formation to the work done at the Jamaica School of Drama,[3] where much cultural exploration took place under the leadership of Jamaican director/writer Dennis Scott, between 1976 and 1982.[4] Her mother, Anita Stewart, who was a student there, was the only woman in Poets in Unity, a group of poets whose work, like that of Mikey Smith and Oku Onuora, evolved out of reggae rhythms and was marked by strong social critique. As a child, anitafrika came along for performances and rehearsals—observing and learning from all that was taking place.

The theatrical style of the school stressed physicality, symbolic minimal-ism, and an aesthetic of scarcity that jettisoned glitz and bling in search of a theatre that would eschew First World excess in a search of a decolonized

---

2   Ronald Cummings, "Queer Marronage and Caribbean Writing" (Ph.D. thesis, University of Leeds, 2012), 6, http://etheses.whiterose.ac.uk/id/eprint/3385.

3   The Jamaica School of Drama is now part of the Edna Manley College of the Visual and Performing Arts located in Kingston.

4   I taught and directed at the Jamaica School of Drama in this period. Anita Stewart performed in a production of *Request Concert*, by Franz Xaver Kroetz, which I directed, and she also performed with Sistren in *Ida Revolt inna Jonkonnu Stylee*, which was part of an exchange of Caribbean popular theatre artists in 1985. See H. Ford-Smith, "An experiment in popular theatre and women's history: *Ida Revolt inna Jonkonnu Stylee*" in S. Wieringa, ed. *Subversive Women: Women's Movements in Africa, Asia, Latin America and the Caribbean* (New Delhi: Kali for Women), 147–64.

mode of address. Here, ring games, riddles, songs, and rhythms from rituals like Nyabinghi, Shango, and Pukkumina frequently became structuring dramatic metaphors in performances of everyday social and political challenges. The Theatre Group for National Liberation creolized versions of Brecht's learning plays while the Jamaican women's theatre collective, Sistren, created autobiographical and documentary scenarios of working class women's lives. Trinidadian director/writer Rawle Gibbons began work on his Orisha plays, and experimented with stickfighting and carnivalesque traditions. The dance and music of sacred traditions like Kumina and Revival, hitherto secret and marginal, found their way into educational settings, improvisational events, and productions of plays by Walcott, Scott, and Soyinka. They even interrupted the flow of Shakespearean iambic pentameter and Greek classics. Poets like Oku Onura, the late Mikey Smith, members of Poets in Unity, and others could often be found rehearsing their performances, chanting to the drum and bass rhythm that was the essence of reggae, adding elements from Burru and Rastafari. Oku Onuora first coined the term "dub tieta" (dub theatre) in his search for a popular performance form that would join the theatrical to the performative sonic reality of reggae. ahdri zhina mandiela, who mentored anitafrika in Toronto, launched dub theatre in Canada with her womanist performance poem *dark diaspora in dub*.[5] mandiela, along with Jean Breeze in Jamaica and Lillian Allen, Afua Cooper, and others, transformed a largely male-dominated poetic form into a womanist performance experience that could move between theatre, dancehall, community, and yard. mandiela's studio b current was the place where anitafrika began to combine performance and poetry.

    androgyne, the play included in this collection, like *dark diaspora,* was originally billed as dub theatre. It is one of anitafrika's earliest pieces and contains the characteristic poetic commentaries of her later work in both *The Sankofa Trilogy* and *The Orisha Trilogy*. But unlike the trilogies, *androgyne* is a play of debate. It stages a dialogue between two women about their relationship, their conflicts around eroticism and friendship, and around reconciling ideas of radical Black identity with queer love. Structured through dialogue, games, and poetry, it tells the story of the evolving and contentious friendship of two young women who come to live in Toronto from Jamaica. The play tackles the topic of internalized homophobia while exploring effects of homophobic community violence. Fear of violence, radical rejection, and isolation structure the possibilities of these two women's lives, but so too do their desires to live joyfully beyond repressive heteronormative confines. *androgyne* is similar to anitafrika's other plays in

---

5   a.z. mandiela, *dark diaspora . . . in dub: a dub theatre piece* (Toronto: Sister Vision Press, 1991).

its use of language, its playfulness, its naming of ancestral forerunners, and its movement between geographic spaces and temporalities. It shifts between Toronto and Kingston; between urban suburb (Scarborough) and inner city yard (Kingston); between remembered childhood past and adult present. These movements call attention to the ways in which the spaces of here and there, region and diaspora, are intertwined in each other's formation. In subtext they also call attention to the ways in which Canada's formation as a nation is always already implicated in the colonial practices that forged what we now call "the global." It challenges mainstream narratives of the whiteness of the Canadian nation by centring the stories of communities of colour.

androgyne's present action takes place in Canada, but it unapologetically privileges Caribbean Canadian and, more broadly, diasporic audiences with its movement between Jamaican and English, and its references to formation at home and in Toronto. It deploys orality, and clearly references the feminist poetry of mandiela, Audre Lorde, and Ntozake Shange. In doing this, the play creates a space of queer marronage from which to assert the existence of alternative ways of being and knowing while asking how it is possible to advance radical justice and radical love. The play answers its own question by portraying struggles taking place in women's movements in the Caribbean and Canada. *androgyne* blurs the boundaries between politics and art as it is about the everyday nature of struggles being waged by activist organizations such as Black Lives Matter in Toronto, the Tambourine Army in Jamaica, and Red Thread in Guyana, who fight gender violence in the Caribbean itself.

While there is a long tradition of scholarship on Black and Caribbean performance traditions in the Americas, it is still far more common in Canada for genealogies of performance and politics to normalize and centre the legacies of the European and North American avant-garde rather than to explore contributions from the context of plantation geographies in the Caribbean, or decolonial cultural struggles across the planet. Forms such as carnival, kaiso (calypso), comic reviews, Jonkonnu, dub, dancehall, or sacred ritual performances of the Black diaspora remain bracketed off as "special topics" within Eurocentric discussions of performance, so that it is still possible for scholars, students, and practitioners to avoid contact with the multiple foundational performance traditions of Black diaspora as a part of their creative and intellectual formation; to see these as "other" rather than intrinsic to geographies of knowledge production through performance.

d'bi.young anitafrika's work challenges all this from outside the academy. She builds on a specific tradition of Caribbean work and on the works of artists like Vera Cudjoe, ahdri zhina mandiela, Sistren, Bennett, Shange, and others to develop a particular theatrical approach. Ric Knowles proposes that mandiela, anitafrika, and Rhoma Spencer of Toronto have created "a heterotopic, transformative space within which they can work at the intersection of nations, sexualities and performance forms."[6] Such a space is enunciated through the resonant presence of anitafrika's embodied performances, and through the sonic space invoked by her use of orality, music, song, percussion, and vocal experimentation.

anitafrika also teaches her approach, most recently through the Watah Theatre school where she mentors young artists and performers, creating and consolidating knowledge made in and through performance. In the midst of joyful and committed resistance to colonial violence of all kinds, students learn to study and perform the raw material of their lives, to place the body at the crossroads of multiple traditions of communities of colour, working class, and Indigenous communities. Her studio is a place in which the presence of decolonization and the transnational becomes an act or practice that transforms space. She draws on Audre Lorde's notion of biomythography, urging students to create "poetic interpretations of their own lived experience drawing on myth and folklore."[7] She also teaches her Anitafrika Method, comprising the principles of self-knowledge, orality, rhythm, political content and context, language, urgency, sacredness, and integrity. Students learn to be accountable and responsible to communities who are in turn formed by the scenarios that are produced and circulated.

anitafrika's acts of queer marronage place political mobilization, sacred ritual music, the comedic, and the carnivalesque in conversation. She joins radical Black and Caribbean performance into the global cultural networks of meaning-making in the urban setting of Toronto. She borrows the orature and performances of older decolonizing struggles and mixes these with the calls of contemporary movements such as Black Lives Matter. In so doing, her work calls attention to the absences in the known archive of performance and the Black radical tradition. Her work performatively creates scenarios for liberation that move beyond nation, enunciating an inclusive decolonial Blackness and a living, breathing, transnational woman-affirming community.

---

6   Ric Knowles, "To Be Dub, Female and Black: Towards a Womban-Centred Afro-Caribbean Diasporic Performance Aesthetic in Toronto." *Theatre Research in Canada/ Recherches théâtrales au Canada* 33.1 (2012): 80.

7   Knowles, 93.

PLAYWRIGHT'S NOTES

androgyne is a love story between two friends.

in 2004, I was asked by an arts program on CBC Radio to write a review of the opera of Margaret Atwood's *The Handmaid's Tale*. I did not write the review; instead I wrote a poem called *organ-eye-zed crime*, parallelling Atwood's novel with the state of womxn in present-day canada. the piece was rejected by the arts program on the grounds that it was not a review (it instead spoke about prostitutes being dismembered, their body parts thrown into dumpsters in our *fair* country). this was the genesis of *androgyne. organ-eye-zed crime* was developed into a half-hour play focused on the discussion of patriarchy and homophobia, and was presented at Hysteria: A Festival of Women, 2004. Buddies in Bad Times Theatre excitedly came on board as producers of the first workshop process, giving me all the resources I needed to continue my creative process: Moynan King as dramaturg, ahdri zhina mandiela as director/dramaturg, Ordena Stephens-Thompson as gyne, Amber Archbell as stage manager, as well as an incredibly committed and driven production team. for the second draft of the script I decided to create another storytelling character because I wanted to focus more intimately on the way Black womxn give and receive love, particularly where sexuality is concerned. I created this play through experiments with my creative praxis now known as the Anitafrika Method.

organ-eye-zed crime (first draft of *androgyne*) was first presented as a staged reading at Hysteria: A Festival of Women at Buddies in Bad Times Theatre on November 10, 2004, with the following company:

playwright, storyteller, androgyne: d'bi.young anitafrika
costume design, makeup: Amina Alfred
set design: Las Krudas—como.where.when painting

androgyne (second draft) was next presented as a workshop reading at Buddies in Bad Times Theatre, June 2006, with the following company:

playwright, storyteller: d'bi.young anitafrika
storyteller: Ordena Stephens-Thompson
director: ahdri zhina mandiela
dramaturg: Moynan King
stage manager: Amber Archbell
set design, costume design: ahdri zhina mandiela
lighting design: Adrien Whan
sound design: Nick Murray
"Pass Fe White" poem: Louise "Miss Lou" Bennett

androgyne (third draft) was next presented as a workshop reading at b current theatre's rock.paper.sistahz festival, April 2007, with the following company:

playwright, storyteller: d'bi.young anitafrika
storyteller: Ordena Stephens-Thompson
director/dramaturg: ahdri zhina mandiela
"Pass Fe White" poem: Louise "Miss Lou" Bennett

CHARACTERS

gyne: a twenty-eight-year-old queer/homophobic womxn
andro: a twenty-nine-year-old homophobic/queer womxn
young gyne: a seven-year-old girl
young andro: an eight-year-old girl
gyne's lover
andro's lover

SETTING

kingston jamaica summer past
scarboro canada winter present
toronto canada spring present

PROPS

a futon bed (also a couch) with ochun-coloured sheet and two pillows
pieces of paper with poetry written on them
a Black female doll
a bottle of red merlot
two wine glasses
a container of weed
a lighter
a pack of rolling papers
a wooden chair

COSTUMES

gyne's costume conveys a womxn who is comfortable in her body. she is sexy and aloof. andro's costume conveys a womxn who is sexually outgoing yet there is an air of conservatism to her.

SCENE OF PLAY

set in a humble malvern scarborough condominium in winter. down centre stage is a futon bed (couch as well). there is a coffee table in front of it with a bottle of merlot, two wine glasses, a container of weed, a lighter, and a pack of rolling papers. there is a wooden chair centre stage left. childhood flashback scenes take place in summer 1995, in whitfield town, maxfield avenue, jamaica. there is also a flashback to spring 2016, in andro's toronto condominium.

androgyne: a person who feels that they do not fit into society's binary gender boxes of masculine and feminine.

PRE-SHOW

DANCEHALL

inside an apartment in canada
two womxn are in bed
the lights are dim
dancehall music plays while the audience enters
a cool romantic vibe is in the air
squeezed up against the forceful dancehall
a half-hour soundtrack of songs that chant intermittent homophobic lyrics plays
atop two female bodies lying on a bed slightly down centre stage
the womxn are asleep wrapped in ochun-coloured sheets
throughout the half-hour they change positions:
spooning, cuddling, separating, hugging, etc.

SCENE 1

INNA DI MIDDLE A DI NIGHT

dancehall fades and a cacophony of city sounds emerge:

streetcars, subways cars, various horns, people yelling profanities

a scratchy-signalled radio station breaks through the confusion

inside the apartment

the womxn in bed are awake

they move about each other, slowly at first

then desperately, in the throws of passionate lovemaking

a news station forces its signal through the scratchy channels

a news report is in progress:

NEWS REPORT: . . . *as the rate of organized crime climbs, police are challenged to invent new ways to combat this growing problem . . .*

. . . reports said she was viciously beaten by her husband . . .

. . . womxn stabbed to death at local td bank . . .

. . . there have been over two thousand reported rapes in the last three years . . .

. . . this just in: man shot dead at train station. moments before, he fired several shots at his wife and then proceeded to beat her in the head with a sawed-off shotgun . . . one college report claims that date rape has quadrupled since the beginning of the year . . . ex-stripper alleges that she was sexually assaulted by law-abiding fifty-two-year-old judge . . . gays now have the right to marry . . .

. . . rape victim will spend two years in jail awaiting trial. it was discovered that she is an illegal immigrant. after the case she will be deported back to where she came from . . .

. . . a new law proclaiming that womxn of the sex trade industry cannot press charges for rape has just been passed . . . five more prostitutes were found dismembered and thrown in a dumpster in the downtown area . . . patrons of local restaurant were disgusted by a breastfeeding mother. both mother and baby were quietly asked to leave the establishment . . . in order to combat welfare fraud the amount of money to single mothers will be cut in half . . .

. . . no means yes in certain countries and in certain situations . . .

. . . when questioned on why he did it, the man said she was asking for it . . .

. . . and in the battle for baby eli, father claims he deserves custody because mother is a lesbian . . .

   the womxn make love to the soundtrack of the newscast

   at the end of the newscast

   the dancehall fades back up

   atop the music a womxn moans from ecstacy

   we see her writhing in bed from orgasm

   as her cum fades so does the dancehall

SCENE 2

THE KISS

   scarboro winter present

   GYNE and ANDRO are long-time jamaican friends

   they were raised in the same neighbourhood of

   whitfield town, maxfield avenue in the '80s

   they moved to canada in the early '90s

   after both their parents immigrated

   GYNE is a poet and ANDRO is a law clerk

   they are best friends

   friday night inside GYNE's humble malvern apartment

   down centre stage is a futon couch with a small coffee table in front of it

   on the table is a bottle of merlot and two glasses

   a container of weed, a lighter, and a pack of rolling papers

   to centre stage left is a wooden chair

   the womxn have a bi-weekly ritual of hanging out

   at each other's apartments

   ANDRO is GYNE's testing ground for new poetry

and is often the first to witness GYNE'*s creative process*

ANDRO *is the memory machine of the relationship*

she often recounts stories of them growing up

GYNE *stands performing her newest poem "the kiss," for* ANDRO

ANDRO *sits on the couch listening*

GYNE: mi cyaan believe weh mi did do
last night without a fright
mi did kiss a Black girl
inna di middle a di light

    ANDRO *is attentive*

now mi know it taboo fi true
mi first kiss wid a girl
mi naw put mout agrung and talk
mi haffi tell di world

    ANDRO *listens*

all mi try, couldn't close mi yeye
lip dem curl toward mi
mout sweet like ripe breadfruit
nevah know wha lick mi

    ANDRO *realizes that* GYNE *is talking about herself and a womxn*

dis was not when yuh kiss a bwoy
lock yuh yeye dem tight tight
play pretend you is a princess
and him is a white knight

    ANDRO'*s gaze is piercing as the story unfolds*

no dis time it was different
from all others before
fi har lip and mine intertwine
a yearn for more and more

    ANDRO *is anxious to cut in*

    she fidgets

a caress di tip of her teeth
den a caress her gum
taste dis womxn sweeta dan man
wid di tip of mi tongue

unable to hold her tongue

ANDRO cuts into GYNE's poem

SCENE 3

MISS LOU

toronto canada. present day

in GYNE's scarboro condo

ANDRO jumps into GYNE's poem

seizing the chance to entertain her as well

ANDRO: *(accusingly at first)* wait wait wait wait wait wait a minute! I recognize that style.

(relaxed and excited) that's like miss lou poetry.

she hops up from the couch and begins

performing miss lou's poem "Pass Fe White"

both GYNE and ANDRO are teary-eyed from laughing

a memory ensues

SCENE 4

RING DING

flashback

summer past whitfield town, kingston jamaica

inside GYNE's house

GYNE and ANDRO are reciting miss lou's poetry

one of their most-favourite pastimes

YOUNG ANDRO: *(pretending to cry)* . . . she hope de gal no gawn an tun

YOUNG GYNE & YOUNG ANDRO: no boogooyagga white

YOUNG GYNE: some people tink she pass B.A.

YOUNG ANDRO: some tink she pass D.R.,

YOUNG GYNE: wait till dem fine out seh she ongle

YOUNG ANDRO: pass de colour bar

   GYNE and ANDRO join hands twirling around in a circle

YOUNG GYNE & YOUNG ANDRO: wait till dem fine out seh she ongle
pass de colour bar
wait till dem fine out seh she ongle
pass . . .

YOUNG GYNE: wait wait wait andro. ring ding wid miss lou starting pon t.v. yuh hear it?

ANDRO: ring ding! ring ding! ring ding!

GYNE: maybe she will call our name today and read our lettah. come mek we go watch.

YOUNG ANDRO: when she call your name and my name we gwine perform fi di whole of jamaica.

YOUNG GYNE: auntie say, if we want to deh pon ring ding, we have to practice di poem ovah and ovah and ovah.

YOUNG ANDRO: mi know gyne. mek we practice again.

YOUNG GYNE: ring ding first. come, andro, it going to start right now.

SCENE 5

WHAT'S FUNNY

GYNE's *apartment*

moments later

ANDRO: *(exasperated)* ring ding with miss lou every saturday morning. oh my god. *wait till dem find out seh she ongle pass de colour bar.*

GYNE: that's a political poem you know. I nevah noticed that growing up. miss lou, revolutionary. we were so young. dem times

ANDRO: I know. we just used to repeat di words, sing dem cuz dem sound nice and catchy. I haven't heard anything like that in donkey years.

GYNE: me neither, since we leave home, basically.

ANDRO: but what ever happened to miss lou?

GYNE: you don't know!

ANDRO: know what?!

GYNE: she died, andro.

ANDRO: she died?
but last I heard she was living here in canada.
eglinton west area. right?

GYNE: yeah. there first, I think. and then she died just di oddah day. she was living here inna scarboro too. one big funeral they had for her. how come you miss dat? it was all ovah everyting. and yuh claim that you are a lawyer. yuh really nevah hear bout it?

ANDRO: nooo. dat mus be the time mi did guh wey pon di long business trip. how come yuh nevah tell mi?

GYNE: mi nevah know seh yuh nuh know. sorry.

ANDRO: miss lou gawn to rahtid.

long pause

(changing the subject) so what it's name?

GYNE: what? mi new poem? . . .

ANDRO nods

. . . "the kiss."

ANDRO: "the kiss" is your latest poetic adventure?

GYNE: I guess you could call it that.

ANDRO: you guess?

GYNE: yuh like it?

ANDRO: eehee.

   she nods her head

but you do realize that your subject matter is, how shall we say . . . different.

GYNE: no shit, sherlock. yeah.

ANDRO: soooooooo poetic license or yuh really give some womxn mout-to-mout resuscitation?

GYNE: mout to mout.

ANDRO: you kissed?

GYNE: that's what I just said.

ANDRO: well well well. story come to town. you're a lesbian now? extra extra read all about it. gyne leave har nice nice jamaica and come turn lesbian inna canada. no, inna foreign. you put a new spin to "rich and switch." "butch and swutch."

GYNE: are you trying to be funny?

ANDRO: no. you my friend, my best friend, are the *funny* one.

   she makes a shaky hand gesture with her right hand

next ting you know, I am guilty by association.

GYNE: well it was just a kiss. don't hold your breath on di wedding.

ANDRO: gay marriage legal now yuh know. so you can go right ahead with your vows at the courthouse and nobody can throw a bottle or a stone. police will come lock them up for homophobic discrimination. well on second thoughts maybe not. the way how tings going in toronto wid the Blacklash after the Pride march they just might let di niggahs kill themselves. then we can see just how much Black Lives Matter.

   she laughs

she Black, right?

   GYNE shoots her a dirty look

GYNE: I am hardly gay for one kiss. And for your information, I was there at the sit-in during Pride.

ANDRO: yes, I went with my new friend. to support the cause you know.

GYNE: your new friend. your new *girl* friend. you are an activist now?

ANDRO: you know when we stopped in the middle of the parade for the moment of silence, then we started to share our perspective on Pride's relationship to Black people and People of Colour and the most marginalized amongst us, people started booing and shouting swear words. it was so scary.

GYNE: you better be careful you know. mind CSIS don't round you up on behalf of nice white people who are not about to relinquish any power they have in this country. And would prefer to see a silent nigger, translation, a dead nigger.

how much time am I going to tell you don't refer to me as *nigger.*

ANDRO begins to sing and dance

ANDRO: all my niggahs in da house say yeah
all my niggahs in da house say hell yeah
all my niggahs . . .

GYNE is not impressed

it's a joke, gyne. bwoy *lesbian* can't tek joke.

she laughs again

but you have to be careful with this Black Lives Matter ting you.
you ever hear about the MOVE 9. the american government bomb them in broad daylight because of their political action, kill children, womxn. it didn't matter. be careful.

they look at each other for a long while

ANDRO switches up the topic to clear the air

did I tell you that I got the promotion?

GYNE: yuh get it?! suh you are HEAD law clerk?

ANDRO brushes her shoulders off

fi real yuh get it? dem know what good fi dem after all.

ANDRO: yeah. after waiting six fucking months for the review. but yeah dem give it to me. all fifteen cents per hour of it.

GYNE: are you for real, they gave you a fifteen-cent raise?

ANDRO: I don't know what they expect me to do with this. I couldn't even buy a lotto ticket at the end of the day to mek mi get rich quick and quit dem stupid no-brainer job.

GYNE: well, weh dem say back home: give tanx fi small mercies?

ANDRO: small indeed.

GYNE: at least yuh have job with benefits. security and teet plan.

ANDRO: *(jokingly)* yuh know they have another name for *teet plan* yuh know.

picking up on her snootiness

GYNE: oh really what?

ANDRO: *dental* plan, dear. it's called a *dental* plan.

they both laugh

which I better make damn good use of now. cuz if it were up to the corporate agenda I wouldn't have anything, not dental, not drug plan, not benefits, and not health care. everyting outta pocket.

GYNE: mi a tell yuh. I feel it for all the single moddahs dem. you know they threatening to cut back on child care benefits and give families some fuckery like twelve-hundred dollars a year for daycare. tings dread.

ANDRO: fuckers. sometimes mi really don't why we pack up and come here enuh. is like yuh jump outta fryin pan and jump inna fyah . . .

GYNE: more like jump outta fryin pan and jump inna . . .

GYNE & ANDRO: freeza

they both laugh

ANDRO: suh gyne, tell mi really and truly, yuh going to do dis womxn pon womxn ting now?

SCENE 6

DICK AND JILL

flashback

whitfield town, kingston jamaica past

evening time inside GYNE's humble wooden house

GYNE and ANDRO are seven and eight years old

they have been best friends for three years

they are playing dick and jill hide and go seek

ANDRO kneels, covering her head

while GYNE looks for her

YOUNG GYNE: dick? dick? dick? mi soon find yuh. dick where are you.

she pounces on ANDRO on the floor

mi find yuh.

YOUNG ANDRO: again again again!

she grabs GYNE's hands and twirls around

they play a slapping-hands game

YOUNG ANDRO & YOUNG GYNE: dick and jill went up the hill to fetch a pail of water
dick fell down and broke his crown
and jill came tumbling after
dick yuh dead?
no no no
mi under di bed wid di chimmey pon mi head

YOUNG ANDRO: sanki, is your turn to hide.

this time it is GYNE who bends over

covering her head while ANDRO pretends not to see her

dick? dick? which part yuh deh? mi soon find yuh. suh you can gwaan hide.

sees GYNE hiding on the floor and pounces on her

ANDRO: dick dick dick dick dick! find yuh! dolly house! dolly house! dolly house!

YOUNG GYNE: remember mi auntie said we musn't play anymore dolly house.

YOUNG ANDRO: wid the boys dem remember. di boys dem not here. suh dat mean seh me and you can play dolly house. yuh waan play?

YOUNG GYNE getting excited at the thought but still cautious

YOUNG GYNE: no mush. we musn't play dolly house cuz mi auntie say is nastiness. and mi don't want har to beat mi like the last time. plus she will tell yuh moddah and yuh won't get to come ovah here anymore and den we won't get to play dolly house, or dick and jill, or brown girl in da ring, or my playmate . . .

YOUNG ANDRO: . . . wid the boys dem remember. she seh not to do nastiness wid the boys dem. di boys dem not here, sanki. suh dat mean seh me and you can play dolly house. she nah guh beat yuh. yuh waan play?

YOUNG GYNE: alright mek wi play

YOUNG ANDRO: yeah yeah yeah ·

they chase each other laughing, then stop abruptly

YOUNG GYNE & YOUNG ANDRO: but me get to be di moddah!

they break out giggling, looking at each other innocently

they fondle, tickle, and roll around on the floor

SCENE 7

WHAT DO YOU MEAN, LIKE

friday night in GYNE's apartment

an hour later

both womxn are drinking wine

GYNE: suh, andro, you want to tell me of all the womxn friends dem that you ever had, you never liked one of them before.

ANDRO: like, what you mean by like? like dem like dem? like like like dem how?

GYNE: like like dem.

ANDRO: like like dem? what you mean?

GYNE's voice deepens with emphasis

GYNE: like dem! mi mean like dem! you know.

ANDRO: no I don't.

GYNE: andro, come on and stop play dumb. you know what I mean.

ANDRO: yuh mean like dem fi deh wid dem?

GYNE: yes.

ANDRO: gyne, I'm not funny like that.

GYNE: stop going as if yuh never do anything wid a girl before.

ANDRO: do anything like what?

GYNE: feel dem up. kiss dem.

ANDRO: di only girl I ever kissed was you.

GYNE: and feel up too.

ANDRO: *fondled.*

GYNE: see.

ANDRO: see what?

  GYNE responds non-verbally

that don't count. we were little girls. all little girls and boys do dem things.

GYNE: suh that mean seh everybody start out *funny* then—

  she repeats the same shaky hand gesture

or at least bisexual.

ANDRO: oh really now.

GYNE: well if a part of the definition of *funnyness* is indulging in sexual activities with those of the same sex . . .

ANDRO: here we go.

GYNE: . . . and kissing and fondling are most definitely sexual activities. then by definition everybody start out *funny.*

ANDRO: what exactly is your point, gyne?

GYNE: that we all have it in us.

ANDRO: say what?! speak for yourself. funny.

SCENE 8

THE FAT WOMXN

GYNE: folds
undulating
hills and valleys
writhing her riddim of flesh
I saw her today
musk clouded and firm
a temple
she stole
nature's sacred form
inna cyclical balance
your mounds in
I want to be comforted

SCENE 9

TRIPLE STANDARDS

ANDRO: okay it's not so much about di womxn dem. a mean. but just di thought of a man putting his ting into another man batty jus seem really nasty to me yuh know. doodo come out a batty. how yuh aguh push yuh ting inna something dat doodo come out of.

GYNE: anal sex, andro. it's called anal sex. and man and womxn have anal sex, too.

ANDRO: yow, gyne, star we can't tolerate dem kinda nastiness deh.

GYNE: but see yah! you going on as if you nevah have anal sex before.

ANDRO: who me. no sah.

GYNE: why yuh suh lie, andro.

ANDRO: me nevah do dem tings before.

GYNE: andro. didn't you call me bout, what now, two or three years ago saying yuh tink yuh need to go to the doctor because something wrong with yuh bottom . . .

ANDRO: what!?

GYNE: . . . and mi ask yuh what coulda wrong with yuh bottom, and yuh tell me dat me musn't tell nobody but dat yuh tink, a who yuh did a see dat time now? germaine.

ANDRO sighs from recollection

right. yuh tell mi dat yuh might have catch something from germaine. 'cause yuh do it unprotected and now yuh have some infection in yuh . . .

ANDRO: . . . alright alright mi remembah. yuh don't haffi a tell di whole of scarboro mi business. and dat don't count cuz is not a everyday, lifestyle choice. it was only di one time and mi nevah do it again. man putting his dick . . .

GYNE: if the sex part wasn't anal you would still have a problem with it?

ANDRO: maybe maybe not.

GYNE: andro, you don't find it slightly hypocritical to say alright yuh don't have such a big problem with the womxn dem but yuh have a problem with the men?

ANDRO: no!

GYNE: isn't it the same premise? sex with the same gender. why does the sexual act have to be under scrutiny?

ANDRO: c'mon, gyne, you don't tink di whole idea of dick inside of something is kinda weird.

GYNE: what do you mean?

ANDRO: I don't know. I mean. it just always feel so funny yuh know.

GYNE: what, having a penis inside? I thought you love to fuck.

ANDRO: I do. is just di penetration part. man a penetrate man. man a penetrate womxn. penetrate. how come me don't get to penetrate.

GYNE: you could. two sex shops at queen west of bathurst. one on the north side and one on the south.

ANDRO: hahaha.

GYNE: dem have whole heap of penis to choose from.

she laughs

. . . but, andro, you are serious. you don't like how penetration feel? how come you never tell me this before?

ANDRO: well is not that mi don't like it. mi like it, trust me. is just that sometimes it hurt. and seem so repetitive. in out in out in out, round and round, in out in out in out round and round. even when you change position.

laughing, ANDRO throws her pelvis back and forth and around

mocking penetrative sex

SCENE 10

IN AND OUT THE CLOSET

flashback

kingston jamaica past

YOUNG GYNE and YOUNG ANDRO one behind the other

YOUNG GYNE's hands hold YOUNG ANDRO's waist firmly as they snake in and out

of an imaginary circle

playing a ring game

YOUNG GYNE: in and out the closet

YOUNG ANDRO: in and out

YOUNG GYNE: in and out the closet

YOUNG ANDRO: in and out

YOUNG GYNE: in and out the closet

YOUNG ANDRO: in and out

YOUNG GYNE: to see a . . .

YOUNG GYNE confronts YOUNG ANDRO

arms raised above her head, she pretends to be a monster

YOUNG GYNE & YOUNG ANDRO: . . . fairy monster
ahhhhhh!

YOUNG ANDRO runs in the other direction

YOUNG GYNE runs behind her

this time, YOUNG ANDRO leads as YOUNG GYNE holds on to her waist

moving through the imaginary circle

YOUNG ANDRO: in and out the closet

YOUNG GYNE: in and out

YOUNG ANDRO: in and out the closet

YOUNG GYNE: in and out

YOUNG ANDRO: in and out the closet

YOUNG GYNE: in and out

YOUNG ANDRO: to see a . . .

> YOUNG ANDRO *stops and confronts* YOUNG GYNE
>
> *arms raised above her head, she pretends to be a monster*

YOUNG ANDRO & YOUNG GYNE: . . . fairy monster
ahhhhhh!

> YOUNG ANDRO *and* YOUNG GYNE *now face each other*
>
> *hands joined they twirl around in a circle*

YOUNG GYNE & YOUNG ANDRO: skip and take a partner
skip again
skip and take a partner
skip again
skip and take a partner
to see a fairy monster!

> YOUNG ANDRO *tickles* YOUNG GYNE *again*
>
> *they fall to the ground laughing*
>
> YOUNG ANDRO *continues to tickle her*

YOUNG GYNE: auntie auntie auntie. make mush stop.

YOUNG ANDRO: auntie auntie auntie. make mush stop.

SCENE 11

ON BEING FULL

GYNE: full
full of you
a harvest moon
bleeding like a blood orange
you peel patiently
wrapping your mouth
around its fleshy surface
allowing your teeth and tongue and lips
to press and pull into it
until you separate parts of the whole
not violent
not forceful
and those separated parts become
what makes you a complete human being

SCENE 12

TRIGGERS

flashback

toronto, one month prior

ANDRO's bedroom

ANDRO is with her LOVER

she moans

LOVER: is true you don't know star. if I could wrap myself in you like a live blanket, tings would be nice.

ANDRO: suh tell me how come you get to be so sweet . . .

LOVER: like green june plum and salt . . .

ANDRO: ha ha ha. what you know bout dem tings deh?

LOVER: come here and gimme a kiss.

ANDRO moans

ANDRO: don't bite my tongue so hard. what yuh tryin to do, draw blood?

LOVER: I like how it feel.

ANDRO: me too. don't stop.

LOVER: who carries the sage secrets of loving . . .

ANDRO: don't stop.

LOVER: what elders and children . . .

ANDRO: don't stop.

LOVER: walk with the old-time knowledge . . .

ANDRO: don't

LOVER: of a courageous love . . .

ANDRO: stop

LOVER: unapologetic love . . .

ANDRO: stop!

the meaning of her word begins to change

LOVER: an uncompromising love . . .

ANDRO: stop!

this takes on new meaning

LOVER: an integritous love . . .

ANDRO: don't! stop!

LOVER: a healing love . . .

ANDRO no longer wants to continue

ANDRO: no no no no.

embarrassed and apologetic

it's not you it's me . . .

LOVER: tell me who . . .

ANDRO: sometimes I just go to a different place . . .

LOVER: and I will sit studently by the rivers of their feet washing away all the unkowing that I have come to know . . .

ANDRO: my spirit don't really feel the vibes right now to do it again . . .

LOVER: relearning a language of honesty
scribed on our tongues and hearts
by the ancients whom I have forgotten . . .

ANDRO: maybe we can try again later . . .

LOVER: somewhere between a dream and a timelessness . . .

ANDRO: but I just said I don't feel like doing that now . . .

LOVER: across the ocean waters . . .

ANDRO: just cool and listen to me nuh . . .

LOVER: Black sons and dawtahs . . .

ANDRO: come on, man, stop . . .

LOVER: Black moddahs and fadahs . . .

ANDRO: stop it . . .

LOVER: Black auntie uncle sistah and bredah . . .

ANDRO: stop it. please don't . . .

LOVER: stretch love fabric . . .

ANDRO: come on stop it . . . don't do this . . .

LOVER: thick and thin . . .

ANDRO's pleas turn into a real physical struggle

ANDRO: no stop . . .

LOVER: we trodding . . .

ANDRO: don't do this . . .

LOVER: trying to heal the scars . . .

ANDRO: please stop . . .

LOVER: of broken fibre . . .

ANDRO: no. get off of me . . .

LOVER: that stick up inna we . . .

ANDRO: stop. stop . . .

LOVER: like macka . . .

ANDRO: stop!

ANDRO continues to resist

we no longer hear her words

ANDRO attempts to call GYNE: GYNE's phone rings

she glances over at it

and lets it ring out

GYNE'S VOICE ON MACHINE: hi you've reached gyne. leave me a message and i'll call you later. beep.

ANDRO does not leave a message

she is curled up on the floor crying

ANSWERING MACHINE: beep

ANDRO hangs up the phone

SCENE 13

WHAT IS REVOLUSHUN

ANDRO: lesbian cannot produce pickney.

GYNE: they've been doing it for years.

ANDRO: is some weirdo white people business, gyne. you tink seh inna afrika dem have dem foolishness deh.

GYNE: wait wait wait. when did we start to talk about afrika and afrikans. and when did you turn continental expert? . . . and in any case sexuality on the continent is as complex and diverse as the people. so what is *your* point?

ANDRO: is not a matter of expert but I know . . .

GYNE getting very annoyed

GYNE: what do you know? site your sources. gimme names of books, research papers, other experts in the field that can corroborate your story.

ANDRO: well . . .

GYNE: that's what I thought. and all of a sudden you and afrika and afrikans are friends when you wouldn't be caught dead making people refer to you as afrikan. because you are jamaican first. canadian second. and afrikan last if at all.

ANDRO: I beg to differ on that one. I know I used to say that but not anymore, gyne.

GYNE: alright fair enough. sorry.

ANDRO: gyne, look at where our community is economically. we don't have anything to show fi centuries of labour we put into this place. no capital. and the primary reason for that, other than gross disorganization, is institutional racism.

GYNE: I agree with you on that. but that fact don't change the other *fact* of institutional homophobia.

ANDRO: hold on a minute. you talking 'bout dis as if yuh give it whole heapa thought. all your points dem just line up suh.

GYNE: *(chuckling)* yeah I have been thinking about it for a while. but even you just mention gay marriage inna canada. is something the community has to deal with sooner or later.

ANDRO: mi notice more and more Black womxn doing dis lesbian thing.

GYNE: and you have to ask yourself why?

ANDRO: maybe is a man-hate some-umn?

GYNE: c'mon, andro, you can't just regurgitate the same fucked up argument 'bout lesbians because it's our cultural party line. dat would mean dat lesbian hate all their sons, and uncles and cousins, and fadahs and bredahs. bwoy mi find that really hard to believe.

ANDRO: I don't. the way how man stay sometime, you haffi work hard fi like dem.

GYNE: and more and more Black men doing di gay ting, down low or not. you tink dat's new? no sah. just more publicly.

ANDRO: tell me seh we really have time to *choose* to luxuriate in dis gay ting when our same Black youths dying in the streets.

GYNE: it's not one or the other. these same youths committing suicide because they're gay and there is no room for them. other youths perpetuating homophobia by gay-bashing. all of that is violence against the youth.

ANDRO: but being Black is not a choice, gyne.

GYNE: I know that. but whether or not someone chooses to live as an out gay person. whether or not they have the choice to be gay, everybody should be able to live dem life, without fear of punishment for who they are. that's the whole idea behind revolushun for equality, right?

ANDRO: is a matter of focusing energy on the worst of all the evils. which is racism. you love to talk bout revolushun but which revolushun you really fighting for, gyne?

GYNE: we been through persecution
and now we persecute
missa youth whatta gwaan
come and gimme likkle truth
mi nuh know how fi understand di situation
how mi fi hate mi bredah man because him love anoddah man
how mi fi hate mi sista gal because she love anoddah gal
is there room for hate inna revolushun

ANDRO gives GYNE a sarcastic round of applause

ANDRO: listen dis a not a performance poetry event suh don't try to use your poetry on me. I never said anything about hating anybody. suh don't put words into my mouth.

GYNE: you don't find that there is a relationship between the way Black people were treated by white people inna slavery and today and the way straight people treat gay people?

ANDRO: how suh?

GYNE: hatehatehate
i hate those fucking homo bastards

ANDRO: lord jesus christ

GYNE: hatehatehate
i hate those fucking nigger bitches

ANDRO: you have such a fucking flair for drama you know that . . .

GYNE: hatehatehate
i hate those queer motherfuckers
fire bun dem to all Black niggers
fucking slaves

ANDRO: hello miss drama queen . . .

GYNE: judgment for all batty man and sodomite
you're going straight to hell
hatehatehate
i hate you and you you and you and you and you

ANDRO: gyne you're not listening to me . . .

GYNE: and you know what if i was white i would fucking hate Black people too
as a matter of fact i do
all you fucking dyke
queer
gay motherfuckers

ANDRO: okay fine. you want to give your fucking self-righteous oscar speech.
go ahead without me. I'm leaving . . .

GYNE: okay okay okay.

ANDRO: cho! the answer to your question is no I don't find racism and homophobia equal. maybe similar but definitely not equal.

SCENE 14

TREACHERY

toronto canada

present

GYNE: what language have I
to transcend the treachery
of betrayal
if poetry gives name to
thought
then courage births revolushunaries
of love
these silent spaces sprout seeds
for a mute beginning
and I am left at the end of the circle
contemplating running the track of
my choices yet again

breathless
from fear

SCENE 15

LESBIAN REVOLUSHUNARY

GYNE's apartment

ANDRO: well lesbian revolushunary or revolushunary lesbian. which title yuh want?

GYNE: be serious.

ANDRO: I am. it was nice knowing you for these past twenty-five years.

GYNE: what the hell yuh mean by that?

ANDRO: now that yuh so sure you are a lesbian, yuh won't have any more time fi straight people like me.

GYNE: andro, stop joking and don't be ridiculous.

ANDRO: you'll be hitting all the gay bar dem, and gay movie, and gay dis and gay dat. and yuh new gay girlfriend. and me don't really have any intentions of joining you down that path, so bon voyagey, adios, seh la vie, see yuh latah, inna di morrows, hasta la vista baby.

she laughs

GYNE: this is not funny.

ANDRO: *(really nasty)* mi keep telling you that the only thing here that is *funny* is you.

GYNE: you know what, stop now!

ANDRO: every day is something new with you, gyne. you always having crisis or revelation. and I guess this is the latest downtown artsy-fartsy trend.

GYNE: artsy-fartsy trend. what are you talking about? andro, why are you . . .

ANDRO: you know exactly what I am talking about. all your experimentations. all your travelling. if it's not one thing then it's another. communism. atheism. santeria. spoken word . . .

GYNE: hold on, hold on a min . . .

ANDRO: . . . intellectualism. nationalism. fem-fuckin-ism.

she chuckles

here today. gone tomorrow. suh today yuh gay!

GYNE: what the hell are you talking about? these are not passing phases. everybody have a right to explore dem life . . . explore who they are becoming . . .

ANDRO: *(underneath her breath)* that's what you call it?

GYNE: . . . what? I should be more like you, yeah? wid my bay street job, and my vanzant latest relationship book, which is obviously not helping. and my honda civic, right? . . . oh no you traded that in for a volvo last year. sorry if our priorities are different . . .

ANDRO: . . . you want talk 'bout priorities. you really want talk 'bout priorities. who is and has always been the priority in this friendship eh? . . .

GYNE: what are you say—

ANDRO: when you had yuh pregnancy scare, fifteen, who go hospital with yuh for blood test? and when it positive, who go hospital wid yuh for abortion? . . .

GYNE: andro . . .

ANDRO: when yuh stranded wid di dyam commies inna cuba, after dem tief yuh wallet and yuh passport and yuh camera, who send yuh money to stay longer? . . .

GYNE: what does that . . .

ANDRO: who send yuh money to come home? when yuh friend throw yuh out of her apartment inna *pari*, who yuh call?

she gets more and more emotional

and last year when I was raped to hell where were you!? . . .

GYNE: wait wait wait . . .

ANDRO: where were you!? where were you!? mi call yuh and yuh dyam answering machine come on. yuh nevah there for me. where were you?!

GYNE: answering machine? . . . what are you talk—

ANDRO: don't fucking tell me bout priorities. it's obvious there is only one priority in this friendship and is you . . .

their next set of lines overlap each other

GYNE: what the hell are you talking about answering machine? . . .

ANDRO: . . . suh have a fucking happy lesbian life. and go right ahead and replace me . . .

GYNE: . . . you called me last year? replace you? . . . wait wait wait. what happened last year?

ANDRO: . . . I wasn't even here in the first place.

GYNE: . . . rape? . . . my answering machine? . . . andro? . . . somebody do something to you? . . . you never tell me? . . . eh, andro? eh?

ANDRO: I called you. I called you . . . maybe if you would stay in one place fi longer than a few seconds then you would have an idea of what a going round you.

GYNE: this is not fair. you so damn selfish . . . how something like that could happen to you and you don't tell me? . . .

ANDRO: I called you and yuh nevah there . . . yuh nevah there. so don't bother with the talking. dis a one-sided friendship and I know that all along.

GYNE: that's because you always carrying on as if you don't need nobody's help . . .

ANDRO: yes . . .

GYNE: . . . andro ace the common entrance . . .

ANDRO: yes . . .

GYNE: . . . andro goes to u of t. andro works in a law firm.

ANDRO: . . . yes

GYNE: andro has it all together. you don't need me.

ANDRO: yes I don't need nobody, and the one time, gyne, di one time I ever need you, you weren't there for me. so there, you prove my point.

GYNE: how can you say that? how you could not tell me? andro, who do I love more than you? who do I love more than you? who do I love more than you?

ANDRO turns away

SCENE 16

SORRY

flashback

kingston jamaica past

YOUNG ANDRO *runs toward* YOUNG GYNE, *excited at her new doll*

YOUNG ANDRO: sanki sanki, look at mi new foreign dolly. mi auntie just sent her from canada. she pretty, eh sanki. she so Black and pretty.

YOUNG GYNE: mek mi see har mush. mek mi see har nuh. mek mi see har.

YOUNG ANDRO: yuh haffi wait, sanki. mi haffi comb her hair first suh dat she can look prettier.

YOUNG GYNE: mush mek mi hold har nuh. just fi a likkle bit. mi promise mi going to hold her gentle and mi won't make her hair untidy. please.

YOUNG ANDRO: alright yuh can look at her.

she holds the doll arms outstretched but does not give her to YOUNG GYNE

see her here.

YOUNG GYNE goes to take the doll and YOUNG ANDRO *pulls it away*

YOUNG GYNE: mek mi see her nuh. mi want to hold her.

YOUNG ANDRO again holds her out then pulls her away when YOUNG GYNE *tries to take her*

YOUNG ANDRO: here she is. take her if you want her.

YOUNG GYNE: mush stop doing dat. let me see her. stop doing dat.

YOUNG ANDRO keeps repeating this action until YOUNG GYNE, *frustrated*

grabs the doll out of her hand

the doll breaks in two

YOUNG ANDRO holding one half

and YOUNG GYNE *the other*

YOUNG ANDRO: look at what you did. you just broke my dolly. you broke my brand new dolly.

she turns away and begins to cry

YOUNG GYNE: mush sorry. sorry mush. I didn't do it on purpose. sorry.

YOUNG ANDRO continues to cry

YOUNG GYNE goes to her and takes the other half of the doll

she gets some tape and awkwardly tapes the two halves together

YOUNG ANDRO watches her in secrecy

look mush, I fix her back for yuh.

YOUNG ANDRO: a lie yuh a tell.

YOUNG GYNE: look I fix har back fi yuh. see har here.

she offers YOUNG ANDRO the doll. YOUNG ANDRO takes her and stops crying

I never mean to break her it was a accident.

she awkwardly hugs YOUNG ANDRO

SCENE 17

ANOTHER PLACE NOT HERE

GYNE: my eyes
black holes of
figments of construction
dance
flicker like desperate stars
fighting the inevitable dawn
eager and frustrated

if my stare stalks yearnings
it is because of an unruly memory
auction blocks and divided destinies
womxn here men there
children nowhere

and yes
I feel I may not survive
another
loss of you

to another place
not here

SCENE 18

KISS FOR ANDRO

inside GYNE'*s apartment*
the air is tense and silent
GYNE *and* ANDRO *are in separate spaces*
both silent and contemplative
ANDRO *having heard* GYNE'*s "who do I love more than you"*
reconsiders all the things she said
and contemplates the implications of GYNE'*s statement*
GYNE, *also having heard her own declaration*
grapples with what that could mean for their friendship
ANDRO *breaks the silence*

ANDRO: suh yuh going to finish the poem?

GYNE: what, "the kiss"?

ANDRO: yeah i'd like to hear the rest of it.

GYNE: alright

> ANDRO *finds the paper with "the kiss" written on it*
> *and gives it to* GYNE

thanx

> ANDRO *manages a smile*
> GYNE *picks up from where she left off*
> *the poem's earlier "miss lou" rhythm has shifted*
> *it is still in nation language*
> *but now is entirely in* GYNE'*s style*
> *her read of the rest of the poem differs from the earlier read*
> *she is less performative*
> *she is open, vulnerable, and honest*
> *her words fall upon* ANDRO

caressing her, comforting her, reassuring her

ANDRO *listens with an open heart*

smiling in recognition of GYNE's *non-verbal offering*

and dem mi realize
stop dead inna mi trak
so mi nearly ketch up
heart attack
is a Black girl
mi did a kiss

wid two breass
a roun rump
broad hips and two dark lips
like mine
har skin brown and shine
like mine
har leg dem strong and thick
like mine

with the absence of that dick
powah play was a trick
standing dere wid mi best frien
mi wish dis feeling nevah end
cuz there was no powah play

in some small part of mi mind
mi wish mi could freeze dat feeling in time
tek it out when mi feel dispossessed and oppressed
cuz inna disya powah structure
di Black womxn deh a di bottom a di laddah

when mi kiss dat Black girl
I could see her and she could see me bright
me and andro inna di middle a di light
a di first time mi feel sexuality wid some real equality

SCENE 19

KISSING ANDRO

in GYNE's *apartment*

ANDRO *and* GYNE *are sitting on the bed*

after GYNE *has finished reading her poem "the kiss"*

ANDRO: I like the poem, gyne.

GYNE: thank you. I was thinking about you when I wrote it.

ANDRO: you were thinking about me when you were kissing some womxn. that's some serious multi-tasking, gyne.

GYNE: I woulda have preferred to be kissing my best friend but word on di street is dat she is not funny like dat . . .

she makes a shaky hand jesture

in one smooth, uncalculated movement

ANDRO *moves into* GYNE *and kisses her long on the mouth*

GYNE *leans with surprise and pleasure*

and kisses her back

GYNE *eases away from* ANDRO

looks deeply and compassionately at her

andro, how come yuh didn't tell me bout di rape?

ANDRO: mi did want to tell yuh. mi try fill tell yuh. but every time mi tink mi was going to do it mi couldn't. sometime by the time wi finished talking it was morning and time to go home, change mi clothes, and guh to di office. sometime yuh nevah here inna di country and sometime . . .

GYNE: andro, mi nuh care which part mi deh. on the other side of the globe, please please please trust mi enough to tell mi anything, anything like dat as soon as it happen, otherwise how mi going to be yuh real and true friend. look how long wi know each other. mi love you more than anything inna di whole world. you know that.

ANDRO: mi know mi shoulda tell yuh. mi shoulda tell yuh. and mi know that you love me. and me love you too.

she pauses

me love you too.

SCENE 20

CLOSETED

flash forward

inside ANDRO's apartment

identical to GYNE's

one year later

the lights are out

there is a loud knock at the door

ANDRO gets out of bed and turns the lights on

the knocking continues

ANDRO: but who in their right mind could be knocking me up at this time? . . .

she grabs her bathrobe and hurriedly puts it on, meanwhile a key turns in the door

but wait!?

GYNE emerges

she is five months pregnant

however her belly is masked completely

at the beginning of the conversation

GYNE: *(entering)* yuh tek too long to open the door, man. look how long mi a knock.

ANDRO: you have a key. you don't have to knock. are you okay?

GYNE: yes I am okay. I couldn't sleep again tonight. no matter how I turn I can't get comfortable in the bed and I can't get any sleep. you on the other hand, you are sleeping just fine, while I am tossing and turning.

ANDRO: no I'm not. if you can't sleep. I can't sleep. cuz yuh come right ovah come wake me up!

GYNE becoming more upset

GYNE: that's not fair. that's not right! . . .

ANDRO goes over to GYNE and guides her to the couch. GYNE's belly is revealed.

ANDRO: alright, gyne, calm down. it was your idea to keep two apartments remember. I still think that we could save by getting one place together but you want to maintain your independence and space. it still does not make sense to me. we spend half the time coming over to each other's places in the middle of the night anyways. we might as well live together.

GYNE: no. every partner I have lived with it hasn't worked out. space is good.

ANDRO: gyne, we are pregnant and you have *never* lived with *me*.

GYNE: *I* am pregnant and you are . . .

GYNE she realizes what ANDRO she just said

ANDRO: not! gyne, you are the one carrying the baby, because you *chose* to carry the baby. we are living in separate spaces because *you* want it that way. I'm trying and you have to give me some credit. mi say this already and mi will say it again, I think we should get one place together. that way I can help, and we can spend less time and money in the luxury of *separate living spaces*. and save us both the journey of trekking in the middle of the night. I don't understand this setup.

GYNE: and my mother wouldn't understand any other setup. or my father, or my brothers, or my cousins, or granny, or any . . .

ANDRO: yuh nuh tell dem yet?! I thought you said you told dem when I told mom?! gyne, really?!

GYNE: hell and powder house now.

ANDRO: hell and powder house is right! you mean to tell me that after six months you still have not told yuh family. and you lied! and *I* told mommy! and you lied! gyne, really?!

GYNE: listen I am pregnant and I really cannot deal with the stress right now!

ANDRO: you think you are the first pregnant womxn on the planet! our great-great-grandmothers cut cane with baby inna belly so at the very least you can have a discussion with me about honesty miss *proud to be a lesbian*!

SCENE 21

NAMING

GYNE: I am lesbian
out of practice
identifying always as queer
bottled by fear
of being found out

ANDRO: I love womxn
I am afraid of womxn
I am afraid of the power
of the intimacy
of loving womxn

I am lesbian
afraid of seeing myself
unveiled
who do I become
afraid of being put on fringes
without my choosing

ANDRO & GYNE: she hugged me in bed
and I thought
how dare she be intimate with me
a womxn

ANDRO: I felt the blood
of the urgency of fear
rush to my head
my heart
my feet
frozen!

ANDRO & GYNE: *how dare she know*
how dare she name me
out me

   end

ABOUT THE CONTRIBUTORS

Kamee Abrahamian (uses she/they pronouns) was born in an immigrant suburb to an Armenian family by way of the SWANA region. They arrive in the world today as a mother and an interdisciplinary creator, producer, and facilitator. They have a BFA/B.A. in film and political science (Concordia University), an M.A. in expressive art therapy (European Graduate School), and are currently working toward an M.A./Ph.D. in community, liberation, eco, and Indigenous psychologies (Pacifica Graduate Institute). The bedrock of Kamee's artistic background is in classical ballet and dance, theatre, and visual art. Their work is primarily collaborative, spiralling into and out of fragmented time/place/being through ancestral reclamation, diasporic futurism, and radical imaginaries. They have published both literary and academic work; internationally exhibited and presented visual and digital artwork, films, and staged performances; curated art spaces and events; and facilitated workshops across Canada and the USA. Most recently, Kamee has been working under Saboteur Productions (founder) and collaboratively through Kalik Arts (co-founder).

Finalist for the 2017 Ontario Premier's Awards for Excellence in the Arts, **d'bi. young anitafrika** is a triple Dora Mavor Moore Award–winning playwright-performer, director-dramaturg, and emerging scholar. One of two hundred Canadian artists to receive a New Chapter grant to produce her critically acclaimed environmental musical *Lukumi: A Dub Opera*, anitafrika has been recognized as a Canadian Poet of Honor, with the YWCA Women of Distinction Award, the Toronto Arts Foundation Emerging Artist Award, a Vital People grant, a K.M. Hunter Artist Award, and the Sheri-D Wilson Golden Beret Award. She is an internationally celebrated arts educator and the founding artistic director of the Watah Theatre. anitafrika is also the instigator of Spolrusie Publishing, a unique micro press that publishes original works by Black and QTIPOC creators. A Toronto Arts Council Leaders Lab fellow, anitafrika is the originator of the creative-leadership praxis and intersectional liberation framework the Anitafrika Method, which has been utilized by the Stephen Lewis Foundation, the Banff Centre, the University of Toronto, the MaRS Discovery District, Women's College Hospital, and other institutions globally. She is the author of seven books, nine plays, and seven dub albums and has toured her work nationally and internationally. anitafrika is about to embark on postgraduate studies in London, UK, where she will be researching the use of theatre to address generational trauma in the Black body.

Art Babayants is a Toronto-based theatre artist, educator, and researcher who has worked in Canada, the US, Great Britain, and Russia. His research looks at the phenomenology of multilingual acting and spectating as well as the concept of multilingual dramaturgy. In 2015 Art, along with his colleague Dr. Heather Fitzsimmons Frey, published his first edited collection, *Theatre and Learning*, which focused on contemporary applied theatre practices in Canada and abroad. In 2017 he co-edited with Nicole Nolette the first issue of *Theatre Research in Canada/Recherches théâtrales au Canada* fully dedicated to stage multilingualism and multilinguals. As a theatre practitioner, Art has presented his work at various Toronto festivals such the Toronto Fringe, the SummerWorks Performance Festival, and Nuit Blanche. Since 1997 Art has been developing theatre projects integrating acting and second-language teaching. His most recent ESL/drama creation called *Embodied English* is a sought-after course for advanced ESL learners and is offered through his theatre company Toronto Laboratory Theatre, www.torontolab.org.

lee williams boudakian (uses they, them, their pronouns) is an interdisciplinary artist, writer, producer, facilitator, and consultant based in Vancouver, unceded Coast Salish territories. They work across the disciplines of film and video, theatre and performance, digital media, contemporary arts, and literature. lee's work emerges from their experiences as a queer, trans, mixed-race settler raised in an immigrant Armenian family. Their work is critical and necessarily intersectional. lee is invested in art and storytelling that integrates ancestral and cultural herstories, grapples with our current worlds, and visions into futures that centre the lives and stories of those of us currently living on the fringe and in the margins. lee works under ShapeShift Arts (founder) and Kalik Arts (co-founder). Recent projects include *Dear Armen*, an interdisciplinary performance and media project; *Setting Bones*, winner of 2017 Fringe New Play Prize; and *World of Q*, a collaborative filmmaking initiative.

Peter Dickinson is a professor at Simon Fraser University, where he holds a joint appointment in the School for the Contemporary Arts and the Department of English. He is also Director of SFU's Institute for Performance Studies and Associate Member of the Department of Gender, Sexuality and Women's Studies. Peter has published extensively on queer Canadian theatre and performance and his produced plays include *The Objecthood of Chairs* and *Long Division*.

Sunny Drake is an award-winning playwright, theatre creator, and performer. He has toured his theatre works to fifty-five cities across Canada, Australia, the US, and Europe, bringing challenging work to a wide range of audiences, from elderly ladies in regional theatres to queers in underground warehouses. His plays and performances have been translated into four languages. Sunny was also Director of the Emerging Creators Unit at Buddies in Bad Times Theatre from 2015 to 2018. He was born in Australia, on Jagera-Turrbal land (Brisbane), and has lived in Toronto since 2011.

Honor Ford-Smith is Associate Professor in Community and Environmental Arts at the Faculty of Environmental Studies, York University, Toronto. Her research focuses on performance, race, gender, and social justice in the Caribbean. Her publications include *3 Jamaican Plays: A Postcolonial Anthology (1976–1986)* (Paul Issa Publications) and, with Sistren, *Lionheart Gal: Life Stories of Jamaican Women* (University of the West Indies Press). Since 2006 Ford-Smith has been working on *Letters from the Dead*, a performance cycle that mourns and remembers those killed by police or by armed strongmen in Jamaica and the Black and Caribbean diaspora.

Born, raised, and based on the unceded traditional lands of the Coast Salish peoples (Vancouver), Filipino Canadian author **C.E. Gatchalian** writes drama, poetry, fiction, and non-fiction. His plays, which include *Falling In Time, Broken, Motifs & Repetitions*, and *People Like Vince*, have appeared on stages nationally and internationally, as well as on radio and television. A two-time finalist for the Lambda Literary Awards, he was the 2013 recipient of the Dayne Ogilvie Prize, awarded annually by the Writers' Trust of Canada to an LGBT author of merit. Formerly Artistic Producer of **the frank theatre company**, he is the recipient of

two Jessie Richardson Theatre Awards for his work as a theatre artist and producer. His non-fiction book, *Double Melancholy*, is due out from Arsenal Pulp
Press in Spring 2019. Please visit his website, cegatchalian.com.

Thomas Morgan Jones is an award-winning director, playwright, movement
coach, dramaturg, and teacher. For over fifteen years he has created theatre
nationally and internationally with companies and schools that include the
Stratford Festival, Theatre Direct, Theatre Passe Muraille, the Charlottetown
Festival, Carousel Players, Cia EnvieZada (Brazil), the National Theatre School,
and Sheridan College. He holds a B.A. from the University of Guelph, an M.A.
from the University of Toronto, and has trained with SITI Company and the
Suzuki Company of Toga in the United States, France, Spain, Italy, Japan, and
Canada. A former artistic director of Theatre New Brunswick, he is currently
the artistic director of Prairie Theatre Exchange in Winnipeg, Manitoba.

Minh Ly is a Canadian actor/writer based out of Toronto, ON. He trained at
Studio 58 in Vancouver, BC. Since graduating from his alma mater, Minh has
worked in film/TV in Toronto and Vancouver. Selected credits include *Cardinal*
(CTV Network), *Mayday* (Discovery Channel), *Star Falls* (YTV/Nickelodeon),
Nikita (CW Network), *Fringe* (Fox Network), and *Psych* (USA Network). He
has also worked largely in professional theatre, appearing in *Hana's Suitcase*
(Magnus Theatre), *Jade in the Coal* (Pangaea Arts), *Thoroughly Modern Millie*
(Gateway Theatre), *Banana Boys* (Firehall Arts Centre), and *Salome* (Leaky
Heaven Circus). Joe jobs of his have included, but are not limited to, being a
Product Demonstrator (inside department stores), Serving/Bartending (too
many to list), Brand Promotions (he probably handed you a flyer), and working as
a Flight Attendant (you might have seen him do a safety demo). Minh's first full-
length play, *Ga Ting*, has been produced twice in Western Canada, and was first
published in spring 2017 by Scirocco Drama. He loves crossfit and its principles
of endurance and stamina; keep on going to achieve your goals when there is no
end in sight. If you've read this far, you know him pretty well. www.minhly.ca.

Bobby Noble is an associate professor of sexuality studies and the principal investigator on the Feminist Porn Archive and Research Project at York
University. He has published numerous articles and is the author of the book
Masculinities Without Men? (UBC Press); co-editor of *The Drag King Anthology*,
a 2004 Lambda Literary Award finalist (Haworth Press); and is the author of the
monograph *Sons of the Movement: FTMs Risking Incoherence in a Post-Queer
Cultural Landscape* (Women's Press).

Kathleen Oliver's first play, *Swollen Tongues*, won the 1997 National Playwriting Competition and has been produced across Canada, in London, and (in a French translation) in Paris. Her other plays include *Carol's Christmas* and *The Family Way*, which were both produced in Vancouver. Kathleen teaches English at Langara College in Vancouver and is a regular contributor to *The Georgia Straight*, where she has been writing about theatre for nearly twenty years. She lives in Vancouver with her partner and son.

Jonathan Seinen is a theatre artist. He is also Co-Artistic Producer of Architect Theatre, Artistic Associate with lemonTree creations, and a founding member of Saga Collectif. He directed *Black Boys*, which was nominated for the Dora Mavor Moore Award for Outstanding Ensemble in a production by Saga Collectif and Buddies in Bad Times Theatre. He was an actor and producer for lemonTree creations's *Body Politic* by Nick Green, which was co-produced by Buddies and awarded the Dora Award for Outstanding New Play. With Architect Theatre he created *Highway 63: The Fort Mac Show*, a collective creation about the oil sands (Theatre Passe Muraille/national tour), and *Like There's No Tomorrow*, a devised work about pipelines in Northern BC (SummerWorks Performance Festival). Jonathan also wrote and directed *Unknown Soldier* (SummerWorks), inspired by the actions of Chelsea Manning, and directed a workshop production of *Boys In Chairs*, for which the cast was awarded SummerWorks's inaugural Jon Kaplan Spotlight Award. He was a participant in the Stratford Festival's Michael Langham Workshop for Classical Direction and was an artist-in-residence with **the frank theatre company**. Born in Terrace, BC, raised in Alberta, and based in Toronto, Jonathan is a graduate of the University of Alberta and the National Theatre School. He is currently an M.F.A. Theatre Directing student at Columbia University in New York. For more information, visit jonathanseinen.com.

Dalbir Singh is a Ph.D. candidate in Performance Studies at the University of Toronto. He taught courses there as well as at the University of Waterloo and the University of Guelph. At Waterloo, he taught the first theatre course exclusively focused on racial identity and Canadian theatre. He has edited five collections of plays and critical essays on topics including Tamil culture and identity, post-colonial theatre, South Asian Canadian drama, and queer Canadian theatre. As a result, he has published the work of such notable writers as Donna-Michelle St. Bernard, Ravi Jain, Guillermo Verdecchia, Anusree Roy, and Yvette Nolan.

Katie Sly is a genderqueer writer, performer, curator, and producer. They grew up on welfare in the borough of Verdun in Montréal, and they hold no degrees.

Katie is Artistic Producer of Tender Container, which produces performance that believes in using what you have at your disposal to build something strong and flexible enough to contain your truth, whatever that truth may be, as nameable or unnameable as that truth is. Tender Container's productions include *Serenity Wild*, *Charisma Furs*, and *How To Self-Suspend*. Katie was the recipient of Buddies in Bad Times Theatre's 2016 Queer Emerging Artist Award and the 2016 Grand Prize Winner of the Wildfire National Playwriting Competition. They were the 2017 artist-in-residence with **the frank theatre company**. Katie is a national advocate for bisexual cultural expression, and since 2014 has been producing and curating *Too Queer: A Bi Visibility Cabaret*, which has held eight events across Toronto and Vancouver. The most recent instalment of *Too Queer* was in February 2018, as part of Toronto's Rhubarb Festival. Katie writes an ongoing column called "Rougher with Feeling" for *Xtra*, in which they explore non-normative expressions of sensuality and intimacy, such as public sex and BDSM.

Donna-Michelle St. Bernard is an emcee, playwright, and agitator. Notable works for the stage include *Sound of the Beast*, *Cake*, *They Say He Fell*, *A Man A Fish*, *The House You Build*, *Dark Love*, *The First Stone*, *Roominhouse*, *Salome's Clothes*, and *Gas Girls*. DM's work has been recognized with a SATAward nomination, the Herman Voaden National Playwriting Competition, the Enbridge playRites Award, a Dora Mavor Moore Award for Outstanding New Play, and nominations for the Governor General's Literary Award, the Siminovitch Prize, and the K.M. Hunter Artist Award. DM is Artistic Director of New Harlem Productions, Co-ordinator of the Adhoc Assembly, playwright-in-residence at lemonTree creations and emcee-in-residence at Theatre Passe Muraille.

Shawn Wright was born the youngest of seven children to Lefty and Regina (Robichaud) Wright in Saint John, New Brunswick. Shortly after graduating from the University of New Brunswick with a degree in English literature, he embarked upon a long and varied theatre career. He made his professional acting debut alongside Gordon Pinsent in a tour of *Cyrano de Bergerac*. Shawn spent seven seasons performing at the prestigious Stratford Festival as well six seasons at the world-renowned Shaw Festival. He was in the Toronto stage premiere of *Jersey Boys*, the Los Angeles premiere of *Mamma Mia*, the world stage premiere of *Lord of the Rings*, and the original Broadway workshop cast of *Ragtime*. Shawn has appeared in leading roles on most of Canada's great stages. He has also appeared on concert stages, original cast recordings, and with the Pacific Opera, Victoria. He has won Toronto's top performance prize, the Dora Mavor

Moore Award; the Tyrone Guthrie Award at the Stratford Festival twice; the Christopher Newton Award for playwriting; and has been nominated multiple times for the BroadwayWorld Award. He is currently a part-time professor of acting at Sheridan College. *Ghost Light* is his first play.

Laine Zisman Newman received her Ph.D. from the University of Toronto's Centre for Drama, Theatre and Performance Studies and the collaborative programs in Sexual Diversity Studies and Women and Gender Studies. Her primary research focuses on queer women's access to performance space in Canada, developing theoretical contributions on gender equity, and *placefullness* (conceived of as the intentional articulation of the politics of place and space). In addition to her research, Zisman Newman is founder and chair of Toronto's Queer Theory Working Group at the Jackman Humanities Institute and co-founder of Equity in Theatre, a national organization that worked to improve equity in the professional Canadian performance industry.

First edition: June 2018
Printed and bound in Canada by Imprimerie Gauvin, Gatineau

Jacket design by Kisscut Design
Jacket image by Cactus Blai Baules

**PLAYWRIGHTS
CANADA PRESS**

202-269 Richmond St. W.
Toronto, ON
M5V 1X1

416.703.0013
info@playwrightscanada.com
www.playwrightscanada.com
@playcanpress

MIX
Paper from
responsible sources
FSC   FSC® C100212
www.fsc.org